Supplement to THE ARMY & NAVY GAZE

GUARDS.

FIELD OFFICER.

Review Order.

PRIVATE.

Undress.

DRUMMER.

Review Order.

UP THE MICKS!

An illustrated history of the Irish Guards

UP THE MICKS!

An illustrated history of the Irish Guards

Foreword by
His Royal Highness the Duke of Cambridge KG, KT
Colonel, Irish Guards

Introduction by
Major General M A P Carleton-Smith CBE
Regimental Lieutenant Colonel, Irish Guards

Dedicated to all who have served in the Irish Guards

Pen & Sword
MILITARY

ACKNOWLEDGEMENTS

No individual claims responsibility for this book and too many people have been involved in its production to name here. However, a debt is owed to Colonel Sir William Mahon Bt who led a team to produce a very successful centenary book in 2000 upon which this publication is based. Since then it has been revised and expanded by a third, largely due to the work of Lieutenant Colonel Brian O'Gorman.

Thanks, though are due to many others from the Regimental Trustees and Council to serving and retired Micks who have contributed their time, advice and material to produce this record of life in a family Regiment. Assistance from others including the Guards Museum and Headquarters London District and the Ministry of Defence was also greatly appreciated.

Every effort has been made to find all the copyright holders of the pictures in this book. In some cases this has not proved possible but no infringement is intended.

Only the Regimental Charitable Funds benefit from any profits from this publication to provide, as the statue in Windsor states, – for Past, Present and Future Irish Guardsmen. Quis Separabit.

First published in Great Britain in 2016 by
Pen & Sword Military
an imprint of
Pen & Sword Books Ltd
47 Church Street
Barnsley
South Yorkshire
S70 2AS

Copyright © The Irish Guards, 2016

ISBN 978 1 47383 563 4

Typeset in Bergamo by
Mac Style Ltd, Bridlington, East Yorkshire
Printed and bound in China by Imago

Pen & Sword Books Ltd incorporates the imprints of Pen & Sword Archaeology, Atlas, Aviation, Battleground, Discovery, Family History, History, Maritime, Military, Naval, Politics, Railways, Select, Transport, True Crime, and Fiction, Frontline Books, Leo Cooper, Praetorian Press, Seaforth Publishing and Wharncliffe.

For a complete list of Pen & Sword titles please contact
PEN & SWORD BOOKS LIMITED
47 Church Street, Barnsley, South Yorkshire, S70 2AS, England
E-mail: enquiries@pen-and-sword.co.uk
Website: www.pen-and-sword.co.uk

CONTENTS

Endpapers: Front – Richard Simkin (1850–1926) was employed to design recruiting posters and to illustrate for the Army and Navy Gazette. This picture was published in the Gazette on Saturday 4th January 1902 but had already been used on a recruiting poster. Notice the officers in tunic order are wearing black armbands indicating that it was painted while they are still in Court Mourning following the death of HM Queen Victoria on 4th January 1901.
Back – Painting of the Corps of Drums in Hyde Park by G Merry, 1903.

FOREWORD

KENSINGTON PALACE

The Irish Guards – the 'Micks', as they are known to one and all – are unique. They are steadfast and feared in action. Their battle honours read like a roll call of the world wars and conflicts of the past century, including recent campaigns in Kosovo, Iraq and Afghanistan. And yet, whenever the name of the Micks is mentioned, a smile tends to play across the lips. This is because they are loved, as much as they are feared and respected. They are loved by other soldiers, by other regiments, by all who come into contact with them – except, of course, their enemies on the battlefield.

Why should this be so? They are, after all, Foot Guards, a proud regiment of Her Majesty's Household Division like any other. But they are also Irish - suffused with all the spontaneity, wit, romance and style of that land, birthplace of warriors and poets. This heady cocktail captivates all who sip at it. My great grandmother, Queen Elizabeth The Queen Mother, loved the Micks, and they loved her, to distraction. For me, the moment of realisation that here was something fine and unique came at Sandhurst, where my platoon Colour Sergeant was a formidable Irish Guardsman. To be part of an organisation that boasted men like him became a burning ambition, realised when Her Majesty The Queen paid me the supreme honour of appointing me Colonel of the Irish Guards.

This book captures the essence of what it is to be an Irish Guardsman. It is a superb historical record of a fighting regiment, but its pages also reveal something extra, that something indefinable which makes all who know and love our great regiment cry out in unison:

"Up The Micks!"

Colonel

INTRODUCTION

      This beautifully presented collection of photographs is a unique pictorial record of the fortunes of a formidable fighting Regiment and an admirable tribute and record for all those who have served the Regiment throughout its distinguished history. In its manner and style it is an important addition to the canon of Regimental literature and I am sure it will be widely read and enjoyed by all Irish Guardsmen; past, present and future and by all those interested in the impression and experience of what it is to serve as an Irish Guardsman. The full tapestry and rich colour of the Regimental family is captured here through the camera lens. It reveals an intimate portrait of a Regiment, at home and overseas, at war and during peace, at work and enjoying its leisure. The vivid impression is of the indomitable spirit, panache, courage and humour displayed by generations of Micks.

      This is a second volume bringing up to date an outstanding predecessor which charted the Regiment's genesis to the celebration of the centenary. This magnificent edition continues in similar vein and includes a compendium of additional Regimental intelligence and information as well as striking images from both Iraq and Afghanistan where a contemporary generation has upheld the fighting traditions of the Micks; the same resolve and tenacity is graphically recorded in this most extraordinary recent chapter of our Regimental history. Colonel Brian O'Gorman is to be congratulated and thanked for offering us this remarkable record for posterity. It is something to treasure and enjoy and it will bring back many happy memories for successive generations of proud Irish Guardsmen.

Quis Separabit.

Mark Carleton-Smith

Major General Mark Carleton-Smith CBE
Regimental Lieutenant Colonel
Irish Guards

28 February 1900
Letter to the Editor of 'The Times'

Sir,

May I venture to suggest, through you, to the authorities within whose province it may come, that now is a most opportune time to recognise the distinguished valour of our Irish soldiers who, in the Inniskilling Fusiliers, the Dublin Fusiliers and the Connaught Rangers, have shown to the world such conspicuous bravery in the many recent battles which they have fought with such brilliant dash and daring throughout our South Africa War. Is there not one mark of distinction and honour that can be conferred upon them and their country which belongs to Scotchmen and Englishmen, but is witheld from them? There are Scotch Guards and English Guards – why not add to the roll of glory a regiment of Irish Guards?

I am, Sir,
Your obedient Servant,
Cumming Macdona,
House of Commons

3 March 1900
From The Queen's Private Secretary in reply to the Secretary of State for War.
Windsor Castle,

My Dear Lord Lansdowne,

By a curious coincidence The Queen has during the past week been seriously considering the question of a Regiment of Irish Guards, thinking that the present was an opportunity for its creation. Therefore I am glad to be able to tell you that The Queen entirely approves of the idea ... Her Majesty asked the Duke of Connaught to speak to the Commander in Chief on the subject and hopes that you will therefore find that Lord Wolseley is already in possession of Her Majesty's views.

Yours very truly,
(signed) Arthur Bigge

Army Order 77
1 April 1900
Formation of Regiment of Irish Foot Guards

Her Majesty The Queen, having deemed it desirable to commemorate the bravery shown by the Irish regiments in the recent operations in South Africa, has been graciously pleased to command that an Irish Regiment of Foot Guards be formed.

This regiment will be designated the 'Irish Guards'.

The House of Commons, 1 April 1900

After the Under Secretary of State for War had announced the formation of a fourth Regiment of Foot Guards to be called the Irish Guards, an Irish MP rose to his feet. It was a great day for Ireland and he waxed lyrical: 'And Mr Speaker, Sir,' he pronounced in ringing tones, 'may I assure your Honour that as fine a heart will beat under the tunic of an Irish Guard as under the kilt of a Gordon Highlander.'

The Irish Guards.

We're not so old in the Army List,
  But we're not so young at our Trade
For we had the honour at Fontenoy
  Of meeting the Guards' Brigade.
'Twas Lally, Dillon, Bulkeley, Clare
  And Lee that led us then—
And, after a hundred and seventy years,
  We're fighting for France again!

      Old days! the Wild Geese are flighting
        Head to the storm as they faced it before.
      For where there are Irish there's bound to be fighting
        And when there's no fighting, it's Ireland no more!
            Ireland no more!

The fashion's all for khaki now,
  But once through France we went
Full-dressed in scarlet Army cloth
  The English—left at Ghent!
They're fighting on our side to-day
  But, before they changed their clothes,
The half of Europe knew our fame,
  As all of Ireland knows!

      Old days! the Wild Geese are flying
        Head to the storm as they faced it before.
      For, where there are Irish there's memory undying,
        And when we forget, it is Ireland no more!
            Ireland no more!

From Barry Wood to Gouzeaucourt
  From Boyne to Pilkem Ridge,
The ancient years return no more
  Non water under the bridge.
But the bridge it stands and the water runs
  As red as yesterday,
And the Irish go to the sound of the guns
  Like salmon to the sea!

      Old days! the Wild Geese are ranging
        Head to the storm as they faced it before.
      For where there are Irish the heart is unchanging,
        And when it is changed, it is Ireland no more!
            Ireland no more!

We're not so old in the Army List,
  But we're not so new in the ring,
For we carried our packs with Marshall Saxe
  When Louis was our King!
But Douglas Haig's our Marshall now
  And we're King George's men
And—after a hundred and seventy years—
  We're fighting for France again!

      Ah France! did we stand by you
        When life was made splendid with gifts and rewards?
      Ah France! and will we deny you
        In the hour of your agony, Mother of Swords!
      Old days! the Wild Geese are flighting
        Head to the storm as they faced it before.
      For where there are Irish there's loving and fighting
        And, when we stop either, it's Ireland no more!
            Ireland no more!

March. 17. 1918.

Rudyard Kipling

Rudyard Kipling's close involvement with the Irish Guards stems from the death of his only son John when serving with the 2nd Battalion in Loos in 1915. A young man of infinite charm and merit, known as 'the Joker', his parents never fully recovered from his death. In his memory Kipling wrote his incomparable two volume history of the Irish Guards in the Great War, many extracts from which appear in the following pages.

Chapter One

1900–1914
THE EARLY YEARS

The Irish Guards were raised in April 1900 to commemorate the bravery of the Irish regiments in South Africa in the years 1899 and 1900.

The first British troops in action were a Mounted Infantry section of the Royal Dublin Fusiliers. Irish regiments held the ring before reinforcements arrived and they continued to feature prominently in the campaign as it developed. County Tipperary, with one of the lowest densities of population in the British Isles, had the highest number of Victoria Cross winners.

The campaign in South Africa was characterised by great bravery, and a lack of awareness of tactical changes which new and better weapons necessitated. The masterly fieldcraft of the Boers, coupled with out of date British tactics, brought a rash of humiliating defeats on the British in 1899. Through all this shone the dash and extraordinary courage of the Irish soldier.

This was brought to the attention of Queen Victoria. Simultaneously a number of letters in The Times suggested the formation of a Regiment of Irish Guards. So it came about that on 1 April 1900, the Fourth, or Irish Regiment of Foot Guards was born.

Left: **12 June 1901. Distribution of South African War Medals by Edward VII.** This was the first royal Guard of Honour found by the Irish Guards, and the first official appearance of the Regimental Band. In the photograph The King has just arrived on Horse Guards and is being greeted by a Royal salute but with no Colour available to be lowered. The first Colours were not presented until 30 May 2002.

Applications to join the regiment started at once. C/Sjt Conroy of the Royal Munster Fusiliers was awarded regimental number 1. Irishmen serving in the other regiments of the Brigade of Guards were encouraged to transfer. Very soon that unique blend between the Brigade discipline and the Irishman's wit began to brew the magic that matured into a regiment of infinite daring, ever stylish and brave, and always ready to laugh. Thus, when the call came for Mounted Infantry to go to the war in South Africa there were volunteers a-plenty. The resulting composite companies were instantly nicknamed the Aldershot Mounted Foot. This attitude of healthy irreverence permeated all that went on, behind the formidable wax moustaches of the era. The DSOs awarded to Lord Herbert Montagu-Douglas-Scott and Lord Settrington who served on the staff were instantly christened the 'Dukes' Sons Only'. Rumour, indeed, had it that the delicate shade of St Patrick's blue that Lady Settrington dyed her husband's white Grenadier plume on his transfer to the Irish Guards matched her dainty silken unmentionables.

Meanwhile, the Regiment began to appear in public to the intense interest of the press. Fine men of superb physique, they had good reason to be proud to belong to the most fashionable regiment and one they held to be without question not only the most novel but assuredly the best.

Left: **Field Marshal Frederick Sleigh Earl Roberts of Kandahar, Pretoria and Waterford VC, KG, KP, GCB, GCSI, GCIE.** Lord Roberts was Commander-in-Chief in South Africa. He ordered his ADCs to transfer to the new regiment, both of whom were on the first King's Guard mounted by the Regiment. Lord Roberts was in South Africa when the Regiment was formed, so he was not formally appointed Colonel of the Regiment until 17 October 1900. 'Bobs' (Lord Roberts) was the hero of the hour, his son having been killed earning a posthumous Victoria Cross at Colenso. The news reached Dublin where Lord Roberts was GOC-in-C Irish Command on the same day that he was ordered to proceed to South Africa as Commander-in-Chief. The Irish Guards, as soon as Lord Roberts was appointed Colonel, became affectionately known in his lifetime as 'Bobs' Own'.

Right: **The Original Recruiting Poster.** Note the public recognition of the bravery of the Irish Regiments.

Below: **'My Brave Irish'** – The Irish Fusiliers in South Africa, by Caton Woodville.

Right: **Capt Hubert Francis Crichton**, Adjutant. 19 May 1900–31 Dec 1901, formerly Grenadier Guards. Served under Kitchener at Khartoum, and was ADC to General Sir John French before the Great War. (Died of wounds received at Villers-Cotterets, 1 Sep 1914).

Above: **Six early recruits.** Note the Broderick cap did not carry a cap star, nor was a belt worn in undress uniform.

Left: **Her Majesty's Irish Guards.** A picture of the newly formed Foot Guards Regiment arriving at Chelsea Barracks was reported in the *Illustrated London News* on 29 December 1900.

Ptes White and Jordan, Pirbright 1900. Note the old stand at ease position, and the fact that no regimental buckles have yet been produced for the waist belts, so the universal royal crest pattern is in use. What was called the Slade Wallace buff equipment remained for ceremonial use until the outbreak of war in 1939.

Colonel V.J. Dawson CVO, first Regimental Lieutenant-Colonel, formerly Coldstream Guards (3 Sep 1900–2 Sep 1905). Generations of his family had served in the Foot Guards since the Peninsular War. As a young man he lived at 16 Charles Street, Mayfair, later to become the Guards Club. He served in the Guards Camel Regiment in the Nile expedition in 1884 and left splendid photographs of that time. He had been Commanding Officer of the newly raised 3rd Battalion Coldstream Guards, so was ideally suited to the appointment as first Regimental Lieutenant-Colonel. He was very well known in both Ireland and England and was a personal friend of The King. The caption to a picture of him in the Cavalry and Guards Club states '*He was never known to have left a party early.*'

Above: **Queen Victoria's Funeral.** On 4 February 1901 the Irish Guards marching detachment at Paddington Station. Note the carriage of arms reversed, and the Slade Wallace equipment. For this occasion the Regiment produced its first ever detachment of street liners.

Above: **First Superintendent Clerk at Regimental Headquarters Serjeant Major Dean.** Note that he wears the crown as a badge of rank (Warrant Officer Class II was not introduced until 1914).

Right: **Coronation King Edward VII.** On 2 August 2002, the Battalion provided a Guard of Honour outside Westminster Abbey for the Coronation of King Edward VII. Positioned left of the Royal Navy guard, it was Commanded by Captain T W Wingfield, the Subaltern was Lt Hon M Wingfield and the Ensign 2/Lt Lord A J Hamilton.

The first King's Guard furnished by His Majesty's new regiment of Irish Guards from Chelsea Barracks, Sunday 3 March 1901. When this photograph was taken the war was still in progress in South Africa and medals had not yet been presented nor had the Regiment's Colours. Opinions, then as now, differed on the success of the Guard, one commentator saying: 'The men presented a motley appearance as the uniforms were by no means complete, and certain items of ceremonial equipment were still awaiting issue.'

Officers and Serjeants of the first King's Guard. *Seated L-R:* Capt H.F. Crichton (formerly Grenadier Guards' Adjutant). (Note a Captain then wore two stars.) Lt Lord Herbert Montagu-Douglas-Scott (Lieutenants wore one star) and Lt Lord Settrington (missing in action 13 Apr 1918); Major G.C. Nugent (formerly Grenadier Guards, killed as Major-General, 31 May 1915); 2/Lt W. Brookes, Ensign with no colour belt, and no badge of rank as was the custom for ensigns (killed 7 Oct 1914); and 2/Lt Lord Kingston (wounded 1 Nov 1914). *Standing:* RSM C.A. Burt; C/Sjt Loughran; Sjt Brennan; Sjt Roberts; L/Sjt Brown; D/Sjt Baylis (a Colour Serjeant, wearing a Warrant Officer's tunic).

On 1 March 1900 it had been authorised, as a mark of appreciation of the great gallantry of the Irish Regiments in South Africa, that the Shamrock might be worn on St Patrick's Day, 17 March, each year.

A fortnight after the Regiment's first Guard, on St Patrick's Day 1901, the Battalion was formed up in Chelsea Barracks having just returned from church where they had worn the Shamrock just presented by the Regiment. An orderly from the Palace marched up to the Commanding Officer, Lt-Col R.J. Cooper MVO, bearing a number of boxes. These contained Shamrock, a present from Queen Alexandra herself to the new regiment. Immediately the previous Shamrock was replaced by the royal gift. So commenced an especially treasured tradition which sets the seal on the St Patrick's Day parade which each year repeats its own unique brand of intimacy and informal formality – and not a little poignancy.

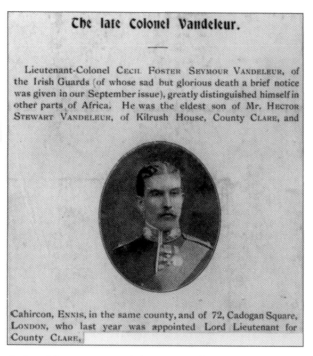

The late Colonel Vandeleur.

Lieutenant-Colonel CECIL FOSTER SEYMOUR VANDELEUR, of the Irish Guards (of whose sad but glorious death a brief notice was given in our September issue), greatly distinguished himself in other parts of Africa. He was the eldest son of Mr. HECTOR STEWART VANDELEUR, of Kilrush House, County CLARE, and

Cahircon, ENNIS, in the same county, and of 72, Cadogan Square, LONDON, who last year was appointed Lord Lieutenant for County CLARE,

Colonel Seymour Vandeleur DSO, formerly Scots Guards, killed in south Africa.

1st Company Guards Mounted Infantry; Irish Guards contingent. Here the Irish Guards contingent in tunics, medals, Broderick caps (with stars) and khaki breeches with puttees, and leather bandoliers pose at Aldershot with Lord Herbert Scott and Major (later General Sir Alexander) Godley. The latter was Baden-Powell's right hand man at the siege of Mafeking, where Captain (later Brigadier General) E.C. FitzClarence won the Victoria Cross.

No 1 Guards Mounted Infantry Company, in South Africa.

Officers of the Guards Mounted Infantry Companies left for South Africa in November 1901. *L-R:* Lt B.G. Van de Wever Scots Guards, 2/Lt J.H.J. Phillips Coldstream Guards, Lt the Hon C.M.B. Ponsonby, Lt H.F. Ward Irish Guards and Capt J. Ponsonby Coldstream Guards. The head dress, uniquely, incorporated the coloured band worn on the soldiers' Broderick and forage caps.

Above: **St Patrick's Day, Tower of London, 1902.** The first occasion when the newly approved Regimental marches were played on St Patrick's Day. After the parade things became more informal. Here the Bigophone Band pose for the camera that afternoon.

Left: **The first Regimental Serjeant Major,** C.A. Burt, photographed at the Tower of London. Serjeant Major Burt transferred to the Regiment from the Scots Guards. He had served in Ashanti and South Africa.

Tower of London 1902. One of the first group photographs of the officers of the 1st Battalion. Of the 28 Officers present 10 were to be killed in action in the Great War in the next decade. *Back row L to R*: Lt Sir M G Crofton Bt, Lt Hon C M P Brabazon, Lt H E Earl of Kingston, Lt Faskally, Lt Hon L J P Butler, Lt Hon J F Trefusis★, Lt I R Viscount de Vesci. *Centre*: Lt C A Tisdall★, Capt R C A McCalmont, Capt W E Lord Oxmanton, Lt G Brooke★, Capt G H C Madden★, Capt J Fowles (QM), Capt R P D S Chichester, Lt Lord A J Hamilton★, Lt Sir S Hill-Child Bt, Lt M I Viscount Powerscourt. *Front*: Lt C H Lord Settrington★, Capt H W E Earl of Kerry, Maj A J Godley, Maj G C Nugent★, Col V J 'Vesey' Dawson, Lt Col R J Cooper, Maj D J Proby, Maj F Stopford, Maj C FitzClarence VC★, Capt H A Herbert-Stepney★

★ – Killed-in-Action in Great War.

Above: **Battalion football team.** Lt-Col R.J. Cooper MVO, the first Commanding Officer, at the Tower of London, 1902. Lt-Col Cooper, from Coolooney, Co. Sligo, served with 2nd Battalion Grenadier Guards in the Egyptian War of 1882. Note the shin pads. Where is the eleventh player?

Below: **Warrant Officer and Staff Serjeants, Tower of London 1902.** Capt Crichton and Serjeant Major Burt are flanked by the Battalion staff (hence the expression Staff Serjeant). They carry a staff cane bearing the regimental insignia.

Above: **The first Bandmaster 1902,** Bandmaster C.H. Hassel, before Directors of Music were introduced. Chosen from over one hundred applicants, he had enlisted at the age of 12 into the old 95th Foot (2nd Battalion The Sherwood Foresters), and then became Bandmaster 4th Battalion The King's Royal Rifle Corps. Promoted Director of Music in 1919, Capt Hassel retired in March 1929, and was awarded the OBE. Over sixty years later, Bandsmen in the Foot Guards were, at the request of Lt-Col 'Jigs' Jaeger, re-styled formally as Musicians.

Above: **The Regimental Band in 1902,** 43 strong. Photographed at Wellington Barracks.

Right: **Coronation Medal.** The commemorative medal issued in 1902 for the coronation of King Edward VII and Queen Alexandra. The military version was only issued to those involved with the coronation.

Below: **Painting of the distribution of South African War Medals on Horse Guards Parade.** Queen Alexandra (who had previously presented the Shamrock for the first time that spring) can be seen on The King's right, in Full Court Mourning after the death of Queen Victoria. (Royal Archives. By gracious permission of HM The Queen)

Muster Roll, incorrectly gives a battle honour for South Africa. Produced after the presentation of colours and probably after 4 Oct 1902 when the Mounted Infantry returned. The draughtsman was ex-Sjt Hicks, a Grenadier Crimean veteran.

Above: **Battalion Swimming Team, Chelsea Barracks, c. 1903.** Capt R.C.A. McCalmont (Adjutant 1 Jan 1904–31 Dec 1906, left, with polished boots and frock coat). Standing second from right: 552 C/Sjt Arthur Munns DCM, (killed 1st Ypres, 17 Nov 1914). Standing, right, in uniform, Serjeant Major Baylis.

Opposite Top: **Change of Quarters,** approaching Aldershot from Farnborough. Until the Second World War, Battalions in England changed barrack location every year, and generally did so by marching to the next destination. Note full Change of Quarter Order, including black leather anklets.

Opposite Bottom: **Settling in.** 1st Battalion Irish Guards having just arrived at Oudenarde Barracks, Aldershot. QM Fowles on the square with sheaf of papers.

IRISH GUARDS

Brian Boru and Handler (photographed at Aldershot in 1906). *The Military Mail* reported in May 1902: 'The Irish Wolfhound Club has recently offered to make the Irish Guards a novel and appropriate presentation in the shape of a young Irish wolfhound as a regimental pet.'

Brian Boru painted by Heywood Hardy, one of a collection of portraits of wolfhounds which hang in the Officers' Mess.

Battalion Tug of War Team, Aldershot, c. 1903. Left in plain clothes Major G.C. Nugent (Commanding Officer 1st Battalion 1908, Regimental Lieutenant Colonel 1909, killed 1915 commanding 5 London Brigade). Centre D/Sjt Hudson DCM (wearing no belt or sword), who won his medal in South Africa with the Mounted Infantry, the Regiment's first decoration, and a bar to his DCM when serving with the Irish Fusiliers at Salonika in the Great War.

Barrack Room, Christmas 1903, Oudenarde Barracks, Aldershot. Whilst at Aldershot the Battalion was under command of the GOC Aldershot, Lt General Sir Horace Lockwood Smith-Dorrien, whose name every man had to know. In addition to his later fame in the Great War, this officer had the distinction of being one of the very few survivors from the Zulu massacre at Isandlwana in 1879, at the time of Rorke's Drift.

No 8 Company's Barrack Room, Oudenarde Barracks, Aldershot, 1904. The trestle tables are ready for a meal, since no mess room had been introduced and meals were collected from the cook house (hence 'come to the cook house door boys'). Beneath each folded bed is at least one soldier's box. The slouch hats are the equivalent of today's combat cap. The small blue plume worn in these hats was later adopted as the pipers' hackle.

St Patrick's Day, Aldershot 1906. Shamrock is being distributed round the companies of the Battalion which are drawn up in mass.

Officers' Mess Cart on manoeuvres, 1906.

In 1906 the Army at Home undertook major manoeuvres. As part of this activity the Irish Guards were involved in a complicated amphibious landing at Southend. Here No 8 Company complete with slouch hats and Slade Wallace equipment goes ashore from lighters.

Pay Sjts 1st Battalion Aldershot, 1906. Each company had a Pay Serjeant, who would now be the CQMS. The Colour Serjeant was the equivalent of the Company Serjeant Major. Silver topped Malacca canes were carried by senior ranks.

The Colours, 1910.
Left: Pte FitzGerald.
Centre: D/Sjt Bracken.
Right: Pte Gilliland.
The Regimental Colour on the right carries the No I Company badge. Originally intended to bear the Royal Cypher, the design VR was submitted to King Edward VII, who wanted his cypher included as well.

Above: **Field Marshal Lord Roberts, first Colonel of the Irish Guards,** mounted at Buckingham Palace for The King's Birthday parade 1913. This photograph was taken specially for personal distribution. Lord Roberts is wearing the sash and star of the Order of St Patrick. His black riding boots are worn outside his overalls as was customary at the time.

Right: **Field Marshal Lord Roberts.** Before the regiment became known as the 'Micks', their nickname was 'Bobs Own' after the Colonel. He died aged 82 in November 1914 visiting the troops in France.

Above: **The Corps of Drums 1911–1912, HM Tower of London.** 34 strong, 8 side drummers (including the boys). *Centre:* Capt & Adjutant The Hon Jack (Hepburn-Scott-) Trefusis (Adjutant 2 Dec 1909–1 Jun 1913) whose letters and war diaries are some of the most vivid ever written.

Right: **Wearing khaki for the first time in London.** An early instance of Military Aid to the Civil Power (MACP). An Irish Guards sentry on duty, complete with bearskin cap, during the railway strike of 1911, at Grosvenor Road railway station.

Presentation of the second stand of Colours, Buckingham Palace, 28 June 1913, by HM King George V.

The King's Colour.

The Regimental Colour.

Boxing Team, 1910–1911, Chelsea Barracks. Capt James Fowles, the first Quartermaster, affectionately known to all as 'Ginger' was an enthusiast in all he did. He was no inconsiderable performer in the ring himself and the real instigator of Army boxing. He also set up the 'Shamrock Minstrel Troupe' which featured large in concerts of the day.

Back Row Standing L-R: Pte Dan 'The Pounder' Voyles, Household Brigade and Army and Navy Heavyweight Champion; Pte Donovan, Light Heavyweight Champion, Household Brigade; Pat O' Keeffe, Instructor and Middleweight Champion of England.
Front Row L-R: Pte P. McEnroy, Finalist Army and Navy Championship; Capt and QM James Fowles; RSM J. Myles; Pte A. Sinclair, Welterweight Champion Household Brigade.

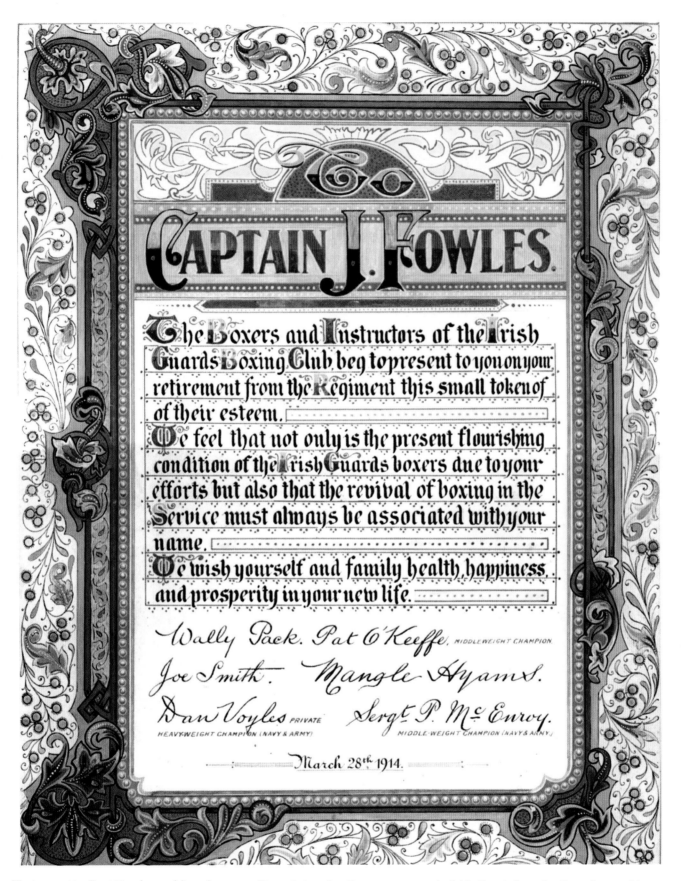

To

CAPTAIN J. FOWLES.

The Boxers and Instructors of the Irish Guards Boxing Club beg to present to you on your retirement from the Regiment this small token of of their esteem.

We feel that not only is the present flourishing condition of the Irish Guards boxers due to your efforts but also that the revival of boxing in the Service must always be associated with your name.

We wish yourself and family health, happiness and prosperity in your new life.

Wally Pack. Pat O'Keeffe, MIDDLEWEIGHT CHAMPION.

Joe Smith.   Mangle Hyams.

Dan Voyles PRIVATE   *Sergt. P. McEnroy.*
HEAVY-WEIGHT CHAMPION (NAVY & ARMY)   MIDDLE-WEIGHT CHAMPION (NAVY & ARMY.)

March 28th 1914.

Testament to Capt Fowles on his retirement. Commissioned as Quartermaster to the Irish Guards from the Grenadiers on 24 May 1900, he nevertheless appeared in his previous role some days later as Regimental Serjeant Major of the 1st Battalion Grenadier Guards providing the Escort to the Colour.

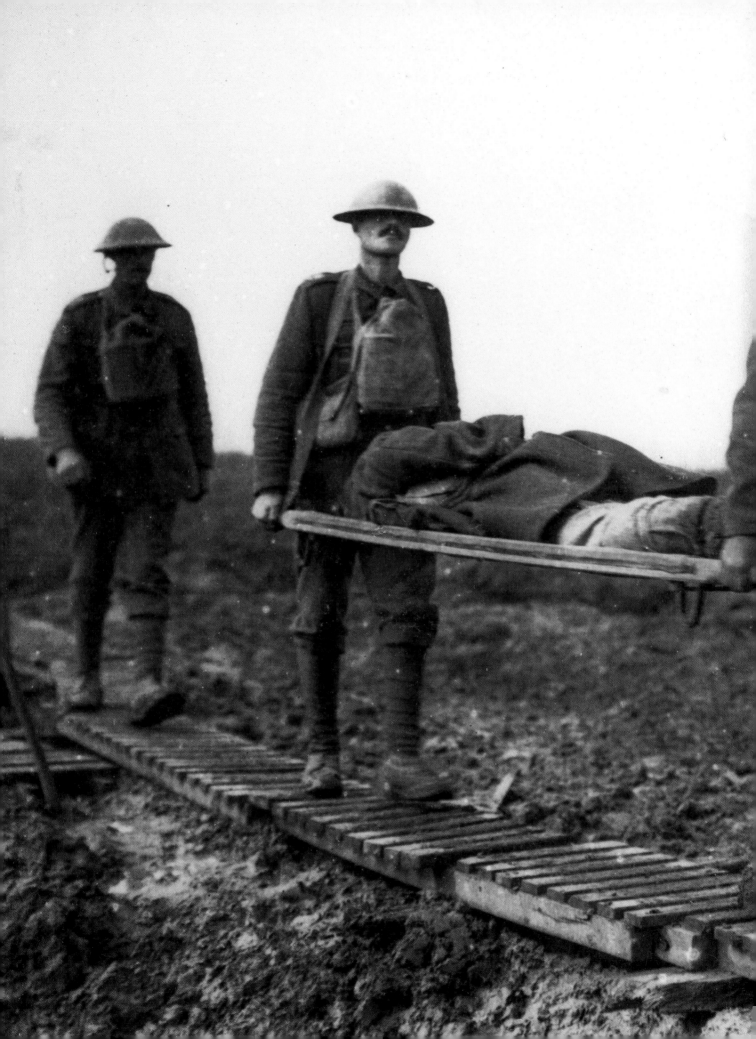

Chapter Two

1914–1918
THE GREAT WAR

War was declared at noon on 4 August 1914. Since dawn that day the boat trains from Ireland had been arriving in London bringing to Wellington Barracks, the home of 1st Battalion Irish Guards, reservists who, anticipating their summons and determined not to miss the "excitement", had boarded the Mail Boats the previous evening. Everyone confidently predicted it would all be over by Christmas.

Four years and three months later, having earned four Victoria Crosses, and after the Regiment had sustained 7,488 casualties (2,349 killed) out of 9,633 all ranks engaged, the 'War to end Wars' came to its exhausted, bloody conclusion. The Victory Medal awarded to each of the survivors was inscribed 'The Great War for Civilisation 1914–1919'.

The Great War brought to an end an era. Its scale (more than four hundred medals for distinguished service or bravery were hard earned by Irish Guardsmen) and the slaughter have engraved images of the savagery and filth of trench warfare in the nation's memory. To remind us, there are, of course, the official accounts, carefully written up after the event. The Regimental Archives is also a priceless source of magnificent photographic cover of much of the Great War. Of the most bloody and tragic parts, however, we only have word pictures in vivid letters and deeply moving dog-eared, smudged, personal trench diaries.

Irish Guards stretcher bearers on duck boards near Ayette/St Leger during the German Offensive, March 1918.

The six stages, as the Regiment saw the Great War, were:

THE FIRST STAGE, 1914. The excitement of mobilization; the long dusty Retreat from Mons to near Paris; confused, fluid fighting in woods; snipers and the first simple trenches; the sacrifice at First Ypres saved the Channel Ports. A sense of newness and unreality.

THE SECOND STAGE, 1915. Hold the line. Stroke and counter stroke in France and Belgium. First use of gas. The Regiment's first Victoria Cross awarded to L/Cpl Michael O'Leary. 2nd Battalion Irish Guards formed 15 July 1915. The Guards Division formed August 1915 under Lord Cavan.

THE THIRD STAGE, 1916. The Somme. The Battle of the Somme was designed to take pressure off the French who were struggling to hold Verdun. In this the British effort succeeded, at huge cost.

THE FOURTH STAGE, 1917. The Hindenburg Line, Passchendaele and Cambrai. The cumulative strain of the Somme and Verdun forced the Germans to withdraw some 15 miles to a prepared defensive line, the Hindenberg Line. The next British offensive was to have been at Arras, but the sudden German withdrawal altered the plans.

Such had been the pressure on the French too, that French mutinies broke out. To give time to restore the French Army, a huge British offensive was rushed ahead, at Ypres. Criticised for being ill-timed on account of the rains, the timing was unavoidable if the French armies were to have a chance to recover. This hideous battle, ever since associated with mud and blood, became known as Passchendale, during which both L/Sjt Moyney and Pte Woodcock won the Victoria Cross.

After Passchendale the Regiment took part in the costly Cambrai offensive which, as so often, had promised so much.

What it remembered was hell in Bourlon Wood.

THE FIFTH STAGE, January–July 1918. The German Offensive. The collapse of Russia in the revolution of 1917 enabled German strength on the Western Front to increase by one third. Sapped by the losses at Passchendale, on the British side every brigade had effectively lost one of its four Battalions, which had not been fully replaced. The Germans broke through, re-capturing every yard of all the Somme gains. An acute crisis developed as the Germans poured through in huge numbers dangerously close to the Channel ports. There were no British reserves. The 2nd Battalion (in 4th Guards Brigade) in an heroic last ditch effort at Hazebrouck, held the German onrush, saved France, and finished off the fighting capability of 4th Guards Brigade for the rest of the War.

THE SIXTH STAGE, July–November 1918. Advance to Victory: Canal du Nord, Hindenburg Line. A British offensive opened on 8 August 1918 and continued to the Armistice. During this phase Lt (Acting Lt-Col) Neville Marshall won a posthumous Victoria Cross whist commanding a Battalion of the Lancashire Fusiliers. The Irish Guards finished at Maubeuge (near Mons, almost where they had started in 1914), arriving on 9 November 1918. Here they heard of the Armistice.

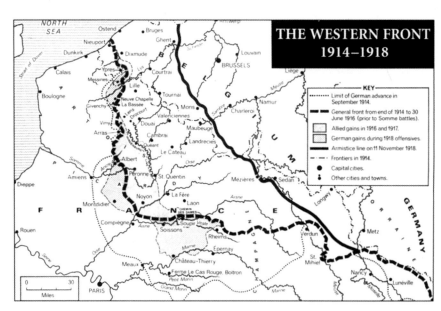

Officers of the 1st Battalion Irish Guards, Wellington Barracks, August 1914, prior to departure for the British Expeditionary Force (BEF), France. *L–R:* Lt the Hon H.G. Hugo Gough (wounded October 1914), 2/Lt E.C. Stafford-King-Harman (killed 6 November 1914 near Ypres), Capt the Hon Tom Vesey (No 3 Company; wounded October 1914), Lt the Hon H.R. Alexander (wounded 1 November 1914) the future Field Marshal, Lt J.S.N, FitzGerald (No 2 Company, twice decorated, served throughout the war without a scratch from August 1914 to 11 November 1918, and then went to Russia). *Seated:* Lt C.A. Walker (No 1 Company).

'Sunday 9 August 1914. Church Parade. In afternoon the Battalion went on a route march – in full war kit (minus ammunition) … marched through Trafalgar Square etc. Crowds cheering the whole time. Halted at Regent's Park, and returned via Hyde Park, Constitution Hill'. Diary of 2587 Pte Kilcoin, a reservist who had just been recalled.

Sjt P. Gallacher marches out like he did in 1914.
Wounded at 1st Ypres in November 1914, he recovered in time to go to France again when the 2nd Battalion went in 1915. He worked in the Shoemaker's Shop, and became the Master Shoemaker.

Irish Guards off to the War, 1914. Here the 1st Battalion Irish Guards (a total of 32 Officers and 1,100 rank and file of which 98 per cent were Irish and 90 per cent Roman Catholic) marches out of the West Gate of Wellington Barracks early on 12 August 1914, heading for Nine Elms Station and Southampton. Each detachment was played off by the Regimental Band, according to Kipling. This photograph bears this out, since the drum is being carried. The Officer is Major H.A. Herbert-Stepney (known in the Regiment as 'Spud') who is leading No 2 Company. When the Commanding Officer and Second in Command both became casualties on 1 September 1914, as the only Major he took temporary command for eighteen hectic days and was killed on 6 November 1914 near Ypres.

Landrecies, 25 August 1914. Scene of 1 Corps and 4th Guards Brigade action '*An unlovely long streeted town in closely cultivated country*' (Kipling). They blockaded the road with '*stones, tables, chairs, carts, pianos*'. One of the drums was later heard going down the main street caught on a galloping horse's hoof. (This is the main street looking south, 1998.)

THE FIRST STAGE, 1914

After the excitement of mobilization and painstaking preparation, 1st Battalion Irish Guards sailed for France and landed at Le Havre. After a long rail journey they arrived at Wassigny, and next morning marched north to head off the anticipated German advance near Mons. No sooner had they approached the Belgian border than it became necessary to withdraw rapidly to conform with the rest of the British Expeditionary Force which was already in danger of being outflanked by the Germans. Thus, unheroically, began the Retreat from Mons (always referred to by veterans as the 'Retirement from Mons'), a most gruelling and testing withdrawal in contact, as much a test of stamina and discipline as anything.

The first serious contact was at Landrecies where a sharp night engagement in the town was followed by further withdrawal.

The day after the Battalion distantly heard what they judged a '*battle in the direction of Le Cateau*' (Kipling), 'Lee Catoo' they called it, but were not involved. The next engagement was a Brigade withdrawal in contact in the beech woods at Villers-Cottérêts on 1 September.

Here, gallantly, 4th Guards Brigade delayed the German advance long enough to prevent the other Division in the Corps from being outflanked. There were grievous casualties, including the Commanding Officer who was killed in the Battalion's first serious action.

The Timber Yard at Wassigny (1998). '*17th August 1914, Arrived at Wassigny (our destination) and detrained in total darkness billeted in a timber yard until daybreak. Had breakfast (bully and biscuits) – Then marched off, destination unknown.*' (Pte Kilcoin's Diary).

Le Murger Farm, near Soucy (31 August 1914). The weary Battalion defended the farm the night before the Villiers-Cottérêts action, but the Germans did not catch up, and they moved off at 2am. The farm, flattened in 1918, has been identically reconstructed and the same family still lives there.

RETREAT FROM MONS

Retreat from Mons, 1914. The woods at Villers-Cottérêts. The Battalion's first serious action was as part of a brigade retirement in contact, with confused and very gallant fighting in the woods. It was imperative to impose delay on the advancing Germans so that the remainder of the exhausted Division could snatch a few hours' rest, and re-group. The Commanding Officer of the 1st Battalion was killed in the first action of the Great War, an event which, cruelly, was repeated in Norway in 1940.

Lt-Col the Hon George Morris, Commanding Officer 1st Battalion Irish Guards. Killed in Action 1 September 1914. Colonel Morris: '*Do you hear that? They are only doing that to frighten you*'. Unknown Private: '*If that's what they're after, Sir, they might as well stop. They succeeded with me hours ago!*' (Kipling). '*We saw him riding up and down, cheering us on, and we only knew he was wounded when we saw the blood coming from his field boot.*' (Recollections of Sjt Gallacher, Master Shoemaker, 1st Battalion).

The Guards Grave at Villers-Cottérêts. Two platoons of Grenadiers fought to the last man, and led by 2/Lt Cecil, with drawn sword, they gave a final bayonet charge. Ninety-three casualties from 4th Guards Brigade (and one other) who fell on 1 September 1914 were buried by the advancing Germans in what eventually became the Guards Grave. Others, including Major Crichton, the Second in Command, are buried elsewhere. Such is the legacy of a fighting withdrawal. Rudyard Kipling, whose son John was trying to join the Irish Guards, helped Lady Violet Cecil in the search for her missing son, and visited the Guards Grave. This, coupled with the disappearance of John at the battle of Loos in 1915, was Rudyard Kipling's inspiration to become a commissioner in the new Imperial War Graves Commission.

MARNE 1914

Ferme La Cas Rouge, Boitron. Battle of the Marne, 8 September 1914. This was the turning point when the German advance from Mons was halted; just east of Paris, and the Allies began the advance northwards towards the Aisne where 1st Battalion Irish Guards crossed by pontoon on 13 September 1914. The 1st Battalion spent the night in this farm after the fighting in the Boitron woods where they captured 90 German prisoners, and 6 machine-guns. They parolled the German officers and invited them to dine on chicken and red wine. The farm, undamaged in either war, remains in the hands of the same family to this day.

Fighting in the woods at Soupir. Heywood Hardy's painting shows the officers wearing their caps backwards to conceal the gold peak from snipers.

AISNE 1914

The Aisne. Le Cour de Soupir Farm. The Connaught Rangers handed over to 1st Battalion Irish Guards (15 September 1914) and 4th Guards Brigade at Le Cour de Soupir Farm. Lt Greer's machine-gun section was lost, and here, crucially, began real trench warfare. As one private put it: '*We was like fleas in a blanket seeing no more than the next nearest wrinkle*' (Kipling). Here too, Lt Hugo Gough, later a celebrated one armed Commanding Officer of the Reserve Battalion in the Second World War, lost his arm. '*The heavily wooded country was alive with musketry and machine-gun fire, and the distances were obscured by mist and heavy rain.*' (Kipling).

Soupir. Capt The Hon Tom Vesey sent his daughter a postcard from Soupir, and marked the places of interest. Situated just behind the Allied line throughout the 1914–18 war, the village was extensively damaged, The Château was destroyed, but the church beside which Tom Vesey had his 'billet' survived.

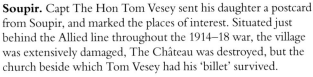

Left: **Aisne. Soupir Village and Woods.** September–October 1914. In these woods which form the slopes of the high Chemin des Dames were fought numerous actions by 4th Guards Brigade. The area became a long term battleground until 1918. Soupir Village today still has its church, and the gates of the Château where they acquired illicit eggs. At the time everybody was familiar with Soupir from the press because of a sensation earlier in the summer when the owner of the Château, imagining herself scandalously libelled by a Paris newspaper, had confronted the editor in his office, produced a pistol from her handbag, and shot him. The case was coming to trial when war broke out, and all were curious to know what happened. The lady was gone by the time they arrived, and other things took their attention … (Reminiscences of Sjt Gallacher, Royal Hospital, 1981)

Above: **Irish Guards Graves at Soupir.** Lord Arthur Hay, Capt Hamilton Berners, and Lord Guernsey, all killed 14 September 1914.

Above Right: **Lt Eric Greer and one of his Maxim gun sections,** August 1914. At Soupir on 14 September 1914 '*A party of Coldstream found some 150 Germans sitting round haystacks and waving white flags. They went forward to take their surrender and were met by heavy fire at 30 yards range, Lt E.B. Greer, machine-gun officer, now brought up his two machine-guns, but was heavily fired on from cover, had all of one gun team killed or wounded and, for a while, lost one gun. He re-organised the other gun team and called for volunteers from the company nearest him to recover it*' (Kipling).

The modern Service Dress cap worn by officers resulted from the German snipers in the Soupir woods. Up to then officers in the Foot Guards wore gold peaked khaki caps with a black band, clearly different from the khaki caps worn by Other Ranks as seen above.

After the bitter fighting on the Aisne, at Soupir in the Irish Guards' case, the British Army moved hastily north to prevent the Germans reaching the sea on the Belgian coast. The 1st Battalion was closely engaged in this critical battle, eventually serving in the remains of 1st Guards Brigade, which had only recently been taken over by Brigadier General Charles FitzClarence vc, their former Regimental Lieutenant Colonel. He was killed and has no known grave.

The situation was so critical that the Adjutant was sent off to Brigade Headquarters to get help. It arrived – eventually. The perilously thin line was still holding out but had suffered terrible casualties, including the Commanding Officer, Lord Ardee, wounded. On 2 November they re-organised into three under-strength companies. On the 7th they lost another Commanding Officer, Major Herbert Stepney. On the 8th they reformed into two small companies. On the 9th they could muster only four platoons. On the 18th, after further losses, they were pulled back for the last time. They were relieved by a company of 3rd Coldstream – and one company sufficed. They had entered the battle over a thousand strong. Eventually eight officers and 390 men recovered. It was so cold the water froze in their water bottles. 'Not a man fell out'.

The 1st Battalion Irish Guards' losses were close on a thousand all ranks killed, wounded or missing. The Battalion had been practically wiped out, partially rebuilt and nearly wiped out again. The remnants were exhausted in mind and body; only their morale and irrepressible humour kept them going.

The famous Christmas Truce of 1914 did not affect the much depleted Battalion. They were in the 'wet dreary' trenches, two hundred yards from the Germans, under occasional heavy bombardment. Two officers and six men were wounded on Christmas Day.

Brigadier General Charles FitzClarence VC at his Brigade Headquarters, France, September 1914.

Royal Irish Constabulary Office,

Dublin Castle,

24th. November, 1914.

Sir,

I have the honour to inform you that, as the result of representations recently made by me, the Government have approved of 200 Constables of the Royal Irish Constabulary being permitted to enlist in the Irish Guards for the period of the war.   From a large number of Volunteers I have selected 200 men who are between the ages of 20 and 35, who are unmarried and are recommended by their officers as being suitable as regards physique, health, intelligence character etc.

Provision is being made, with the sanction of the Treasury, to grant these men privileges as regards the counting of Army service for the purposes of pay and pension on the lines of those conferred on Reservists by the Irish Police Constables (Naval and Military Service) Act, 1914.

I shall be glad to hear from you regarding the following points :-

1. Should the men enlist at the Recruiting Office, Gt. Brunswick Street, Dublin, specially for the Irish Guards, and, if so, will you communicate direct with the Recruiting Officer on this point and also arrange with him to issue passes for each man to proceed to the Regimental Depot at Warley, Brentford, Essex?

2. I presume the men should wear their own plain clothes when en route to Warley and that they will receive instructions from the Recruiting Officer, Dublin, as to whom they should report themselves at Warley ?

3. Will you kindly inform me whether it will be more convenient for you if the men enlist in batches of 50 and proceed to join the Regiment ?   If so, could you draw out a table showing the dates on which the batches of 50 should present themselves for enlistment in Dublin ?

I have the honour to be,
Sir,
Your obedient Servant,

Neville Chamberlain.

Inspector General.

Above: **Warley** 1914, 2/Lts Vivyan Harmsworth (wounded November 1917, MC) and John Kipling (missing Loos, 1915) joined on 15 August 1914 in car, barrack square, Warley.

Irish Guards beat back with Bayonets a German Cavalry Charge

Above: **Fighting on the Marne.** It was reported in *War Illustrated* in October 1914 that the Irish Guards fought off three regiments of German Cavalry on the Marne, '*They threw back at bayonet's point, in utter demoralisation, the Kaiser's horsemen*' it was reported. Nothing loses in the telling.

Below: **Volunteers of the Royal Irish Constabulary** ('*large drilled men, who were to play so solid a part in the history and glory of the Battalion*') who arrived during Neuve Chapelle, following the correspondence between the Regiment and Neville Chamberlain, Inspector General of the Royal Irish Constabulary. Two hundred had been proposed, hundreds more volunteered.

The Germans who had so nearly captured Ypres in November 1914 needed a pause to consolidate. That pause saved the Regiment. So rapidly were the new drafts made available for the 1st Battalion, it spent little time out of action. 'Airoplane Duty' was introduced in the trenches. Freezing men were issued with woollen cardigan waistcoats, and every man received a goatskin coat. Duckboards, too, an omen of things to come, joined improvised jam tin grenades as the novelties of the season. The 1st Battalion took a supporting part in the offensive mounted by the Indian Division near Cuinchy, where there had been brick factories (an indication of the clay in the soil). Stacks of bricks stood waiting to be taken away, when war arrived. Here L/Cpl Michael O'Leary suddenly leapt to international fame when he won Ireland's first Victoria Cross of the war. His fearless dash, which captured a German machine-gun post, and dispatched several other 'Huns', somehow encapsulated all the virtues upon which the regiment prided itself.

Father Gwynne in the trenches early 1915. *L-R:* Sjt McEnroy, Sjt Bennet and Rev Fr Gwynne. Of Father John Gwynne they said: '*He was not merely a chaplain, but a man unusually beloved. He feared nothing, despised no one, betrayed no confidence and comforted every man within his reach.*' He was killed on 1 November 1915 when the HQ dugout was hit. Yet another Commanding Officer, Lt-Col Gerald Madden, was mortally wounded. In the first fifteen months of the Great War 1st Battalion Irish Guards lost five Commanding Officers, of whom four were killed and one was wounded.

Father Gwynne, Capt McCarthy, the Battalion's superb Medical Officer, and 2/Lt Straker examine an unexploded German shell. Straker arrived in the Battalion in time for 1st Ypres, as the new Machine-Gun Officer. He was seriously wounded in April 1915.

'Sleep is sweet, Undisturbed it is divine.' This is reputedly 2858 Pte (later L/Cpl) Green MM.

By March 1915 the jam tin grenade had become obsolete, succeeded by the 'stick grenade of the hairbrush type'. The Mills bomb was not introduced until the autumn of 1915.

Service dress caps, incredibly, were still the normal headdress even in the trenches, until the number of head wounds eventually forced the introduction, in late 1915, of the steel helmet. A 1915 letter to Regimental Headquarters in London thanks for sausages, and asks the Regimental Adjutant to contact George Potter, the Aldershot musical instrument supplier, explaining that the next lot of flutes for the Corps of Drums should be made of seasoned wood; the last consignment had warped in the damp conditions in France. And please to send some more electric cells (batteries) for the electric torches (the Regiment priding itself on being the first to have bought some of these convenient new inventions).

Re-invigorated, the Germans opened the Second Battle of Ypres on 27 April 1915. This coincided with a British attack in the Neuve Chapelle area, the purpose of which was to capture the important Aubers Ridge. The 1st Battalion took part in the offensive in the Festubert Sector, and in a ten-day battle some six hundred yards were gained, but the breakthrough never came. In the attack on La Cour L'Avoue Farm Irish Guards losses were 18 Officers and 461 Other Ranks on 15 May 1915.

The Guards Division was formed in the summer of 1915 and the two Irish Guards Battalions, meeting for the first time, eyed each other with interest. Loos (in the flat coal mining district south of the La Bassée Canal) was the last major offensive of the year in late September 1915. It was the 2nd Battalion's baptism. Like so many other battles, Loos ended tragically and at great cost. It was also the first action of the newly created 1st Battalion Welsh Guards. 'Sleep is sweet, Undisturbed it is divine, So lift up your feet and do not tread on mine.' So read the commanding officer one night, on finding a man deeply asleep with his feet protruding into the fairway. He made no comment, but it was remembered with affection. Despite the horrors the battalions took life with a philosophical calm.

Those who fought in the period from 15 August to 22 November 1914 were awarded the 1914 Star (known as the Mons Star), with a clasp showing those dates. The ribbon bore a silver rosette. The 1914 Star covered all engagements up to the end of the First Battle of Ypres.

Those who fought during the period 5 August 1914 to 31 December 1915, but who had not qualified for the 1914 Star (i.e. those who had been UNDER FIRE in France or Belgium between August and November 1914 within specified dates), were awarded the 1914–15 Star which looks almost identical, but has no clasp on the ribbon (nor rosette), and which bears a single scroll in the centre giving the dates: 1914–15. The clasp worn on the 1914 star, and the rosette on the ribbon, were disparagingly referred to by Gallipoli veterans and many of the arrivals after late 1915 who went to the horrors of the Somme, Passchendaele and subsequent battles as the 'Runners' medal.

The 1914 Star.

THE SECOND STAGE, 1915. Hold the Line

Within the lines life assumed a fearful monotony, but punctuated by moments of sheer terror. From time to time they went over the top – 'popped the parapet', they called it. The technique was the same; before zero hour – or what a German once inappropriately called 'love' hour – the barrage started. Designed to cut the enemy wire on some selected piece of ground, it was of ferocious intensity. Then came the charge, when one machine-gun against you was worth a platoon, and three a company; the consolidation phase awaiting the inevitable counter-attack and, finally, the agonising roll-call.

In these attacks a man's world was the shell-wracked horizon some few yards ahead. Under these conditions comradeship could help you carry on, but it was the discipline that got you started and kept you going. And hanging over everything was that awful pretence of not being afraid.

And it was here or hereabouts that people started to talk of 'The Guards Way', as a benchmark for perfection in all matters military, a message that pervaded the Army through the enormous number of men who rose in the ranks of the Brigade and then were commissioned in other regiments.

The brick stacks at Cuinchy under fire. This is where L/Cpl O'Leary won his Victoria Cross, February 1915. (For full citation see p. 283.)

L/Cpl Michael O'Leary VC. Lady Butler painted a romanticised portrait of the first Irish Guards VC.

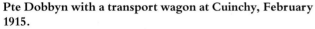

Pte Dobbyn with a transport wagon at Cuinchy, February 1915.

Meanwhile, at Warley, the training for war continued apace.

Above: **Bayonet fighting competition.** Training in the 2nd Battalion at Warley continued with the aim of it becoming a Service Battalion. The bayonet fighting competition, judged by the Earl of Kerry, was an example. 'Points were awarded for speed, and for getting the bayonet through a card on the sacks.'

Left: **Mop fighting competition, St Patrick's Day,** 1915. Training and inculcating regimental spirit went on with the 2nd (Reserve) Battalion at Warley.

The discomforts of a young Officer's life in the early trenches. Vivyan Harmsworth arrived in France with a draft from Warley on 28 November 1914, just after the Battalion had been severely battered at First Ypres. Here he is shortly after arrival, not at all comfortable in Service Dress.

'Irish Guards Resting', Neuve Chapelle, March 1915. Near Aubers Ridge and La Bassée, the Battalion was involved in open attacks from inferior trenches taken over from 6th Brigade. The first very welcome ex-RIC draft arrived during Neuve Chapelle.

Recruits at Warley. As the casualties mounted in 1915 and the army expanded rapidly, equipment became scarce. Hence the RIC man wears his RIC uniform, and shoulder stars are used instead of cap stars.

Sniper's rifle and Pte Connor DCM, April 1915, shortly before the first German chlorine gas attack during the Second Battle of Ypres. Casualties from small arms fire had been increasing because of the sodden state of the parapet. On 10 January 1915 Lt The Earl of Kingston set up a 'telescopic-sighted' rifle. D/Sjt Bracken 'certainly' accounted for three killed and four wounded of the enemy. The War Diary, as Kipling puts it, '*mercifully blind to the dreadful years to come*' thinks '*… There should be many of these rifles used so long as the Army is sitting in trenches.*' Many of them were, and (nowadays) are so used, and this, the father of them all, is in the Guards Museum.

Machine-gun Section 2nd Battalion Irish Guards, Warley, June 1915. *Standing: Back row second from left:* Pte Legiar. *Right hand man standing on the ground:* Pte Gallagher. *Seated L-R:* Unidentified L/Cpl, Sjt Major Price, Capt Hon Tom Vesey (First Adjutant of 2nd Battalion, recovered from his wound at Soupir).

Lord Kitchener's Inspection of 2nd Battalion Irish Guards (now a Service Battalion), 13 August 1915. He expressed his belief they would be a credit to the Guards Division then being formed in France. To the Regiment's delight, the Earl of Cavan (an Irishman who was a Grenadier), who had commanded 4th Guards Brigade, assumed command of the new Guards Division. He later became the fourth Colonel of the Irish Guards.

A Moment of Drama, 1 August 1915. Field Marshal Lord Kitchener's visit to 2nd and 3rd (Reserve) Battalions at Warley before the Second Battalion went to France to join the new Guards Division. In this photograph the new Colonel of the Regiment, Field Marshal Lord Kitchener (a former Sapper) looks annoyed. We now know that Lt John Kipling (known as 'the Joker') had just commented, too loudly, on a grease spot on the top of Kitchener's white cap cover. 'Anybody can see he is not a Guardsman.' Lord Kitchener, unfortunately, heard these words just as the photographer said 'Smile, please, Gentlemen …' and the moment was captured for posterity. The witnesses were Messrs Rupert Grayson and Langrishe, each of whom also heard the remark.

4th Guards Brigade leaving 2nd Division for the newly formed Guards Division in which it became 1st Guards Brigade. No 4 Coy 1st Battalion, Capt Sidney FitzGerald. Pipers visible, Lt-Col G.H.C. Madden (whose son and grandson both served in the Regiment in their generations) had taken over from Lt-Col Jack Trefusis DSO (promoted Temp. Brigadier General) the previous day. This was the day 2nd Battalion left Warley for France.

1914–15 Star.

2nd Battalion Irish Guards leaving Warley for France, 1915 under command of Lt-Col The Hon L. Butler. A family regiment. The lady carrying a child is Mrs Young, wife of Capt G.E.S. Young. The baby, later Brigadier H.L.S. (Savill) Young, won the DSO with the 1st Battalion at Anzio, and his son, too, served in the Regiment in the 1960s.

Above: **Lord Desmond FitzGerald in a shell hole,** probably taken at the Battle of Loos, September 1915. An imperturbable Adjutant, much loved, he was tragically killed in a grenade accident when training on the new Mills Bomb on the sands of Calais in March 1916.

Above: **John Kipling.** This popular, short-sighted officer was missing at Loos. Like so many others, his parents never recovered. His grave was finally identified in 1992.

Left: **Laventie,** 1915. The young officer walking in front of CSM Rankin later became Field Marshal Alex and wears the newly introduced service dress cap. At this stage the two Battalions were together in the trenches between November 1915 and February 1916.

In the trenches, Loos, 1915. After the battle, the two Battalions remained in the trenches and held the section near the Hohenzollern Redoubt 'where they had many bombing encounters with the enemy' (T.H.H. Grayson).

LOOS

Right: **Trench visitors book:** An entry by the future Field Marshal.

'*The worst of this war is not bullets or shells, but the absence of female society that tells.*'

H Alexander.

Later Field Marshal. In later years he became an excellent artist.

Above: **Rev Father S. Knapp,** Battalion priest to both the 1st and 2nd Battalions. After the death of the gallant Father Gwynne, Father Knapp spoke to both Battalions. '*Those that survived that heard it say it moved all men's hearts. Mass always preceded the day's work in billets, but even on the first morning on their return from the trenches the men would make shift somehow to clean their hands and faces, and if possible to shave, before attending it, no matter what the hour*' (Kipling). The Regimental Priest holds a treasured place in the annals of the Irish Guards. Friend to all ranks, he was also an indispensable sounding board of the mood of the Battalion to the Commanding Officer.

In December 1915 Field Marshal Sir John French, later to become the third Colonel of the Regiment, was succeeded by Field Marshal Sir Douglas Haig as Commander-in-Chief of the British Expeditionary Force.

St Patrick's Day at Warley 1916.
When the 2nd Battalion went to France in 1915, the 3rd (Reserve) Battalion was formed at Warley. HM Queen Mary distributes Queen Alexandra's shamrock, watched by HM King George V. John Redmond MP (top hat), whose son was serving, gave the first set of pipes to the Regiment. He was leader of the Irish Party in the Commons. Field Marshal Lord Kitchener, on Queen Alexandra's right, had become the Second Colonel of the Regiment on the death of Lord Roberts in November 1914. He was later drowned in HMS *Hampshire* on 5 June 1916. The Regimental Lieutenant Colonel, Col D J Proby, looks on.

THE AFFAIR OF GINCHY.

Below: **Ginchy Ridge.** To the observer just another piece of undistinguished and indistinguishable landscape in a muddy, bloody world. But to those who took part a very special Hell. And that day the 'creepy-crawlies', the tanks, made their first, and inauspicious, appearance.

Above: **Irish Guards in Prayer before Battle** (Caton Woodville). *'Shortly before dawn on 15 September 1916, Fr Browne of the 1st Battalion came forward and collected half companies or groups of men as he could find them. Together they knelt on the shell churned ground, Protestant and Catholic, bare headed, their rifles with bayonets fixed by their sides while the small seemingly insignificant figure of the priest gave them Absolution. This simple scene seemed somehow to throw into relief the squalor and the filth, the glory and the sacrifice which was their war.'* (Kipling)

THE THIRD STAGE, 1916, The Somme

The Guards Division attacked with two brigades abreast each of four waves no more than fifty yards apart to take advantage of the massive artillery barrage, a guarantee of confusion should a leading wave be held up. To their right lay the Quadrilateral, a formidable German fortification. As was apt to happen, the attacking troops edged away from the point of most resistance thus the right-hand brigade found themselves advancing north rather than north-east and across the front of the other brigade. Soon the whole division had merged into an indescribable confusion of all lines and all regiments. But, as the chronicle records with feeling and not a little pride – 'The discipline held.'

An Irish Guards casualty at Ginchy is helped by Grenadier stretcher bearers during the assault on Ginchy Ridge, 15 September 1916.

Somme. Village of Ginchy, 1916.

It was a time of heroics and great bravery, much of it unnoticed and unsung. Here Lt-Col J.V. Campbell of the Coldstream Guards won the Victoria Cross for rallying remnants of his own Battalion and a remarkable mix of strays of all sorts (with a silver hunting horn).

At Ginchy and in the ensuing fourteen days the two Battalions of Irish Guards lost over one thousand men.

Guards Division Memorial, Les Boeufs, near Ginchy.

Silk Postcards. The women of Northern France were known for silk weaving and embroidery so they adapted their skills to make woven regimental postcards for the troops. Using a hand loom, they made 25 cards to a 75 inch strip of muslin. They were sold for five shillings, a days pay for a JNCO, which made them too expensive to buy for most allies.

Village of Ginchy, 1998. German shells, ploughed up recently. The iron harvest.

Main road through Guillemont. After the Guards Division battle of 15 September 1916.

Back at Warley and the Guards Depot at Caterham, '*Yes, We made 'em – with the rheumatism on us and all; and we kept on making 'em till I got to hate the silly faces of 'em. And what did we get out of it? "Tell Warley that their last draft was damn rabbits and the Ensigns as bad." And after that, it's Military Crosses and DCMs for our damn rabbits.*' (Kipling)

Leitrim Boy receives his Shamrock, St Patrick's Day 1917. Drum Major Fitzgerald looks on as Master Vickers places the Shamrock on Leitrim Boy's collar, which is held by Drummer Titman. The Pipers' (shown here are the 3rd Reserve Battalion, Warley) shoes have no buckles because when the first pipes were presented by John Redmond MP, the Master Shoemaker cut down the second pair of boots of the two pipers, and made the long tongues from the upper which he had removed. He could scrounge no suitable buckles, so to this day Irish Guards Pipers do not wear buckles. (Reminiscences of Sjt Gallacher, Royal Hospital)

Communication trench and grave, west of Ginchy-Flers road. '*German shells bursting in our lines.*'

CSM Toher receives the Military Medal for Bravery in the Field from Lord French who had succeeded Lord Kitchener as Colonel (at Warley on St Patrick's Day, 1917.) CSM Toher was the originator of the ever famous saying with reference to one of our own barrages: '*And even the wurrums themselves are getting up and crying for mercy.*'

THE FOURTH STAGE, 1917.
The Hindenburg Line, Passchendaele and Cambrai

Mainly as a result of the Somme Offensive, the Germans withdrew from the Somme to the Hindenburg Line in 1917, a distance of some 15 miles. This was more sudden than had been anticipated, and preparations were already in place for another offensive at Arras. The Guards Division was not involved, although it was in reserve for the attack on Messines Ridge. At this stage the French Armies were in serious difficulty and mutinies had broken out. To take the pressure off the French and allow them to restore the situation, the British mounted a further offensive at Ypres. This was the Third Battle of Ypres, otherwise known as Passchendaele. Its timing, recognised as critical because of the soil and the climate, was dictated by the urgent need to help the French, not as popular myth would suggest, by the stupidity of the General Staff.

Going up the line, Ypres, 1917 (Passchendaele). Silhouette of figures on skyline.

L/Sjt John Moyney VC. This self-effacing man found himself isolated with his section in no man's land during the 3rd Battle of Ypres (which he called 'Yepree'). With astonishing leadership and daring he held out, and eventually evacuated his section under heavy fire across the perilous Broembeek stream. He left the Regiment after the war, and was for many years the Station Master at Roscrea, Co. Tipperary. He marched on the St Patrick's Day Parade in 1982 at the Guards Depot, 'VC and all!'. He told an Irish newspaper interviewer that the VC had saved his life, for it had made him too famous to murder during the Troubles when ex-servicemen were hunted down in Ireland. (For full citation see p.286)

L/Cpl Thomas Woodcock VC, who lies among his regimental comrades. Thomas Woodcock was part of L/Sjt John Moyney's section, cut off in no man's land. He won his award in the withdrawal over the Broembeek by going back under fire, to try to rescue a comrade who had been with them through their ordeal. LCpl Woodcock was killed in action in March 1918. This portrait must have been taken between October 1917, when his VC was Gazetted, and his death. (For full citation see p.285)

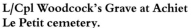
L/Cpl Woodcock's Grave at Achiet Le Petit cemetery.

Passchendaele, 1917.

Aerial photograph of trench systems prior to the main attack and capture of Cambrai, 1918.

Below: **Yser Canal after the attack involving 2nd Battalion,** 31 July 1917. The prodigious difficulties of the Third Battle of Ypres are amply illustrated in these photographs which show the dramatic difference between this battle and so-called conventional trench warfare.

While all this was happening a quiet young officer, Lt Hugh Lofting, was writing home to his young daughter. Allowing his imagination to wander away from the horrors, he composed imaginary conversations and fantasies. After the war these formed the basis for *Doctor Dolittle*, which he duly had published to world acclaim.

Left: **Lt-Col E.B. Greer MC, July 1917, Commanding Officer of 2nd Battalion Irish Guards.** With Eric Greer's death the Regiment lost of one of its very finest officers. But the family connection continues. The photographer with the 1st Battalion Battle Group in Kosovo in 1999 was his grandson, Fergus Greer, who had served in the Regiment and who contributed many of the Balkan photographs.

Lt Neville Marshall (seated behind trophy) with an Irish Guards football team. Acting Lt-Col Marshall MC★ was posthumously awarded the Victoria Cross for his bravery when commanding a Battalion of the Lancashire Fusiliers in 1918. (For full citation see p. 285)

THE FIFTH STAGE, January–July 1918. The German Offensive

The collapse of Russia in the revolution of 1917 closed Germany's Eastern Front, and thus enabled German strength on the Western Front to increase by one third. On the British side every brigade had effectively lost one of its four Battalions, sapped by the losses at Passchendaele, which had not been fully replaced. A new Fourth Guards Brigade was created (there having been but three brigades in the Guards Division), consisting of the 4th Grenadiers, 3rd Coldstream and 2nd Irish Guards. The Germans broke through, recapturing every yard of all the Somme gains, and more. An acute crisis developed as the Germans poured through in huge numbers dangerously close to the Channel Ports. There were no British reserves. 2nd Battalion Irish Guards fought in 4th Guards Brigade in an heroic last ditch effort near Hazebrouck (actually at a village called Vieux Berquin). In the process not only did 4th Guards Brigade cease to exist, but the component Battalions were so severely reduced during the engagement as to merge and blend into one ad hoc group, fighting as tenaciously as Guardsmen ever fought, backs to the wall. They held the German onrush and saved France. 2nd Battalion Irish Guards ceased thereafter to be operational, becoming, until the end of the war, a training Battalion for officers joining the Guards Division at Criel Plage.

Harry Robertshaw

7159 Pte Harry Robertshaw was killed with the 2nd Battalion Irish Guards near Ayette in the last stages of the German breakthrough on 28 March 1918. An Englishman in the Regiment, as had become more common as the war progressed, he had been wounded earlier in the war and evacuated to England. When he had regained his fitness he returned to the 2nd Battalion. The day he departed for the front he said to his sister: 'Please buy my friends a drink.' His sister remembered his words, and nearly seventy years later Mrs Lupton (Harry Robertshaw's sister) left a handsome bequest to the Regiment. Regimental Association dinners, St Patrick's Day drinks, and other special regimental occasions are subsidised by this generous bequest. Every time, a brief explanation of the story is given and the toast is drunk to the memory of Pte Harry Robertshaw. So when the Colours were trooped in 1996, the Irish Guards arranged that all the men on the Queen's Birthday Parade, regardless of regiment, would count as 'friends'. Each was given a specially labelled bottle of beer with lunch, showing the Irish Guards Colours, with the date, and stating that it was in memory of Pte Harry Robertshaw. The custom continues and beer is distributed when the Battalion's Colour is being trooped.

THE SIXTH STAGE, July–November 1918.
Advance to Victory: Canal du Nord, Hindenburg Line

HINDENBURG LINE

The Canal du Nord (not a major battle honour of the Regiment, though one could be forgiven for wondering why not). This photograph gives an indication of the strength of the German defensive position. Here, after the capture, the Irish Guards cooks set up in one of the locks.

Nearing the end. Advance over the canal at Maubeuge, not all that far from where they had first seen action over four years earlier.

ARMISTICE, 11am, 11 November 1918.

They began their last day, half an hour after midnight, marching 'as a Battalion' out of Bavai with their Lewis-gun limbers. Twice they were slightly shelled; once at least they had to unpack and negotiate more mine-craters at cross-roads. It was a populous world through which they tramped, and all silently but tensely awake – a world made up of a straight, hard road lumped above the level of the fields in places. Here and there one heard the chatter of a machine-gun, as detached and irrelevant as the laugh of an idiot. It would cease, and a single field-gun would open as on some private quarrel. Then silence, and a suspicion, born out of the darkness, that the road was mined. Next, orders to the Companies to spread themselves in different directions in the dark, to line ditches and the like for fear of attack. Thus dispersed, the Irish Guards received word that 'An Armistice was declared at 11a.m. this morning, November 11.

Men took the news according to their natures. Indurated pessimists, after proving that it was a lie, said it would be but an interlude. Others retired into themselves as though they had been shot, or went stiffly off about the meticulous execution of some trumpery detail of kit-cleaning. Some turned round and fell asleep then and there; and a few lost all holds for a while. It was the appalling new silence of things that soothed and unsettled them in turn. They did not realize till all sounds of their trade ceased, and the stillness stung in their ears as soda-water stings on the palate, how entirely these had been part of their strained bodies and souls. ('It felt like falling through into nothing, ye'll understand. Listening for what wasn't there, and tryin' not to shout when you remembered for why.')

The two Battalions had lost in all two thousand three hundred and forty-nine dead, including one hundred and fifteen officers. Their total of wounded was five thousand seven hundred and thirty-nine.

They were too near and too deeply steeped in the War that year's end to realize their losses. Their early dead, as men talked over the past in Cologne, seemed to belong to immensely remote ages. Even those of that very spring, of whom friends could still say, 'If So-and-so had only lived to see this!' stood as far removed as the shadowy great ones of the pre-bomb, pre-duckboard twilight; and, in some inexpressible fashion, they themselves appeared to themselves the only living people in an uncaring world.

'But ye'll understand, when everything was said and done, there was nothing real to it at all, except when we got to talking and passing round the names of them we wished was with us.

'But ye might tell that we was lonely, most of all. Before God, we Micks was lonely!'

Kipling

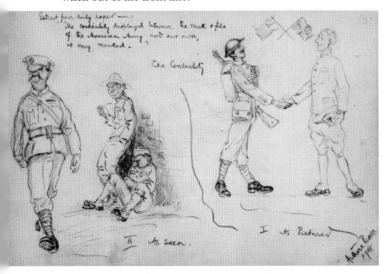

The irrepressible humour throughout the war, as shown by this satirical cartoon in the Officers' Mess visitors' book used when out of the front line.

Announcing Armistice, Capts Barry and Paget 1st Battalion Irish Guards.

Victory Medal. The dates 1914–1919 on the reverse enabled the Victory Medal to be awarded to young soldiers of the Russian Expeditionary Force to Archangel who might otherwise have not qualified for a war medal.

Maubeuge, 1918. Ptes Joseph and Brown, sentries on the Porte de Mons.

The watch on the Rhine. The picture was taken by Fr Frank Browne in 1919 in Cologne where the Battalion was based 1918–20. Fr Frank Browne SJ, an amateur photographer, is best known around the world for his 'Titanic' pictures – he took the last pictures of the doomed liner. He also served with great distinction as an Army chaplain during the Great War. He spent most of the war as Padre with the Irish Guards, was wounded five times and was seriously gassed and much decorated. Every time he recovered from injury he insisted on returning to the Front. His Commanding Officer at the time, who later became Field Marshal Alexander of Tunis described him as *'the bravest man I ever met'*.

Marching towards Germany, halted in the Meuse Valley.

Irish Guards entering Cologne,
15 December 1918.

The Prince of Wales presents silk Union Flag (specifically not a Colour) to 2nd Battalion Irish Guards in Cologne,
14 January 1919. The filial was a spear head, not the royal crest normally borne on Colours.

Triumphal March through London. The world was in an unsettled state in 1919. For several reasons it was deemed sensible to let the capital know that the Guards were back. There was therefore held a magnificent triumphal march through London by the Guards Division. Two Irish Wolf Hounds attended. Many discharged and wounded men were on parade, and the germ of the Regimental Association (first termed The Irish Guards Old Comrades Association) was undoubtedly sown. The King, mindful of the sacrifices and sterling work of the Foot Guards declared that henceforth Private Soldiers of the Foot Guards were officially to be termed Guardsmen. In addition, he decreed that the badge of rank worn by officers of the Foot Guards should cease to be the star of the Order of the Bath, and that each regiment should wear the star of the appropriate order of chivalry. Thereafter the Irish Guards officers have worn the star of the Order of St Patrick. Although the title Guardsman was not formally adopted until The King's decree after the war, the permanent headstones on graves of Private Soldiers of the Foot Guards of the Great War all carry the term Guardsmen. *L-R:* Lt D.A. Moodie, Sgt Lavery, Lt G. Tylden-Wright. Making the laurel wreath borne on the colours on the anniversary of a battle honour was the responsibility of Drum Major. Today artificial laurel wreaths are used.

The British War Medal, known as the 'Squeak'. The 1914 Star was called 'Pip' and the Victory Medal affectionately referred to as 'Wilfred'. Pip, Squeak and Wilfred were popular cartoon characters of the period.

Post Script: Field Marshal Alex at the Dublin Reunion, 1960. The formalities over, he made immediately for two frail, elderly members with marvellous moustaches, 'I remember you at Bourlon Wood,' he said. They beamed. In an instant age fell from those old shoulders. To be replaced by … Pride. Pride of association; Pride of achievement; Pride of Family, and Pride of Regiment.

Chapter Three

1919–1938
BETWEEN THE WARS

One week after the Victory Parade in London, the 2nd Battalion was placed in suspended animation and their Union Flag, presented only eight weeks before in Cologne by the Prince of Wales, was laid up in the Roman Catholic Church at the Guards Depot, Caterham. No one on that emotional day would have guessed that only twenty years later the 2nd Battalion would have to be reactivated for another world war.

The spell at home of the 1st Battalion ended abruptly in May 1922, when they embarked to reinforce the Army of the Black Sea in Constantinople. Returning via Gibraltar they were back in England by April 1924.

Twelve years' home service followed until, in November 1936, the Battalion found itself in Egypt in Kasr el Nil Barracks, Cairo.

Their desert routine was rudely interrupted in July 1938, when they were suddenly ordered to Palestine to help keep order in a land even then of simmering discontent. Four hectic months on internal security duty ensued until, in November that year, they were ordered home.

By then war clouds were gathering and in anticipation of the conflict, in July 1939, the 2nd Battalion was reactivated. Shortly afterwards a Training Battalion was formed at Hobbs Barracks, Lingfield.

In March 1938 the 1st Battalion moved to Mena Camp near the Pyramids.

ST PATRICK'S DAY, 1919

Preparing for the parade. The 2nd Battalions wolfhound, Frank, and handler. Note the white lanyards worn on the left shoulder by the 2nd Battalion until 1919. Also just visible are the two green bars worn on the left sleeve indicating the 2nd Battalion.

Rudyard Kipling with officers and wives. His incomparable two volume *The Irish Guards in the Great War* was published in 1926 and was recently reprinted.

Tug of War. After men's dinners on St Patrick's Day it was traditional for a sports meeting to take place. Over the years this became a less formal affair.

The 2nd Battalion marching to church after the presentation of gallantry medals. The Regimental Serjeant Major and the Guardsman beside him are wearing DCMs, and the right hand man of the leading group wears both DCM and MM. There are six DCM winners and eleven MM winners to be seen leading the parade. No fewer than six members of the Regiment won a bar to their DCM, of whom most unusually two were Privates/Guardsmen.

The 1st and 2nd Battalion wolfhounds, Doran and Frank.

Final parade of the 2nd Battalion, 19 August 1919. Leaving Wellington Barracks, the wolfhound, Frank, leading.

The King's Birthday Parade in Hyde Park, 3 June 1919. Number Seven Guard, Capt the Hon W.S. Alexander DSO; Lt G.L St C. Bambridge MC; Lt E.C. FitzClarence. The parade was held in Hyde Park because Horse Guards Parade was still covered in wooden War Office huts.

Pipe Sergt Atkins.

Battalion cooks c. 1920. Regimental cooks, under the leadership of the Master Cook, attracted many sobriquets. This individual, who is not in the photograph, was a member of the Battalion staff, addressed as 'Sir', and known by one and all as the 'Master Gyppo'.

The 1st Battalion Irish Guards Athletics Team in 1921. They were winners of the inaugural Army Athletics Championship. It was to be 44 years before the Regiment would win the championship again. It is not often that the Commanding Officer appears in athletics team photographs as a competitor. In this picture, Lt Col Harold Alexander, who was a fine middle distance runner can be seen in his running vest seated in front of the trainer in white. That year he won the Mile race in the Army Competition. In 1914 he had been the Mile champion of Ireland and was regarded as a likely candidate for the Olympic Games, which were to have taken place in 1916.

Guardsmen Three – Gdsm A. Duggan; L/Sjt J. Moyney VC; Gdsm P. Dunn.

Capt and Adjutant J.S.N. FitzGerald MBE, MC. Known to all as 'Black Fitz', Colonel Sidney served from before the Great War and was Regimental Lieutenant Colonel for most of the Second World War.

The creation of the Irish Free State in 1922 meant the disbandment of the southern based Irish regiments. So passed into memory such redoubtable names as The Royal Irish Regiment (18th Foot), The Connaught Rangers (88th and 94th), The Leinster Regiment (Royal Canadians 100th and 104th), The Royal Munster Fusiliers (101st and 109th) and The Royal Dublin Fusiliers (102nd and 103rd). These infantry regiments bore reputations for courage and tenacity in the field second to none. The Colours were saved from the fire at Windsor Casde in November 1992, and are now on show in the restored State Apartments, thus fulfilling King George V's pledge to keep them safe.

At a moving ceremony at Windsor Castle the Colours of the old Irish Regiments were formally accepted into safe keeping by His Majesty King George V, 12 June 1922. (Royal Archives. By gracious permission of HM The Queen)

Magnificent silver inherited by the Irish Guards from the old Irish regiments.

Major. the Hon Harold. Alexander. D.S.O.

The Corps of Drums marching at ease on their way to Windsor Station carrying slung rifles.

In May 1922 the 1st Battalion embarked for Turkey to reinforce the Army of the Black Sea endeavouring to keep peace between the Greeks and the Turks.

Preparing to entrain. A soldier's entire possessions travelled in his kit bag. They are seen here piled by companies.

The Commanding Officer, Lt Col Harold Alexander, receives his Shamrock from the Commander-in-Chief, General Sir Charles Harrington, under whom they had served in the Great War.

On arrival, the Drums and Fifes showed the flag at Pera.

TURKEY

A recurring dilemma has always been how to convey the Shamrock for St Patrick's Day to the far flung elements of the Regiment. Strange have been the methods adopted but they almost always succeed. In 1923 the situation was more acute for this was before the days of refrigeration. So it came about that three weeks before the great day, and courtesy of Imperial Airways, a withered and yellowed consignment duly arrived. It was shown to the Commanding Officer, Lt-Col the Hon. H.R. Alexander DSO, MC. Colonel Alex was horrified but the Quartermaster, Capt H. Hickie MBE, MC, rose to the occasion, 'Leave it to me, Sir. I will get it right for the day.'

But as St Patrick's Day loomed there was still no sign of the Shamrock and whenever the Commanding Officer raised the subject the Quartermaster was curiously evasive. At length Alex could bear it no longer. He must see it for himself. So together they wound their way down into the great cool cellars of the barracks to that holy-of-holies, the realms of the Quartermaster. Finally they came on the Shamrock and there it lay as green and as fresh as the day it had left Ireland. 'Hickie, you've achieved a miracle,' Alex exclaimed, 'what did you do?' 'Well, Sir,' came the reply, 'I just gave it some of what you and I like best. I gave it a sup of Irish whiskey.'

Battalion Parade, Tash Kishla Barracks, Constantinople, 1923. On one such parade, the Battalion was entranced by the unexpected appearance of a delicious young lady, who rushed onto the square seeking her paramour of the night before: 'Eddy, Eddy,' she cried at full voice, 'Have you got my keys?' A very embarrassed subaltern, Eddy FitzClarence, son of the late Brigadier Charles FitzClarence VC, Grandson of King William IV, was never allowed to forget the incident.

Irish Guards Old Comrades Association Dinner, 1927. The Old Comrades Association was formed after the Great War to enable friends to keep in touch with one another and to help members of the Regiment to find employment. The provision of welfare assistance soon began to be necessary, particularly for wounded old comrades. An annual dinner has been held by each branch ever since. The Association, now renamed the Irish Guards Association, continues to fulfil the same role.

Officers of the 1st Battalion Irish Guards, Aldershot, 1926.
3rd Row: 2/Lt V.V. Gilbart-Denham; 2/Lt J.O.E. Vandeleur; 2/Lt Creehan; Rev J. McGuinness, Chaplain; 2/Lt Montagu-Douglas-Scott; Capt and Quartermaster H. Hickie MBE, MC; Lt R.C. Alexander.
2nd Row: Capt T. Nugent; Lt T.A. Hacket-Pain; Lt E.R. Mahony; Lt T.H.H. Grayson; Lt F. Kellet; Lt T. Lindsay; Lt J. Repton; Capt D. Murphy.
Seated: Capt Hon. W. Alexander DSO; Capt W.D. Faulkner MC; Colonel Hill-Child; Field Marshal The Earl of Cavan KP, Colonel of The Regiment; Lt-Col R.V. Pollok CBE, DSO, Commanding Officer; Capt R.B.S. Reford MC; Capt K.W. Hogg.

Winners of the Connaught Cup for Infantry Chargers. Twenty-one teams competed in Aldershot in 1929. The Regiment is nowadays not renowned for its prowess in the horse world with one or two notable exceptions. However, in this photograph the Commanding Officer, Second-in-Command, Adjutant and Company Commanders, all formally mounted officers, competed against the rest of the Army at home. Lt Jim Matthew; Major the Viscount (Hugo) Gough MC; Capt Bruce Reford MC; Lt Moose Alexander; Capt Francis (Pokey) Law MC; Capt Kenneth Hogg; Lt Edward Donner; Major Sidney FitzGerald MBE, MC; Capt Andy Pym, *Standing:* Lt-Col Val Pollok CBE, DSO.

The St Patrick's Day feast. In 1932 there was no central messing so this meal was held in barrack rooms. The Victorian Barracks in the Marlborough Lines at Aldershot did not have mess rooms at this time. Capt Tris Grayson with his Company.

King's Birthday Parade, 1932. Numbers 5 and 6 Guards found by the Battalion.
<u>5 Guard</u>
Capt C.LJ, Bowen; 2/Lt the Hon B.A. O'Neill; Lt H.C. McGildownay.
<u>6 Guard</u>
Major the Hon W.S.P. Alexander DSO; 2/Lt D.H. FitzGerald; Lt H.M. Taylor.

Many of those on Parade were later to form the backbone of the Battalion in Norway in 1940.

Father McGuinness.

Lieut. J.B. Keenan.

St Patrick's Day Ball, 1933, Aldershot. The etiquette of the time required booking partners for dances during the evening.

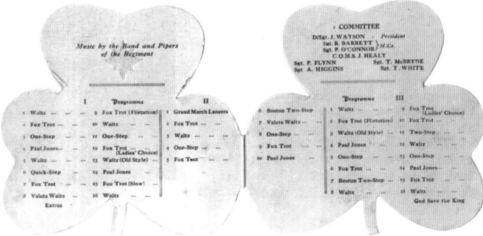

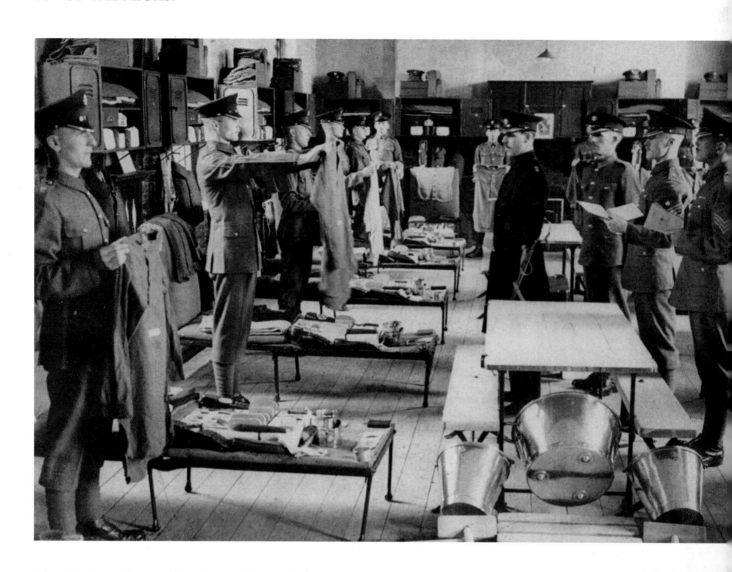

Above: **Kit Inspection,** c. 1930s. The Guards Depot, Caterham contained a company from each regiment of Foot Guards which was totally manned by staff from the regiment. No 5 Company Irish Guards had the role of converting raw recruits into Guardsmen, a task involving drill, fitness (PT), weapon training (rifle, bayonet, and 36 Grenade), discipline and meticulous attention to detail. Here a company officer carries out a formal kit inspection. Note the burnished tea buckets and the gleaming larger bucket (with small feet) in the centre.

Right: **Officers and Other Ranks still serving, who went to France with the 1st Battalion,** 12 August 1914–12 August 1934, *Standing:* Gdsm (Pte) J. O'Connell; Gdsm (Pte) D. Foran; Gdsm (Pte) J. McInerney; Gdsm (Pte) P. Seagrave; Sjt P. Cronin. *Seated:* D/Sjt (L/Cpl) J. McGann; Lt QM (CQMS) P. Mathews; Lt-Col (Lt) J.S.N. FitzGerald MBE, MC; RSM (L/Cpl) J. Linnane MM; Sjt (Sgt) R. McCabe MM.

MASCOT DESERTS THE IRISH GUARDS

AND JOINS UP WITH THE COLDSTREAMERS

BY THE CULPRIT

I had a rare bit of fun to-day.

I am a wolf-hound, and, though I say it myself, as fine a wolf-hound as you'll find anywhere. The Irish Guards have adopted me as their mascot. I go on parade with them, and behave very solemnly. You know what parades are, and how fussy the Guards are about them.

To-day a drummer boy who often takes me out said, "Come along, Tiny" (I am so big that of course I have to be called Tiny), and took me in what I think you call the dickey seat of a motor-car.

    •   •   •

Just as we got to Buckingham Palace I heard a band. The Changing of the Guard. I wanted to have a look, to see if the Coldstreamers are as smart as our

Here I am, bolting through the gates of the Palace.

fellows. (Our fellows always swear they're not.) But the car wouldn't stop.

So out I jumped, dragging the drummer boy with me.

I soon shook him off, and, dodging sentries and policemen, ran into the courtyard of the Palace and started to watch the Coldstreamers. The crowd at the Palace gates who had also come to watch the Coldstreamers stopped watching them to watch ME!

Just as I was getting interested in the "Old Guard, Present Hipe!" "New Guard, Present Hipe!" stuff I noticed the drummer boy and several policemen approaching.

I bolted.

    •   •   •

Into the Green Park, round the Victoria Fountain, up The Mall I went. By this time lots of ordinary people were after me, and just as I was wondering what to do I saw a batch of Coldstreamers marching down The Mall and had an IDEA.

As they reached me I fell in with them and solemnly marched along at their head, just as though they were my own mob.

I was enjoying the situation thoroughly when that pesky little drummer boy stole up at my back, grabbed my collar, and yanked me back to barracks. Bad cess to him!

Still, I'd had my fun.

    •   •   •

REFLECTION: Lucky for me I'm a mascot, not an "other rank." What a charge-sheet there'd be to face in the morning—"Absent from parade," "Unsoldierly conduct," and goodness only knows what.

Above: **Silver Jubilee Medal.** 6 May 1935 was the Silver Jubilee of King George V and Queen Mary. He was unwell by this time and died some eight months later.

Above: **Cruachan goes absent!** Evidently a considerable character, he unfortunately developed a strong dislike for the Italian Ambassador's poodle and, after savaging it one day in Hyde Park. Some weeks later he went further and killed it. So followed his premature retirement. No replacement was sought until 1942.

Right: **The King's Birthday Parade,** 1935. The last attended by King George V. His Majesty, seen here wearing the star of the Order of St Patrick, accompanied by the Regimental Lieutenant Colonel, J.S.N. FitzGerald MBE, MC. (Royal Archives. By gracious permission of HM The Queen.)

Farewell to the Horse, August 1936. The Transport Platoon became the Mechanical Transport Platoon. The change took place at Pirbright (the old black huts are visible in the background). The Transport Platoon under Lt A.S. Lockwood comprised one General Service Wagon (centre), the Battalion cooker (right), incorporating a Sawyer stove introduced after the Crimean War, and the ammunition limber (left). The Field Officers' chargers are in the front. The platoon commander, as a mounted officer, wore boots and breeches.

Welcome to the First Mechanical Transport Platoon. The platoon grew to 38 strong and contained four 15cwt trucks known as Bugs, as well as two dispatch riders ('Don Rs') and three Austin Seven convertible cars with civilian registration numbers. No longer a mounted officer, the platoon commander reverted to puttees.

One day in 1936, with the Adjutant on leave and a soporific air settled over the Battalion, the acting Adjutant, nosing under the blotter on his desk, came on a highly disturbing letter. To everyone's horror it revealed that in thirty-six hours The King himself was coming to witness a first demonstration of the change from drilling in fours to drilling in threes. No one knew of this, no one had tried it out, no one had practised it. The result, however, was deemed highly satisfactory!

Col.
R.C.A.
McCalmont.
D.S.O.

Postscript: *Seizing on the moment in a rehearsal for the 1939 King's Birthday Parade, when the Guards unwind after a form, the German press made much of the fact that the Irish Guards appeared unable to keep their dressing. To refute this monstrous accusation and show that in fact the Micks could and indeed were wont to march in straight lines, the* Daily Mail *unearthed the previous picture.*

EGYPT

In November 1936 the Battalion embarked for Egypt. They were stationed at Kasr el Nil Barracks, Cairo.

Training in the desert had its peculiarities.

Below: **Semaphore.** Semaphore, favoured by the Royal Navy, was a much practised art. In this picture of training in Egypt a Signal Platoon semaphore team of Sender, Reader, Runner and NCO in charge can be seen.

Above: **The Signal Platoon in training near the Pyramids using heliographs.** This method of using Morse code by flashes of sunlight from a mirror was exceptionally effective and allowed brief messages to be sent prodigious distances in a very short time. Regiments of the Indian Army wore polished flat waist belt clasps, pierced with holes (which normally accommodated a regimental brass insignia), which when taken off could be used as heliographs. Old soldiers may remember the small metal shaving mirrors issued with a hole in the centre which were designed for the same purpose.

Above: **Coronation Medal 1937.** Although the 1st Battalion was serving in Egypt at the time of the Coronation of King George VI, a number of medals were presented to Irish Guardsmen.

Below: **The Intelligence Platoon** under Capt J.O.E. Vandeleur who had previously commanded a Camel Company in the Sudan. On his left, Drummer Thackrah who was later awarded a Military Medal in Palestine, and went on to become a Regimental Serjeant Major in The Gloucestershire Regiment during the Second World War.

PALESTINE

The desert routine was interrupted in July 1938 when they were suddenly ordered to Palestine where an uprising was simmering. Four months of intensive internal security operations followed.

The wireless lorry was the only communication with base.

Principal transport were the commandeered donkey lorries seen here full to overflowing with the Instant Response Platoon.

The ubiquitous donkey was the universal carrier. The Battalion was allocated thirty of these beasts and had 'found' an extra one during an operation in the hills – 'the strongest and most obstinate donkeys in all Palestine', they declared. When normal urging was unsuccessful they resorted to lighting dried grass under their bellies. The effect was electric! The sun helmets carried a bronzed and enlarged cap star.

Patrolling. The last man carries a grenade launcher on his rifle. The uniform looks to the modern eye to be unsuitable for patrolling in rough, hot, prickly country. Full 1908 pattern web equipment wearing Khaki Drill with shorts, boots, puttees and hose tops (with blue–red–blue tops) and sun helmets!

Cars were meticulously searched at checkpoints manned by the Battalion …

… sometimes yielding a rich haul, in this case of ancient firearms, bandoliers and landmines.

One fighter was shot down, the pilot and observer both killed. To destroy the aircraft, its bomb and armaments and prevent them falling into the rebels' hands, Capt Michael Gordon-Watson ran down under heavy sniper fire and set fire to the machine. He was awarded the first of his three Military Crosses.

Ambush. At this point in the track near the town of Safid an Irish Guards Platoon truck with a Lewis Gun and a Rolls Royce armoured car of the 11th Hussars ran into an ambush. The leading truck was blown up by a mine and one man was killed and five wounded. The SOS platoon was called up, and with air support from the RAF, 15 rebels were accounted for.

In November 1938 the Battalion returned to England.

Left: **Guardsmen returning from training at Pirbright** in 1938. Here the newly issued 1938 Pattern blancoed web equipment has replaced the 1908 pattern. The helmets are still painted a pale (Palestine) colour, and bagged bearskins are part of the standard equipment when the Battalion is in London District. (Pirbright was part of London District until the 1990s.)

Below: **On return from Palestine the Battalion was stationed in the Tower of London,** just as it had been shortly before the Great War. Here Capt Basil Eugster (later General Sir Basil Eugster KCB, KCVO, CBE, DSO, MC Colonel of the Regiment 1969–1984) leaves Waterloo Station (wearing his newly won first Military Cross ribbon) at the head of No 1 Company as they march to the Tower of London.

General Service Medal.
Clasp Palestine.

In the Foot Guards it was customary to spell Serjeant with a 'j' until 1939. However, the rest of the Army preferred to use a letter 'g'. In an urge to modernise and standardise the Foot Guards reluctantly decided to conform in 1952.

With the crisis in Europe deepening, war clouds gathered once again. In expectation of conflict the 2nd Battalion was reformed.

Military Medals being presented at the Tower of London by the Major-General, A.RA.C. Thorne CMG, DSO. *L-R:* Sjt. T. Millar; L/Cpl J. Thackrah; L/Cpl D. Murphy; L/Cpl W. Rooney. The Major-General having been received with a General Salute is addressing the parade. The Commanding Officer, in a frock coat, has his sword drawn (not easy to return when the scabbard is unslung).

Field Marshal the Earl of Cavan KP, GCB, GCMG, GCVO, GBE. In 1922, the fourth Colonel, a widower of 27 years, married Lady Joan Mulholland, herself widow of an Irish Guards Officer. She had married Lt Hon A F S Mulholland on 10 June 1913 but he was killed at the first Battle of Ypres on 1 November 1914 having never met his daughter, Daphne. He was CIGS, aged 57, when they married and they had two daughters, one of whom was a bridesmaid to The Queen in 1947. The Queen Mother was the Godmother to the other daughter, Joanna, who died in 2011. Lord Cavan, himself, died in 1946 and the Countess of Cavan in 1976.

Chapter Four

1939–1945
THE SECOND
WORLD WAR

When war was declared on 3 September 1939, both Battalions were at Wellington Barracks. Rumours were rife as to where the Irish Guards might be first committed. It turned out to be Norway where the 1st Battalion was to suffer a devastating first blow.

While the 1st Battalion was so engaged, the 2nd Battalion found themselves acting as covering force for the evacuation of the Dutch Royal family and Government from the Hook of Holland. Ten days later they were helping with the evacuation of the BEF from Boulogne.

As part of the the build up to the eventual invasion of Europe, it was decided to create the Guards Armoured Division. So in the autumn of 1941 the 2nd Battalion converted to tanks.

While the 2nd (Armoured) and newly created 3rd Battalions trained in England, the 1st Battalion once more embarked for foreign shores on 1 March 1943. This time to North Africa, where the Regiment earned immortal fame at the Battle of the Bou.

The invasion of Sicily and later mainland Italy left the 1st Battalion unaffected until the amphibious landing at Anzio thirty miles south of Rome in January 1944. Here, in a short campaign of unexampled ferocity, while adding new laurels to the Regiment's name, the 1st Battalion effectively ceased to exist.

On D+17, the Guards Armoured Division landed in Normandy, and from then until the end of the war eleven months later, the 2nd and 3rd Battalions saw almost unceasing action in France, Belgium, Holland and finally Germany itself. Early in the conflict it was decided to create regimental groups each consisting of an armoured and infantry Battalion. So it was as the Irish Guards Group that the Regiment latterly fought in Northwest Europe.

Right: **Presentation of Colours to the 2nd Battalion** by His Majesty King George VI, Wellington Barracks, London, 16 February 1940. Major T. G. Lindsay; 2/Lt G.G. Romer; Lt J.D. Hornung; Major E.R. Mahoney. An unusual order of dress was the wearing of a blue-grey greatcoat over Service Dress with field boots and breeches which took the place of home service clothing in war time. This photograph was taken during the 'Phoney War' when the British Expeditionary Force was in France, and the Germans had not yet invaded France, Belgium or Holland. In the next few weeks both Battalions of the Regiment earned major battle honours in Norway (1st Battalion) and at Boulogne (2nd Battalion).

Left: **The Regimental Band in Hackney,** 1940. The Regimental Band wore the old pattern Service Dress and Service Dress caps.

Right: **1939–45 Star,** awarded for six months'★ service in an operational command, except for service in Dunkirk, Norway, some specified commando raids, and other services for which the qualifying service was one day. The ribbon, as with the whole series of Second World War campaign stars, was selected by The King. The 1939–45 Star (originally known as the 1939–40 Star) represents the colours of the three armed services in equal proportions.

★For the purposes of the Army, a month has thirty days when it comes to medals!

Mounting King's Guard at Buckingham Palace. The 1st Battalion wear steel helmets and carry respirators. Memories of gas in the Great War, and speculation on German capability to deliver gas attacks from the air brought about the insistence that civilians as well as the armed services carry respirators at all times. Since the respirator was worn slung over the left shoulder and crossed the Sam Browne belt's cross strap, the strap was temporarily taken out of use.

NORWAY

Both the Battalions were in Wellington Barracks, London when on 10 April 1940, to the chagrin of their sister Battalion, the 1st Battalion went to Norway. Speculation had been rife as to which Battalion would go to war first, and where it would go.

Arctic Star. In 2013, 73 years after the events, it was announced that the medal would be awarded for operational service north of the Arctic Circle. Those on the *Chobry* qualified but sadly few were alive to receive it. For all bar the Arctic Star the campaign star ribbons were designed by His Majesty King George VI, who decided that each ribbon should be coloured in a way so as to be identifiable with the campaign it represented. This principle was followed for the belated issue of the Arctic Star. Its ribbon represents the colours of the armed services (Navy blue, Army red and RAF light blue) separated by a theme colour, in this case white for the snow.

Seeing off the Battalion. The Adjutant, Capt the Hon B.A. O'Neill; Commanding Officer, Lt-Col W.D. Faulkner MC and the Second-in-Command Major C.L.J. Bovven. On the evening of that day the Battalion paraded on the square in their new battledress and piled aboard Green Line buses scrawled with such messages as 'To Norway', 'See the Midnight Sun', 'The North Pole Express'. So Norway it was to be. To the well-used valediction 'Keep your head down, Mick' from their comrades, the 1st Battalion were piped away from barracks. This was the first public airing of the new battledress.

The ubiquitous 'puffers', the local fishing boats, were used to ferry the companies ashore.

Capt F.R.A. Lewin, later killed in the *Chobry*, and 2/Lt G.P.M. FitzGerald in Arctic order.

THE *CHOBRY*

On 13 May 1940, the same day that the Germans invaded the Low Countries, the Battalion sailed south from Narvik on board the former Polish liner, *Chobry*, to reinforce the flimsy line attempting to hold the inexorable German advance up through Norway. It was the time of perpetual daylight in those latitudes and at midnight they were attacked by a force of Heinkel bombers. Striking amidships, all the bombs exploded near the senior officers' cabins, killing the Commanding Officer, the Second-in-Command and the Adjutant. Of the five company commanders, Major T.A. Hacket-Pain and Capt J.R. Durham-Matthews were killed outright. Major V.V. Gilbart-Denham died later, while both the other company commanders were wounded. Three Guardsmen were also killed in the attack.

A blazing inferno now divided the ship and the Regimental Sergeant Major, Johnnie Stack, formed up the Battalion on the foredeck awaiting rescue. The one officer present was the Battalion priest, Father 'Pop' Cavanagh, and so, on a burning ship in the Arctic, bare-headed, the Guardsmen said the prayers they had learned in the quiet churches and farmsteads of Ireland, as their forebears had once done on the battlefields of France.

With great gallantry, and expecting *Chobry* to blow up at any moment, the attendant destroyer HMS *Wolverine* pulled alongside. Using gangways and ropes the Battalion filed aboard. Command devolved on the senior surviving fit officer, Capt D.M.L. Gordon-Watson MC.

'I never before realised what the discipline of the Guards was … There was no confusion, no hurry, and no sign of haste or flurry … Their conduct in the most trying circumstances, in the absence of senior officers, on a burning ship, open at any time to a new attack, was as fine, or finer than, the conduct in the old days of the soldiers on the Birkenhead. *It may interest you to know that 694 men were got on board in sixteen minutes.'*

Extract from a letter from the late Commander Craske, RN, Captain of HMS *Wolverine*.

RSM Stack who was awarded the Military Cross for his outstanding leadership that day. The sole warrant officer in the Regiment to be awarded the Military Cross in World War Two.

Father 'Pop' Cavanagh.

Chobry after the German attack. The Captain of *Chobry*, a gallant Pole, asked Commander Craske of HMS *Wolverine* to take a photograph of *Chobry* lest he be falsely accused of abandoning his ship unnecessarily. It can be seen that the bow and the stern of the ship are separated by the inferno amidships.

HOOK OF HOLLAND

The 2nd Battalion had been formed as an infantry Battalion in 1939 as the threat of war became obvious. Some eight months later it saw action for the first time. On 12 May 1940, the day before the 1st Battalion sailed south from Narvik, Norway in the *Chobry,* the 2nd Battalion hurriedly embarked at Dover bound for some unknown destination and task although now dignified with the name 'Harpoon Force'. The destination turned out to be the small port of Hook of Holland and it transpired they were to cover the evacuation of the Dutch Royal Family and the Dutch government in face of the advancing German Army. After two days of being under constant air attack they succeeded and returned to Dover aboard HMS *Whitshed*.

BOULOGNE

Eight days later, they were off again, this time to Boulogne, together with the 2nd Battalion Welsh Guards, to try to buy time for the British Expeditionary Force's (BEF) evacuation from Calais and Dunkirk.

The Germans were closing fast and the perimeter shrinking ominously. In this situation of imminent danger the Battalion Padre, Fr Julian Stonor, embarked on his personal crusade. Running from slit trench to slit trench he gave everyone absolution. As he later wrote, *'any number, and not all of them Catholics, told me afterwards that from that moment afterwards they felt no fear.'*

Pressed from all sides and under fire from Germans now dominating the high ground overlooking the harbour, the remains of the two battalions re-embarked again on HMS *Whitshed*.

From a strength of 670 men, the Battalion had lost 5 Officers and 196 Other Ranks killed, wounded or missing. A Royal Navy Officer later broadcast a description of the withdrawal. *'The courage and bearing of the Guardsmen were magnificent, even under a tornado of fire with casualties occurring every second. They were steady as though on parade and stood there like rocks, without giving a damn for anything.'* For this action they were awarded the Battle Honour 'Boulogne 1940'.

In early 1941, it was announced the Guards Armoured Division was to be formed. The news that the Battalion was to be equipped with tanks and become the 2nd (Armoured) Battalion IG was received with enthusiasm and some trepidation. As expected, they served with distinction adding another 10 Battle Honours to the Colours.

Ships Emblem. HMS *Whitshed* presented her Bridge Emblem to the Battalion as a memento of the day. Her close support during the evacuation from the port was crucial.

The dockside at Boulogne as the Battalion deploys in support of the BEF.

HMS *Whitshed*, a Dover Destroyer supported the Battalion in both operations. As it returned from Boulogne, a Guardsman climbed to the ship's bridge and deposited a bottle of champagne on the chart table. *'Thanks for the double ride'*, he said and disappeared.

The Distinguished Conduct Medal.

The King awarded DCMS to L/Cpl J. Wylie; Gdsm T. Callaghan; Gdsm M. O'Shea and Sgt W. Johnstone; also a bar to his Military Cross to Capt D.M.L. Gordon-Watson MC. The Distinguished Conduct Medal was introduced to 1854 (i.e. before the Victoria Cross) for 'NCOs and Privates only'. It ranked next below the VC in soldiers' gallantry awards. It was discontinued in 1994. Sgt Johnno Johnstone, Medical Sergeant on the *Chobry*, became a revered Quartermaster in the 1960s. Gdsm O'Shea was orderly to Michael Gordon-Watson throughout the war, a highly hazardous occupation!

His Majesty The King, dressed as Colonel-in-Chief, visited the 1st Battalion in July 1940 at Northwood, Middlesex on their return from Norway.

Wartime use of the Northwood Golf Course.

BUILD UP

Shortly after the Battalion returned from Norway, Lt-Col Edmund Mahony, from Galway, took over command at Northwood. Touring barracks one morning with the Adjutant, Capt Basil Eugster, MC, they were surprised to see a staff car draw up. A self-important, red-tabbed sub area commander emerged. *'Who is this man; are we expecting him?'* asked Colonel Edmund of the Adjutant, *'Show him the latrines!'* and stalked off. One did not call on the Irish Guards uninvited.

Bayonet Practice. *L-R:* Capt Michael Gordon-Watson with blackthorn walking stick, The King, Colonel Edmund Mahony.

Purposeful PT wearing steel helmets decorated with a stylised regimental blue plume on the right.

TRAINING BATTALION

The Training Battalion had been formed in April 1939 to handle the immense number of recruits now pouring in. Shortly after, they moved to Hobbs Barracks, Lingfield in Surrey which was to be their home until near the end of the war, with a brief interlude in July 1940 on anti-invasion duties at Dover.

St Patrick's Day, 1941, Hobbs Barracks, Lingfield. Lt (QM) A. Ashton; Lt-Col the Viscount Gough MC, Commanding Officer; Lt J.D. Moore, Adjutant; General Sir Alexander Godley GCB, KCMG (who had trained the Regiment's Mounted Infantry for the Boer War); Lt Col M. Marchant ATS; Major J.O.E. Vandeleur; Capt A.R. Pym; Capt D.J.B. FitzGerald; Capt G.A.M. Vandeleur; CSM Twomey; CSM McKenna; CSM White.

At Lingfield the reinforcements for all three service Battalions were 'taught to become', above all, Guardsmen and Irish Guardsmen before being passed to holding units in the various theatres of operation. Not all remained as Irish Guardsmen, however. Others, including such luminaries as Spike Milligan, were given their basic training and then moved on to other regiments.

Presiding over the Training Battalion in his own inimitable way was Lt-Col the Viscount Gough, who was the first officer to be decorated in the Regiment in the Great War, who lost an arm and won the Regiment's first Military Cross. Those who came under his influence remember their time with deep and abiding affection.

One day a Guardsman was brought before his Commanding Officer on a charge of being drunk and disorderly. He was no stranger to this court of justice, this giant of a man from County Clare, who later proved to be a fine fighting Mick.

In a weary tone Lord Gough enquired, *'So just how drunk were you this time, O'Donovan?'*

Came the winning reply: *'I thank you for leave to speak, my Lord; I was as drunk as a lord, my Lord.'*

The case was dismissed.

Admirers!

Lt-Col the Viscount Gough MC.

SECOND BATTALION

In the autumn of 1941 the 2nd Battalion, then stationed at Woking, converted to tanks as part of the newly created Guards Armoured Division.

The doubters, of which there were a few, declared that Guardsmen could not physically fit inside tanks nor ever adapt to the swiftly moving panorama of armoured warfare. They were proved generally wrong on the first count and triumphantly wrong on the second.

The first tanks were Covenanters Mark I, very second-hand, flogged near to death, but the pride of the whole Battalion. Their first inspection was an armoured review in front of the Major-General. The four tanks behaved impeccably and only a few ill-humoured spectators remarked that they had seen rusty water coming from one of the barrels when dipped in salute!

The Commanding Officer's tank was christened 'St Patrick', seen here with Sergeant Bob Gorton, its driver until the end of the war. The Adjutant's was 'St Columb'; Second-in-Command's 'Ulster'. The three squadron commanders, 'Munster', 'Leinster' and 'Connaught'. Within the squadrons, Number 1 had names beginning with 'A'; Number 2, 'B'; Number 3, 'C'. Troop Commanders in Number 1 Squadron used the prefix 'Ard…'; Number 2, 'Bally…'; Number 3, 'Castle…'. It was a simple, easily understood system which allowed for no confusion and it served the Battalion well.

The carriers of the Carrier Troop for forward resupply and casualty evacuation were named after places in Ireland beginning with the letter 'C' – here 'City of Cork'.

The dingo scout cars of the Recce Troop used the letter 'D'.

The tanks continued to arrive, all second-hand at first, then one day a brand new one appeared and with that the Battalion reckoned their existence had been properly acknowledged.

The Covenanter weighed 18 tons, with a top speed of 31mph, but armed with a pea-shooter of a gun, a puny 2-pounder. Later Marks had a 6-pounder but experience in North Africa had already shown this too was no match for German armour.

There was a brief interlude with Crusaders, sleek, low-silhouetted, very fast with a wonderful suspension but still armed with the 6-pounder. Then one day, after returning from an exercise at Thetford in Norfolk, they found to greet them sixty gleaming new American Sherman tanks.

Much higher, with a crew of five rather than the three of Covenanter and Crusader, the Sherman was a different prospect altogether. Moreover, it was armed with a very fine 75mm gun. The Sherman, despite its tendency to 'brew up' when hit, served the Battalion well, being able to deal with any enemy armour until in due time they came up against the monster German tank, the King Tiger.

The Colonel of the Regiment, Field Marshal The Earl of Cavan KP, GCB, GCMG, GCVO, GBE, takes the salute from a Crusader of the 2nd Battalion.

The Queen with Lt-Col Gerald Verney MVO, Commanding Officer 2nd Battalion Irish Guards. The censor has obliterated the divisional signs from the sleeves of battle dress and the tactical signs have been removed from the tanks to prevent identification. When the Guards Armoured Division went to Normandy, 2nd Armoured Battalion Irish Guards formed part of 5 Guards Armoured Brigade. Its tactical sign was the Ever Open Eye and the white number 53 on a red background. Gerald Verney's son, Major Peter Verney, who served 1950–1974, wrote the book *The Micks – The Story of the Irish Guards* in 1970.

2nd (Armoured) Battalion Irish Guards Battalion Headquarters, Spring 1942. This Battalion wore black berets, of which they were very proud.

From L–R Front Row (seated): RSM Robin Hastings; Lt Ronnie Robertson; Capt Will Berridge (Adjutant); Lt-Col Gerald Verney MVO; Capt George Dennehy; Lt Patrick Pollock; Sgt Cross.
Second Row: L/Cpl Bricky Cardwell; Gdsm Laverick; L/Cpl Doran; Sgt Bob Gorton; Gdsm Lawless (transferred to Parachute Regiment); Gdsm Jock O'Neill, Gdsm McGuinness; Gdsm Spatcher.
Third Row: Gdsm Ernie Lloyd (Despatch Rider); Gdsm Jack Bettam (Despatch Rider); Gdsm Hughie Williamson; Unidentified; Sgt Matt Fitzsimmons; Gdsm Yates; Gdsm Thackham; Gdsm George Knight (Driver of 'Erin').
Back Row: Gdsm Ken Shaw; Sgt Chamberlain; Gdsm Victor Crampton.

Forming up on the drive of Fonthill House. The road to the training areas on Salisbury Plain passed through the charming village of Wylye. Wylye's Days of Horror, as the ensuing period was known, became memorable to the long-suffering inhabitants who stoically endured the vagaries of Mick tanks. Many of the drivers had never driven anything in their lives, and the steering of the Covenanters was notoriously unreliable and prone inexplicably to fail altogether. Hence, as the Regimental history cheerfully records, hardly a day passed without the Battalion leaving its mark.

On one occasion a tank slewed uncontrollably off the road ending up in the front room of a house where two old ladies had been quietly having tea. When asked to remove his offending monster the tank commander was forced to point out that were he to do so the house would assuredly fall down. Whereupon the imperturbable pair invited him and his crew to join them for tea! In 2010 a nearby village requested financial support to repair a local war memorial allegedly damaged by the 2nd Battalion. Being entirely plausible, given the expertise of our drivers, Regimental Headquarters contributed to the refurbishment. Six months later, an apology was received in the post that they had incorrectly identified the Micks as the culprits. The Regimental Council smiled but no-one felt inclined to ask for the money back.

Tommy Gun Practice at Fonthill. Lt Mick O'Cock receives instruction from Capt Terence O'Neill (later Prime Minister of Northern Ireland, Lord O'Neill of the Maine).

Building a footbridge under the watchful eye of Lt Oliver Chesterton and to the huge amusement of everyone else.

The Defence Medal was awarded for service in non-operational areas subjected to air attack or closely threatened, provided such service lasted for three or more years. Its ribbon, flame coloured with green edges, is symbolic of enemy attacks on 'our green and pleasant land'. The two black stripes represent the black-out.

The intrepid Capt Paul Stobart, known as 'The Beak', goes first.

Capt Morrogh O'Brien.

Skulking.

HOME DEFENCE

Purposeful home defence exercises formed an integral part of training in England. With a fine sense of the ridiculous, one such exercise was held at Woking in which the 2nd Battalion was required to flush out pretend German parachutists and Fifth Columnists (spies). It will be noted that in the photograph showing the prisoner under escort the Guardsmen are wearing respirator cases and side caps.

Under escort, Major Jack Thursby.

Interrogation about to commence.

Rumbled.

NORTH AFRICA

On 1 March 1943 the 1st Battalion embarked at Liverpool on board the P&O liner *Strathmore*. Their destination was North Africa as reinforcement to 1st Army which had landed the previous November. In conjunction with the 8th Army, operating from the south, it was conducting a massive pincer movement designed to squeeze the Germans out of North Africa and Tunisia in particular.

Preliminary operations involved patrolling, followed by a gallant night attack by No 2 Company on Recce Ridge. The company, lacking proper intelligence, set off quietly across the plain at dusk to attack the feature. The Battalion heard wild firing in the distance, and then nothing. Several weeks later it took a full Divisional attack to capture Recce Ridge. Only a handful of Irish Guardsmen, mostly wounded, had survived and they were taken prisoner. The full story of Recce Ridge was not known until after the war when the prisoners came home. The minor battle honour, not carried on the Colours, *Medjez Plain*, was awarded for the operations. The key to the town of Tunis, and ultimately to Tunisia itself, was the narrow neck of the Medjez Valley some thirty miles west of the town. At its eastern end the valley is some four miles across but dominated by a major feature, Djebel Bou Aoukaz, the 'Bou'.

Towards the end of 21 April, Guards Brigade, comprising 1st Irish Guards, 1st Scots Guards and 5th Grenadiers, were committed to clearing the corridor. On 27 April the Irish Guards were ordered to capture two important features, Points 212 and 214.

The attack was straight up a plain dominated to the left by a well established enemy. It had originally been planned for the night of the 27th, but at noon this was brought forward to four o'clock in broad daylight in the heat of the afternoon.

The Africa Star was awarded to 1st Battalion Irish Guards with the clasp First Army, with a silver figure 'I' worn when only the ribbon is worn.

Memorial Cross erected on Point 212 to commemorate those Irish Guardsmen who gave their lives taking and defending the Bou.

Sgt Desmond Lynch DCM. Awarded his DCM at the Battle of the Bou, Desmond Lynch was RSM at the Indian Military Academy and then at both Eaton Hall and Mons Officer Cadet Schools under the then Brigadier Basil Eugster. His last appointment after retirement was Assistant Adjutant RMA Sandhurst.

JEBEL BOU AOUKAZ, 27 April 1943

With their approach dominated by the high ground to their left, the Battalion suffered appalling casualties in the cornfields and well-defended olive groves in the open ground. *'They threw everything but their cap-badges at us. Guns, mortar, and those abominable machines the six-barrel mortars, everything within miles let drive. The platoons spread out into open order and plunged into the waist-high corn. The fire intensified and the whole cornfield was ripped and torn. Part of it was burning smokily. Amid the tall poppies that stood out over the corn there sprang a new crop – rifle butts. They appeared so suddenly, and so quickly, that it was almost a surprise to look beyond them and see the thin line of men plodding steadily on towards the olive grove. "We could not believe it," said a German prisoner afterwards. "We thought no one could cross that plain." A Guardsman put it more succinctly. "Thank God for drill, it keeps you going." (FitzGerald)'* In 1949 D.J.L FitzGerald MC, Adjutant of the 1st Battalion 1943–44, wrote *A History of The Irish Guards in the Second World War*, generally acknowledged as one of the finest military histories of that war. In it he wrote:

At dusk 173 men, all that had survived from four full rifle companies, and forward elements of Battalion Headquarters, struggled up the slopes of Points 212 and 214 beyond, and were promptly cut off by Germans swarming in behind them. Three days later 80 men, which included a smattering of reinforcements who had been able to get through the German cordon to the little beleaguered force, were finally relieved having resisted incessant and persistent attacks to uproot them.

Looking down from Point 212 to the Olive Groves and startline, during a regimental visit to the battleground in 1987.

After the battle. Father Dolly Brookes said Mass with the survivors on Point 212 after the dedication of the Memorial Cross. Father Dolly, Adjutant of the 2nd Battalion in the Great War, priest and friend to all thereafter, had persuaded three Germans, by use of his blackthorn stick, to help him look for the wounded in the cornfield. '*There are not words strong enough to express the shining example Father Brookes gave to all ranks ... he has been in places where the fire was impossibly heavy, and yet has given comfort to the dying without any thought for his safety ... an almost unbelievable devotion to duty and bravery ... never appearing too tired to go to the furthest points to help a wounded man ... the admiration of all. The sight of Father Brookes pacing up and down reading his breviary under heavy fire has restored the confidence of many a shaken man*' (extract from citation for the Military Cross).

In 1987 a regimental tour visited the Bou. Major Sir Oliver Chesterton MC, standing on the top of what had been called 'Oliver's Hill' because he was the first officer to reach the top, said that he had a guilty conscience about the Bou. He had been wounded twice in the cornfield. '*Ducking and weaving like a Welsh fly half, I was.*' He was carrying a Tommy gun and a grenade. He pulled the pin from the grenade with his teeth, like a film star, and fought his way to the summit. Then, seeing two Germans in a shell scrape, he chucked it at them. '*And I've always felt guilty about that. We'd lost so many men, and we were angry, but they weren't actually harming anyone then.*' From among the veterans present on the tour came a voice: '*Don't worry any more Sir. That grenade never went off. You hadn't cleaned it!*' It was Gdsm Crawford, his orderly from 1943, who had travelled from Australia to be there. Lt-Col Andrew Montagu-Douglas-Scott was awarded an immediate DSO as was Capt Colin Kennard who had so dominated the defence of Point 214 and had been recommended for a VC. Also given were two Military Crosses, four DCMs and seven Military Medals after an epic which was to go down as one of the great stands in the Second World War.

Then in August they heard that L/Cpl John Kenneally (now L/Sgt) had been awarded the Victoria Cross. (For full citation see p. 287.)

Marching to the Victory Service in Carthage Cathedral, May 1943. As the noise of the pipes was heard one of the white-robed priests sprang from his stall and rushed down the aisle crying. '*I must see the boys, I must.*' His religious name was Pere Angelicas but he had been born Flynn and came from County Westmeath, Ireland.

On 27 August General Alexander made the presentation. The Battalion was formed up on three sides of a square and, after carrying out a full inspection, L/Sgt Kenneally was marched out to receive his ribbon. Then with Kenneally standing on the saluting base to his right, the Battalion marched past. RSM McLaughlin and L/Sgt Kenneally VC.

ANZIO

In July 1943 the invasion of Sicily commenced.
On 9 September took place the first landing
on 'Fortress Europe' at Salerno. Then
winter clamped down on Italy and stalemate
ensued. To break the stalemate, to by-pass
the opposition and make use of the available
landing craft before they left the Mediterranean
bound for home, OPERATION
OVERLORD and D-Day, an amphibious
operation was mounted thirty miles south
of Rome at the seaside resort of Anzio. To
veterans of that campaign in the Italian spring
of 1944 the name recalls memories of death in
appalling conditions of mud and cold, and of a
battle so nearly lost. The Germans described it
as the Allies' 'Epic of Bravery'.

A scene of peace! The first morning, General Alex, Supreme
Allied Commander, and the Naval C-in-C, Admiral Troubridge,
on the beach as a member of the pioneer platoon sweeps the ground
they are standing on for mines!

Above: **The hell hole of Anzio and the notorious Wadis.**
Here in a world of savagery their skill at arms, pride of
Regiment and sheer bloody-mindedness brought them through.

Below: **The Road to Rome.** View of the Via Anziate taken
five days after the landing. An inviting prospect and only thirty
miles from Rome but overlooked from the Alban Hills behind,
with a water-table only just below the surface and opposed by a
resourceful foe – recipe for a bitter war.

Above: **L/Cpl Doak** with two German prisoners.

On 27 February the remnants of 1st Battalion Irish Guards were withdrawn from Anzio, a total of no more than 20 officers and 247 Other Ranks. In five weeks they had lost, killed, wounded or missing, a total of 32 Officers and 714 Other Ranks.

This vicious fighting earned the Regiment three further battle honours: Aprilia, Carroceto and Italy 1943–44. It is sad, but understandable, that the number of battle honours to be carried on the Colours of any regiment had to be limited to ten (as in the Great War). Difficult choices had to be made after the war, and Anzio was selected as the 'generic' battle honour to cover this bloody episode in the Regiment's history.

There were no more reinforcements in Italy. Casualties in North Africa and at Anzio for the Irish Guards were as severe as they had been in the early stages of 1915. In the Second World War there was no possibility of completely rebuilding a Battalion more than once. This had happened after North Africa, ready for Italy. History repeats itself, for in 1918 the 2nd Battalion was removed to Criel Plage having ceased to be effective on account of constant heavy casualties. Then at Anzio the 1st Battalion's casualties were so severe, it too ceased to be an effective fighting Battalion for the remainder of the war.

Christmas in Italy. The Regimental Band performing at Foggia near Naples under the direction of Major George Willcocks (Director of Music 1938–1948).

The survivors celebrated St Patrick's Day at Massalubrense near Sorrento where General Alex, after presenting Gallantry awards won at Anzio, distributed the Shamrock. Major Savill Young was awarded the DSO for Anzio. Like the Scotts, his father had served in the Great War, and his son followed the tradition. Capt H.F. McKinney; Quartermaster; General Alex; the Commanding Officer and Capt G.H. Willcocks, Director of Music.

Lt-Col Andrew Montagu-Douglas-Scott DSO. His father, already holder of a DSO, fought in South Africa in 1901 with the Irish Guards Mounted Infantry Section. Colonel Andrew won his first DSO commanding the 1st Battalion and his second commanding a Brigade. His son also served in the 1st Battalion after the war. (Mercifully there was no war, so no DSOs, for the third generation.)

Medal, Italy Star. The Italy Star was awarded to those who fought in Italy at any time between 11 June 1943 and 8 May 1945. The colours of the ribbon represent the Italian colours. After the war a few soldiers of the North Irish Horse transferred to the Irish Guards. They, unusually, were permitted to wear a small maple leaf on the ribbon of the Italy Star, their regiment having served with distinction in a Canadian formation in Italy. The last of the North Irish Horse 'maple leaf' men was L/Sgt Cairns who ran the Battalion PRI shop at Hübbelrath in 1962.

The 1st Battalion was not to serve again in the Second World War. The survivors returned home to be absorbed into the other two service Battalions. Some, though, stayed in Italy. Foremost was Lt-Col Andrew Scott who was required to command 28th Infantry Brigade, and subsequently 1st Guards Brigade. Father Dolly became General Alex's Senior Religious Adviser. When General Alex went to call on the Pope in Rome he took Father Dolly with him. Waiting outside to be shown in to the presence, Father Dolly produced a small bakelite comb from his pocket. *'Dolly,'* said the General, *'how could you? Put it away!'*

In June 1945 Field Marshal Alexander insisted Fr Dolly Brookes accompany him on an official visit to Rome to meet with Pope Pius XII.

The Warrant Officers of 1st Battalion Irish Guards. CSM Pestell; CSM Micky Moran MM; CSM Gilmore; CSM Stewart; CSM Paddy Mercer MM; D/Sgt Kenny; RSM McLoughlan; D/Sgt Bill Rooney MM; CSM George Stone.

Only surviving members of The 1st Battalion Irish Guards from Palestine in 1938 to Anzio in 1944. *Back Row:* Gdsm. P McCarthy; Gdsm R. Adamson DCM; Gdsm J. Lavery; Gdsm P. O'Shea DCM; Gdsm J. Getbings; L/Sgt C. Englishby; Gdsm E. Davis; Gdsm E. Rooney; Gdsm E. Moore; L/Cpl D. Murphy; L/Cpl T. O'Connell; Gdsm J. Ryan MM. *Middle Row:* Gdsm W. Gormley, Gdsm M. Lawton; Sgt A. Hughes MM; Sgt P. Hatche; Sgt M. McCarthy; L/Sgt C. Weir MM; L/Sgt P. McNally, L/Cpl R, Ashton; L/Sgt D. Smith; L/Sgt J. Sweeny; Gdsm S. Robinson; Gdsm G Prentice. *Front Row:* L/Cpl S. Carr; Sgt R. McConnell MM; CQMS W. Wallace; CSM W. Pestell; D/Sgt M. Moran MM; Major D.M.L. Gordon-Watson MC; RSM W. Rooney MM; Major H.L.S. Young DSO; CSM G. Stone; Sgt O' Sullivan; L/Sgt P Freeman; L/Cpl G. Currie.

NORMANDY 1944

Whilst waiting near Eastbourne to go to France, the 2nd and 3rd Battalions heard of the destruction of the Guards Chapel at the start of Morning Service on Sunday 18 June in which Major John Gilliatt and three other members of the Regiment were killed. Then on D+17 (23 June 1944) the first elements of the Guards Armoured Division sailed for France; the 3rd Battalion, with 'X' Company Scots Guards attached to make up numbers, in 32nd Guards (Lorried Infantry) Brigade; the 2nd Armoured Battalion as part of 5th Guards Armoured Brigade. Before departure each troop was issued with a Firefly tank, a Sherman mounting an 18-pounder gun. Called a tank-buster it was a formidable weapon which was to prove its worth on many occasions in the months ahead.

En-route to France. Officers of 3rd Battalion. Lt Robin Hastings; Capt Desmond Kingsford (later MC, killed in Normandy); Major Ivo Reid and the Medical Officer.

Major 'Feathers' Steuart-Fotheringham, Company Commander of the redoubtable 'X Company Scots Guards. Note the Guards Armoured Division sign on the battle dress sleeve. This was a variation on the Great War design which was more stylised and on a different shield, showing the Ever Open Eye. After this design is named the Household Division yacht, *Gladeye*.

The France and Germany Star was awarded to the Army for participation in any land operation in France, Belgium or Holland between 6 June 1944 and 8 May 1945. The colours of the ribbon are symbolic of the Union Flag and those of France and the Netherlands. The colours of Belgium could not be included in the ribbon, since they were the same as those of Germany. The Dunkirk and Norway operations were not eligible for the France and Germany Star. They qualified for the 1939–45 Star only.

Taking part in a massive armoured thrust east of Cagny (OPERATION GOODWOOD), Lt John Gorman, a troop commander in 2nd Armoured Battalion was probing forward in his tank 'Ballyragget' when he suddenly found himself broadside on to a massive German tank which no one had ever seen before, the King Tiger. He fired one round from his 75mm gun which bounced off the German's armour. 'Ballyragget's gun then jammed, and seeing the beast's massive gun slowly traversing in his direction, John Gorman gave the order to ram.

'Ballyragget' struck the enemy amidships disabling the tank and causing its crew to bale out hurriedly. At this moment an artillery stonk came down.

After seeing his own crew to safety Lt Gorman commandeered a Firefly, 'Ballymena', whose commander had been killed, and completed the destruction of the King Tiger with his 18-pounder gun. He was awarded the MC, his driver, L/Cpl James Baron, an MM. The battle honour *Cagny* was awarded for the Regiment's part in OPERATION GOODWOOD.

These photographs were taken in early 1945 and were presented to the Irish Guards by Monsieur André Lechipey, who as a boy is seen sitting on the massive 88mm gun of the King Tiger, accompanied by his sister, with the disabled 'Ballyragget' in the foreground. Through diligent research members of the German tank crew were eventually identified and contacted in the 1990s and the existence of these photographs was discovered with the Germans providing the introduction to M. Lepichey.

The first King Tiger Tank seen in battle. A photograph taken, we assume, nearer the time of the incident – the wireless aerials are intact.

Sgt James Baron as a Chelsea Pensioner.

Commander and Driver meet again. On the left Sir John Gorman CVO, CBE, MC, the Troop Commander meets Sgt James Baron MM, his tank driver, at an Irish Guards Association function some 50 years later although both had maintained their friendship in the intervening years.

In August the Guards Armoured Division was switched to the right of the British sector to exploit the penetration by 6th Guards Tank Brigade into the German defences at Point 309, christened Coldstream Hill after the exploits of the 4th Armoured Coldstream. Equipped with Churchill tanks they were able to deal with the massive high banks surrounding tiny fields that characterised the bocage country of Normandy – the only tanks that could do so.

Here, around the villages of St Martin des Besaces, St Charles de Percy and La Marvindière, the two Battalions of the Irish Guards suffered heavy casualties. The 3rd Battalion took part in a furious frontal attack down a forward slope at Sourdeval, under intense fire, as part of a brigade advance. Their losses were immense.

Around now 'X' Company Scots Guards left the 3rd Battalion. Theirs had been a successful and harmonious marriage and both sides were genuinely sad at parting. Their place was taken by an entire Number 4 Company created from the Mediterranean veterans of the 1st Battalion.

Few Micks who were in Normandy had ever heard of Mont Pinçon. It was the overall battle honour awarded for the first phase of the breakout from the Normandy landings bridgehead. It went to eight armoured regiments, two Yeomanry regiments, all five regiments of Foot Guards and to twenty-seven Infantry regiments.

Lt Hugh Dormer who was awarded the DSO for his remarkable undercover work in occupied France. After returning to his beloved 2nd Battalion he was killed in Normandy. In the last entry before D-Day in his recently republished diary – a moving testament by a deeply religious man – he wrote: *'God knows no man ever set out more happily or gladly before – and lead where it may, I follow the path in ever-mounting spirits. God grant me the courage not to let the Guardsmen down, knowing as I do how much they count on me. I only ask that He do with my life as He wills – if I should be privileged to give it on the field of battle, then indeed would the cup be full.'* Hugh Dormer was killed in a trivial incident in a Normandy orchard and as a brother officer wrote: *'He was buried with the others by the roadside and the Guardsmen came with bunches of flowers for his grave. They loved him because they knew he loved them.'*

Number One Company of the 3rd Battalion seen moving towards St Martin des Besaces accompanied by a Sherman of the 1st Armoured Coldstream, 2 August 1944. The second Guardsman carrying a shovel is Major Tony Brady, later the Regimental Archivist.

3rd Battalion's children's party at Montilly. Thirty local children were invited but in fact 110 turned up. When their guests were stuffed with food CSM Bill Gilchrist DCM organised Jeep rides.

Lt-Col J.O.E. Vandeleur. Commander Irish Guards Group. He was awarded two DSOs in North West Europe.

At the end of August 1944, with both Battalions at Douai, a major reorganisation of Guards Armoured Division took place when Regimental Groups were formed each consisting of an infantry and an armoured Battalion of the same Regiment. Thus came into being the Irish Group. As senior Commanding Officer Lt-Col J.O.E. Vandeleur assumed overall command with his cousin, Lt-Col Giles Vandeleur, who had recently taken command of 2nd Armoured Battalion, remaining in command of the armour.

This marriage of infantry and tanks from the same regiment was to prove a battle-winning factor in the months ahead.

All 'spoke the same language', all had the same background and most had known each other all their military lives. There was perfect accord and complete mutual trust and the combination was to become renowned.

The Guards Armoured Division took no further part in the battles of Normandy. On 30 August they crossed the Seine amid growing fervour and increasing signs of enemy rout.

The evening after the new union Lt-Col J.O.E. gave out his first orders as Group Commander: *'The Irish Guards will dine in Brussels tomorrow night.'*

BRUSSELS

That night the crews worked until midnight and beyond. The distance to Brussels was little short of ninety miles. Would the engines, the tracks and the bogies take such punishment, let alone what nasty surprises a still determined enemy might have in store along the route?

Dawn on 3 September. A squadron of the Household Cavalry and the Welsh Guards Group pass through to take up the running. Then they were off …

'The 2nd Battalion had no mechanical trouble that day; for years they had been preparing their tanks for a day like this. Through the Belgian villages roared "St Patrick", "Ulster", "Leinster" and "Connaught", "Achill", "Bantry", "Cloneen" and sixty-seven other Irish villages and towns. The rattle of tank tracks on the cobbled streets brought the astonished inhabitants out of their houses to wave flags and cheer wildly … Opposition was bypassed or ignored.' (FitzGerald)

Amid a welcoming hail of hydrangeas and unripe apples the Irish Group reached the outskirts of Brussels around six o'clock.

Outskirts of Brussels. The crew of a Sherman of the 2nd Battalion beginning to sample the rapturous reception of Liberation. History repeated itself in Pristina, Kosovo in 1999.

The Liberation scenes in Brussels were soon a distant memory as the advance continued. Although supposedly in full retreat the German resistance was fierce and sometimes fanatical. North of the Albert Canal the enemy were in great numbers, Panzer Regiments (brigades), SS Regiments and, nastiest of all, SS Panzers. To make matters worse the country was ill-suited to an armoured dash, a succession of broad canals or rivers, few bridges and these approached by narrow roads usually riding above the generally soggy landscape. On many occasions they were advancing on a single tank front with no means of getting off the road without getting bogged in the swampy ground.

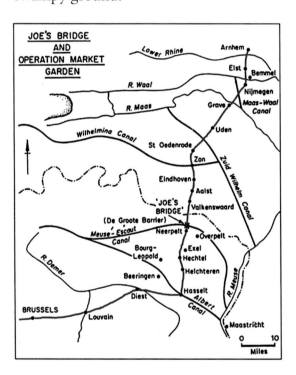

THE ATTACK ON JOE'S BRIDGE

On 10 September the wide-ranging reconnaissance scout cars of the invaluable 2nd Household Cavalry Regiment reported a brand new military road between Exel and Overpelt. More significantly, they reported that the bridge over the considerable Meuse-Escaut Canal at De Groote Barrier, although mined and strongly held by 88mm guns, was still intact.

Lt Desmond Lampard's troop of Shermans and the platoon of Lt John Stanley-Clarke were detailed to take the bridge under the covering fire of every tank in the Irish Group for they were beyond the range of any artillery support. It was nearly dark

'It was after eight o'clock when the waiting crews saw the Very light burst green at the top of its arc (signal for maximum covering fire). Something or somebody had set fire to a large brick house on the right of the bridge. Whatever was inside it, it burnt remarkably well and the flames lit up the bridge and banks like a theatre set. For two minutes every gunner kept his foot hard down on the firing button that controlled his Browning machine-gun. All co-drivers who could see, and some who could not, fired their main guns. The red Very light went up (signal for the assault) and Lt Lampard's troop charged. In moments they were through and over the canal as were the platoon racing after them on either side of the bridge ignoring the fierce Spandau fire which broke around them. Then a very brave Sapper officer, Capt Hutton, with four Guardsmen, while bullets were rattling round them on the girders, removed the detonators from the charges. Capt Hutton was awarded the Military Cross, his four assistants Military Medals.' (FitzGerald)

Again and again the Germans tried to regain the bridge whose capture had so unpinned their defence; again and again they were beaten off.

The bridge over the Meuse-Escaut Canal at De Groote Barrier is now named 'JOE's Bridge' in honour of its captor.

Memorial to the Irish Guards Battle Group at JOE's Bridge.

The taking of JOE's Bridge.

MARKET GARDEN

With JOE's Bridge secured on 14 September, they pulled back to regroup at Overpelt. Here they learned of OPERATION MARKET GARDEN. The 'Market' element was an airborne assault by the Americans on Nijmegen, the bridge over the massive Mass-Waal Canal, and the River Waal itself, and that of the British 6th Airborne Division further on at Arnhem. 'Garden' was the link up by ground forces. The Irish Group were given the dubious honour of leading the latter.

Above: **Breakout from the Escaut Canal Bridgehead.** 2nd Battalion tanks advancing across the Escaut Canal over the Bailey bridge constructed beside the original JOE's Bridge captured intact on 10 September.

Above: **Infantry cross by JOE's Bridge.**

Above: **The remains of a German 88 mm which had once defended it.** These powerful guns were also used in the lower register in an anti-tank role.

Below: **Consolidating in the main square of Valkenswaard** before resuming the advance. At that stage, Allied air superiority was total so 'bunching' was not such a sin as it had been.

NIJMEGEN

Following close on the American airborne assault on Nijmegen, the bridge over the River Waal was stormed and captured intact by the Grenadier Group. On 21 September the Irish Group passed through and took over its defence.

The purpose of OPERATION MARKET GARDEN was for the ground troops to link up with the Airborne Division which was gallantly holding Arnhem. It proved to be impossible to link up in time because of the very narrow front and strong resistance. [This is the origin of the expression 'A Bridge too Far', later the title of an American epic film to the intense irritation of those who had participated in 1944. The only entertainment was that Colonel J.O.E. Vandeleur was played by Michael Caine, with whom he got on famously. The Irish Guards Group managed to link with the US 101st Airborne Division at Zon, and reached Nijmegen. They were awarded a further battle honour, *Aam*, for the actions of 1–4 October 1944 clearing eastwards up the River Maas.

The Divisional Commander, Major-General Sir Allan Adair, who led the Guards Armoured Division with such distinction, inspects the warrant officers of the 3rd Battalion somewhere in Holland. Watching, the Commanding Officer, Lt-Col Dennis Fitzgerald and Adjutant; D/Sgt 'Tommo' Thompson; D/Sgt Jack Thackrah MM; CSM 'Johnno' Johnstone DCM; Capt Jimmy Quinn.

Meeting up with the American 101st Airborne Division on 18 September at Zon, north of Eindhoven where the bridge across the massive Wilhelmina Canal had been destroyed.

A Sherman of the 2nd Battalion consolidates the position.

A 6-pounder anti-tank gun, 20 September, at the approaches to Nijmegen road bridge. Quiet reigns and a Guardsman has his hair cut.

Nearing the end in Germany. Shermans in a typical German village. Surrender was imminent.

Gdsm Edward Charlton VC.
(For full citation see p. 288–9)

Mrs Charlton, Gdsm Charlton's mother, on 28 May 1956 presenting her son's Victoria Cross to the Regiment.

NEARING THE END

The battle now moved across the Rhine into Germany, meeting furious resistance from fanatical German defenders. The honour *Hochwald* was awarded for the 2nd and 3rd Battalions' fighting between 24 February and 4 March 1945. Similarly awards were made for the *Rhine*, 25 March–1 April 1945, and *Bentheim*, 2–3 April 1945.

On 21 April, while probing forward by the village of Wistedt near the town of Elsdorf, a troop of Shermans and its supporting platoon were caught in a German counter-attack. With his tank disabled Gdsm Edward Charlton, the co-driver, dismounted his Browning machine-gun in full view of the enemy and advanced firing from the hip to cover the withdrawal of the remainder of the little force. Wounded in the arm he propped the gun on a gate and continued to fire with the other until, hit again, he fell. Despite every effort of the German doctors he later died of his wounds.

This incredible deed was unrecognised until a Guardsman who had temporarily been taken prisoner escaped to tell what had happened. This was later confirmed by a captured German officer who, like his men, had been astonished by the Guardsman's courage.

Gdsm Edward Charlton was posthumously awarded the Victoria Cross, the last in Europe during the Second World War.

Above: **Victory Parade, Luxembourg, May 1945**. His Royal Highness Prince Felix of Luxembourg; Her Royal Highness the Grand Duchess Charlotte of Luxembourg; Prince Jean Hereditary Grand Duke of Luxembourg, Lieutenant Irish Guards, and from 1984 to 2000 the 7th Colonel of the Regiment. He was the first to stand down, rather than the decision of the 'Grim Reaper.' The Irish Guards contingent led by CSM Jock Monks with, L-R: Sgt George Hare and Sgt J. Cain MM.

Far Right: **Brigadier Derek Mills-Robert** DSO, MC★ was in the Supplementary Reserve of Officers before the war. After serving with the 1st Battalion in Norway, he transferred to the Commandos. He commanded 6 Commado in North Africa (1943) and then 1st Commando Brigade in North-west Europe. For many years he chaired the North of England Branch of the Irish Guards Association.

Right: **War Medal.** Awarded to all full time servicemen who had completed 28 days of service before 2 September 1945. The ribbon is a variation of red, white and blue from the Union Flag.

THE END

On 29 June 1945, at Rotenburg Airfield in Germany, the Guards Armoured Division paraded for the last time with their armour. At 11.30 Field Marshal Montgomery arrived and, after inspecting the parade in a half-track, took his place on the saluting base.

Then the columns of tanks advanced and counter-marched across the ground, each tank commander traversing his turret and saluting. The columns turned and swung away over the hills in the background. As they disappeared the bands broke into the strains of 'Auld Lang Syne'.

There followed a short pause. Then coming over the crest of the hill could be seen the marching columns of the former armoured Battalions. To their regimental marches played in succession by the bands, they came striding down the arena to join their comrades of the Foot Guards below.

As the old familiar tunes rang out what memories must have been stirred in those present that day! Of Cagny; of the costly fighting in the Bocage; of the welcome on the gallop to Brussels; of the great liberation scenes themselves; of the Escaut Canal, MARKET GARDEN and the bitter fighting before reaching Germany. Of individual acts – John Gorman's ramming of the King Tiger in Normandy; Desmond Lampard's dash at JOE's Bridge and Gdsm Charlton's incredible personal battle for which he was awarded the Victoria Cross. And memories of so many more whose endurance and example and skill at arms had added one more passage to the fighting record of the Regiment.

In the Second World War the Irish Guards lost in all 734 dead, including fifty-nine officers. They were awarded two Victoria Crosses; seventeen DSOs; eighteen DCMs; thirty-three MCs and seventy-two MMs.

NORTH-WEST EUROPE 1944–45

The Farewell to Armour Parade.

Guards Chapel. After it was destroyed by a VI rocket on 18 June 1944, it was rebuilt in a modern style in the 1960s. Each Regiment now has its own side chapel and alter. There is also a Regimental Book of Remembrance in the cloister. And to the Guards Memorial, facing Horse Guards Parade, scene of peacetime glory, has been added a modest commemoration of those who gave their lives in the Second World War and in campaigns thereafter.

Chapter Five

1946–1965
POST WAR YEARS

In 1946 the remnants of the 3rd Battalion were incorporated into the 1st and a few months later the 2nd Battalion was once more placed in suspended animation. Prior to that, the 1st Battalion had been sent to Palestine to help keep some semblance of peace between Jews and Arabs before the British Mandate expired.

This was the most intense Internal Security situation yet experienced. So it was with mixed feelings that, in company with the other British forces, the Battalion pulled out in June 1948.

An all-too-short few months in Tripoli: Libya were succeeded by home service until, in 1951, they found themselves in Germany at Hubbelrath near Dusseldorf with 4th Guards Brigade.

1953 was Coronation Year and to the Regiment's great pride, a picked contingent, brought back from Germany, provided the Guard of Honour outside Buckingham Palace.

The German tour ended in 1953 and was immediately succeeded by a spell in the Canal Zone in Egypt before home service took over again for several years. 1958 was interrupted by four months active service in Cyprus including security operations against EOKA.

With heightening East-West tension, the regiment found itself in 1961 at the heart of the Cold War, in West Germany.

Returning in 1964 to a rebuilt Chelsea Barracks, apart from Battalion training in Libya, public duties absorbed their time.

1st Battalion Irish Guards, Nefisha Football Ground, Canal Zone, Egypt, 1955. Commanding Officer, Lt-Col H.L.S. Young DSO.

Amalgamation of the Officers of 1st and 3rd Battalions, 20 August 1946.
Back Row: 2/Lt G. Rooney; 2/Lt M.H. Vernon; 2/Lt G.B.A.F. Rowell; 2/Lt M. Levine; Lt M.E.H. Mullholland; 2/Lt M.N. Garnett; 2/Lt M.C. Robinson; Lt C.K. Atkins; Lt P.A. Filmer-Sankey; 2/Lt Martin.
Middle Row: 2/Lt T.C.P. Whidbourne; Lt A.I.S Boyd; Lt T. Crowe; Capt R.D.C. Bacon; Lt A.S. Reid; Capt M.J. de R. Richardson; Lt B.S. Dale; Lt A.C.B. Millar; Capt J.C. Crewe MC; Capt J.V. Taylor MC.
Seated: Capt G. Gordon-Shee; Capt P.A. McCall; Capt P.C.H. Pollock; Major D.H. FitzGerald DSO; Colonel C.A. Montagu-Douglas-Scott DSO; Major J.D. Hornung OBE MC; Major H.L.S. Young DSO; Major A Bell MC; Capt (QM) J, Keating MBE.

In October 1946 a detached company moved to Hillsborough, the first time the Regiment had been stationed in Northern Ireland.

Inspection of the Governor's Guard by His Excellency The Earl Granville, Governor-General of Northern Ireland.

Laying up the Colours of the 2nd Battalion at Colchester, July 1947. *L-R:* Capt J.D. Chichester-Clarke (later Prime Minister of Northern Ireland); Major J.D. Hornung OBE, MC, Regimental Adjutant; Lt-Col B.O.P. Eugster DSO, MC, Commanding Officer, Colonel J.O.E. Vandeleur DSO, Regimental Lieutenant Colonel; Capt P. Foden Patterson; Capt A.G. Reid.

The Colours of the 2nd Battalion being marched on to parade for the last time. The only occasion upon which a Warrant Officer carries two Colours.

Guard Mounting at Buckingham Palace in battledress, February 1947. Note the presence of the subaltern of the St James's Palace detachment (later dispensed with) as well as the subaltern of the Buckingham Palace detachment. The Guard wears Great Coats and woollen gloves, with service dress caps. The 1938 pattern webbing braces are being worn outside the great coats, and the officers carry a .38 pistol in a webbing holster on the right side. Web anklets were worn, a custom which later ceased in Battalions in London District and at the Guards Depot.

The King's Colour.   The Regimental Colour.

PALESTINE

In the spring of 1947 the 1st Battalion was once again in Palestine. This time its role was to preside over the expiring UN Mandate and to attempt to keep Jew and Arab apart – so being heartedly disliked by both sides. The ensuing months saw the most bitter and intensive Internal Security operations ever undertaken by British forces up to that time.

Enforcing the curfew in Haifa, 15–18 April 1947.

Jerusalem, 28 July–30 September 1947. Search of Givat Shaul.

House searching.

Arms cache found under a stone wall.

Road block.

A load of straw looks suspect.

GSM Palestine
1945–48.

Above: **The Battalion unofficial mascot** 'Capstar' with Capt Bill Churchill.

Presiding over the affairs of the 1st Battalion, as he had those of the 2nd Battalion during the War, was the Quartermaster, Capt Jack 'K' Keating. A native of Ballyragget in County Kilkenny he was a man of infinite charm and instant wit. The name Ballyragget has a place of its own in the Regiment. In a David and Goliath action, a tank of that name rammed a giant King Tiger. Keating's son, Ted, also joined the Regiment as a Guardsman and like his father achieved a commission.

Above: **Battalion sports at Rosh Pinna.** The Commanding Officer, Lt-Col D.H. FitzGerald DSO, competing in the bicycle race.

Left: **Rosh Pinna, St Patrick's Day** 1948. *L-R:* CSM Smart; the Quartermaster, Capt J. ('K') Keating MBE; Sgt Maxi McComish MM.

Right: **CQMS Jack Pestell; CSM Paddy Mercer MM; CSM Micky Moron MM; RSM George Howe.**

Donkey Power, CQMS Jack
Pestell giving encouragement.

**The pipers playing
at Safad**, an area of
some risk. Unusually,
the Drum Major
leads the pipes, and
the pipers' caubeens
are won at an angle
that is no longer
fashionable.

After a lapse of nearly ten years, in 1949 the Brigade of Guards returned to tunic and bearskin.

Above: **The first guard to be mounted by the Regiment at HM Tower of London in full dress**, 15 May 1949. The Drum Major, for whom no gold-laced Drum Major's tunic was available from the pre-war stock, is wearing a warrant officer's tunic with the four large inverted chevrons of the Drum Major's appointment on his sleeve.

Below: **In July 1949 a serious national dock strike saw the Battalion working in the docks.** Unskilled men could never match the performance of the experienced dockers, so ran the theory. The Guardsmen, enjoying the novelty and relishing the opportunity to prove a point, astonished the port authorities by the speed at which they were able to unload huge tonnages with relative ease.

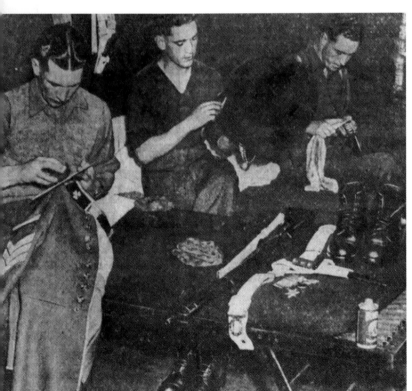

Above: **Preparation, Kings Birthday Parade**, 1949. Sgt F. Beattie and Gdsm P. Duffy (later Major Pat Duffy MBE).

A well decorated group. RSM Bill Rooney MM (Palestine 1938); D/Sgt Micky Moran MM (Anzio 1943) and D/Sgt Johnno Johnstone DCM (Norway 1940).

Fiftieth Anniversary, St Patrick's Day 1950

The Golden Jubilee Ball. In keeping with tradition, a dance programme was produced.

Royal Attendance. Her Majesty The Queen and HRH The Princess Elizabeth accompanied by HRH The Princess Mary, The Princess Royal attended St Patrick's Day with the King for the Regiment's 50th Anniversary.

An aerial view of the march past at Chelsea Barracks after the distribution of the Shamrock by His Majesty King George VI.

Left: **Presentation of Colours**, 27 July 1949 at Buckingham Palace. The King is seen talking to the Colonel of the Regiment. *L-R:* Lt-Col T.E.G. Nugent MVO, MC; Major P.F.I. Reid, Regimental Adjutant; Capt the Lord Plunket, Equerry; The Colonel of the Regiment; The King; Colonel T.W. Gimson, Regimental Lieutenant Colonel. Two of the Ensigns who carried the Colours, Pat and Micky (late Archbishop of Southwark) Bowen, were sons of John Bowen, killed on the *Chobry*. The Colours presented on this occasion displayed only the honours awarded for the Great War. The battle honours awarded to the Regiment for its service in the Second World War were authorised in 1956, and only then were honours added to the Colours. On the King's Colour they were set in two columns of ten, one on each side of the central device. On the Regimental Colour the twenty honours were arranged in two columns of five on each lateral arm of the cross. These are now in the Guards Chapel.

Below: **Field Marshal The Rt Hon the Earl Alexander of Tunis and Errigal in the County of Donegal** KG, PC, GCB, OM, GCMG, CSI, DSO, MC, Colonel of the Regiment (1946–1969), then Minister of Defence, lays the Regimental wreath at the Guards Memorial, 1952.

Below: **Contingent from the Battalion for the funeral of His Majesty King George VI**, 1952. Sixteen officers were brought back to London to form one watch for the Lying in State of King George VI. Officers of the Household Division share with His Majesty's Bodyguard of the Honourable Corps of Gentlemen at Arms and the King's Bodyguard of the Yeomen of the Guard the privilege of guarding the coffin of the Sovereign continuously while it lies in state in Westminster Hall. Each period of twenty-four hours is divided into four watches of six hours. Each watch consists of a minimum of sixteen officers and the Officer Commanding the watch (not below the rank of Lieutenant Colonel). Four officers are on duty together round the coffin, and two officers are always in waiting, of whom one stands at the top landing of the steps and one remains dressed and ready for duty if called upon. (Standing Orders for the Brigade of Guards, 1952.)

Above: **The Regimental Band playing in the City Hall Grounds, Belfast,** after the Coronation under Major C.H. 'Jigs' Jaeger OBE, Director of Music 1948–1969.

Left: **Coronation of Her Majesty Queen Elizabeth II**, 2 June 1953. Guard of Honour found by 1st Battalion Irish Guards outside Buckingham Palace. *L-R:* Capt C.W.D. Harvey-Kelly; 2/Lt J.E.L. Nugent; Lt R.A.C. Plummer.

Coronation Medal 1953. A medal for the Coronation of HM Queen Elizabeth II was issued to 71 members of the Battalion who were involved in the event. Henceforth, only HM The Queen features on medals as Prince Philip is her Consort and not King.

THE CANAL ZONE, EGYPT

From 1954 to 1956 the Battalion formed part of
the British Garrison in the Canal Zone, Egypt.

A Family Regiment. Sons and Grandsons of former members of the Regiment serving in the
Canal Zone in 1955.

Canal Zone Clasp. In June
2003 it was announced the
'Canal Zone' clasp for the
GSM 1918 was to be awarded
to those who served in the
Suez Canal in Egypt during
the period 16 October 1951
to 19 October 1954. The
Battalion qualified, and
would have been pleasantly
surprised, as they arrived
in January 1954 as garrison
troops for three years.

Left: **The Queen's Birthday Parade,
Moascar,** June 1954. Regimental Sergeant
Major Micky Moran MM, with drawn
sword, receives the Regimental Colour
before handing it over to the Ensign. Note
the use of the Regimental Colour on a
parade when the Sovereign is not present.

Below: **Berwick Camp, Fanara.** Company Lines.

Christmas Day 1955

The Sergeants' Mess Team arrives by trailer train towed by an Austin Champ. Christmas was traditionally celebrated overseas in the pre-television age, with an Officers v Sergeants football match and sports. Every subterfuge was employed to ensure a Sergeants' Mess victory, and the atmosphere was mischievous. The Officers always claimed to have 'been robbed!'.

After the Commanding Officer was tackled by D/Sgt Dai Evans, in a moment of forgetfulness that he was now playing soccer, things became confused.

Stella (Beer) Cup.

The two teams, and assorted hangers-on. In the picture: Tony Ross (lying in front); Maxie McComish (in djellaba); Ibrahim, the Sudanese cook; Keith Thomas; Major Mark White; Capt Tony Plummer, Adjutant; Major Stephen Langton, Second-in-Command; Capt John Ghika; Lt Richard Barrow; Major Bobby O'Grady; Lt-Col Savill Young, Commanding Officer; Tom Barry; Harry Fanning; Nobby Clarke; Jimmy Wild; ORQMS; Major Paddy Grogan; Capt Denis Grehan; D/Sgt Dai Evans; Dan Moriarty; Martin Campbell; Philip Lucas; Capt John Head; Tom Gaffney.

Irish Guards Boys, Pirbright, November 1955. The front rank includes: CQMS Ramsey, Lt Jan van Moyland; Major Tony Aylmer, CSM 'Tabs' Mahoney, Sgt Donnan; L/Cpl Mallinson.

Boy soldiers had originally been trained as drummers or tailors and were under the guidance of the Adjutant and the Drum Major of the Battalions of Foot Guards. When Battalions went abroad the boys were sent to the Training Battalion at Pirbright. After the Second World War more opportunities for junior entry into the Army became available, so the Foot Guards set up a Boys' Company (later re-named the Junior Guardsmen's Company) at Pirbright. The age of enlistment never went below 15½. Juniors received education and specialist training before graduating to the Guards Depot at the age of 17½. They were trained as drummers, pipers, clerks, grooms, tailors and signallers.

Another stream of Junior Leaders, enlisted with higher educational qualifications, was trained at Oswestry (and later Shorncliffe) in the Guards Junior Leaders (Waterloo) Company, part of the Infantry Junior Leaders Battalion. The success of junior training was spectacular. It yielded a high proportion of the most successful Warrant and Non-Commissioned Officers. With the re-organisation of training resulting from Options for Change in 1991, adult training was re-structured and the Guards Depot, most regrettably, came to an end. Junior Guardsmen and Junior Leaders ceased to be trained, and the Household Division lost a valuable source of high-grade manpower.

Over the first fence in the 1955 Grand National. The Assistant Regimental Adjutant, Major Mike MacEwan, rides 'Minimax' (32). 'Royal Tan' (2) was the eventual winner.

CYPRUS

In 1958, when stationed at Shorncliffe in Kent and without warning, the Battalion was placed at seven-days' notice to move … somewhere …

… This turned out to be Cyprus, for once again the Middle East was in turmoil. On arrival the Battalion was deployed in company groups in the rural areas around the capital, Nicosia, with close support from the armoured cars of The Royal Horse Guards (The Blues). The EOKA campaign was still active with atrocities between Greek and Turk a daily occurrence. Cordon and search operations became commonplace.

Medal GSM Cyprus.

Above: **Number One Company rounding up suspects.** The 1st Guards Brigade sign showing the 'Ever Open Eye' can be seen on the Land Rover.

Support Company on a Brigade Exercise in the Panhandle. The anti-tank platoon equipped with the 120mm Mobat which had replaced the venerable 17-pounder.

Above: **Identification of suspects.** RSM Paddy Mercer MM visiting the cage.

Below (left & right): **Under guard in makeshift cages.**

ST PATRICK'S DAY

Above: **The Shamrock arrives courtesy Aer Lingus.**

Below: **Grandfather and Grandson.** L/Cpl G. Murphy fixing the Shamrock to the hat of his grandfather, Chelsea Pensioner Sgt S.C. Murphy DCM, a veteran of the Boer War. The wearing of Service Dress Caps ceased in 1958.

Above: **Father and son.** The Colonel of the Regiment, Field Marshal Alex and 2/Lt The Hon. Brian Alexander.

Below: **Father and Daughter.** L/Cpl Dodd gives the Shamrock to his daughter. He is wearing two long service chevrons, the crossed flags of a B3 signaller and the Cyprus General Service Medal.

ST PATRICK'S DAY

Above: **Three cheers** for Her Royal Highness The Princess Royal, Windsor 1960. Capt Peter Thomas in front and Sgt Ambrose Latham nearest the camera.

Above: **Her Royal Highness The Princess Royal** presents Shaun with his Shamrock, Caterham 1961. The Royal gift has been presented annually since 1901 – firstly by Queen Alexandra until her death in 1925; then by Princess Mary, later to become The Princess Royal, until 1964. In 1964 Queen Elizabeth The Queen Mother, who first attended St Patrick's Day in 1927, began her long era of presenting the Shamrock - very often in person despite the frequent conflict over dates with Cheltenham Races.

Left: **Company Commanders receiving the Shamrock** for their companies from the Colonel of the Regiment, Chelsea 1965. *L-R*: Capt 'Johnno' Johnstone MBE, DCM, Quartermaster; the Colonel of the Regiment; Major G. A. Allan; Major P.V. Verney; CSM George Shannon; Major J.N. Ghika. In this photograph the Colonel is distributing the Shamrock presented by the Queen Mother.

The Fighting 69th. On a visit to the United States in 1960 a battered Great War bugle was presented to the 69th National Guard Regiment (The Fighting 69th). This Irish regiment had served beside the Irish Guards in the Great War. RQMS Victor Sullivan, Major Giles Allan and Lt-Col Lynch of the Fighting 69th.

Above: **Snow at Windsor.** A photographic opportunity. 2/Lt Paul de Remusat takes the officer's patrol at Windsor. This is one of a series of posed photographs taken for the 1960 Christmas card. Eventually a picture showing the drummer carrying a lantern was selected.

Below: **Guard of Honour at HM Tower of London** for the installation of the Colonel of the Regiment Field Marshal Alexander, as Constable of the Tower of London. His son Brian was the Ensign. 1960.

The Guards Depot moved from Caterham, its home for years, to Pirbright in 1960.

Below: **Review of the Household Troops on the occasion of the State Visit of President de Gaulle, April 1960.** In the Irish Guards contingent were Major William Harvey-Kelly; Capt James Baker, Lt Anthony Wordsworth; Lt Donough O'Brien and 2/Lt the Hon Brian Alexander. RSM Arthur Bell of 1st Battalion Irish Guards was correctly identified by General de Gaulle as the smartest man on parade. The Battalion smiled quietly to itself and wondered what General de Gaulle knew about drill.

Above: **The old .303 Lee Enfield No 4 Rifle** which had served so well for so long was succeeded by the 7.62mm Self Loading Rifle which required a different drill.

Drum Major Keith Thomas BEM marches off the Old Guard, led by Shaun and Gdsm Birmingham.

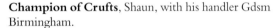

Champion of Crufts, Shaun, with his handler Gdsm Birmingham.

On the way to Gatwick. CSM Jimmy Officer; Shaun; Sgt Ambrose Latham; 2/Lt Willie Mahon.

In 1961 the Battalion returned to Dusseldorf as part of the British Army of the Rhine. This was the first air trooping to Germany by the British Army and was from the newly opened Gatwick Airport. There were not enough married quarters at Hubbelrath for the over strength and heavily married Battalion, So the Commanding Officer, Lt-Col Stephen Langton MVO, MC, decided to solve the problem. To the consternation of the authorities, he somehow obtained a fleet of mobile-home-style caravans which were parked in a back area of the barracks, thus enabling numerous families to be united. It was a good idea; but the climate in winter was not too good. The gesture put a great spark into the powers that were, and soon the quartering situation was resolved. The colour is piped aboard a Vickers Viscount aircraft..

Sgt Lally with the MOBAT anti-tank gun, twining at Sennelager. This was the era of each rifle company having its own support platoon.

Skiing Olympian. In 1960 Capt John Oakes, Army and Combined Services downhill champion for the previous two years, was chosen to captain the British Ski Team at the Winter Olympics in Squaw Valley, California.

C/Sgt Martin Aldridge (a keen amateur photographer and uncle of Major Pat Duffy) is seen here at Vogelsang (a Belgian run training area in the Eifel Mountains) in 'Palmerstown', the Pioneer Commander's APC. The Battalion was equipped with the Humber 1 Ton Armoured, otherwise known as the 'Pig'. Under-powered on account of the armour, and weak in the clutch, the vehicle had a reputation for breaking down and bogging in. The Battalion generated extraordinary hysteria over the loss of red glass tail covers, known as rubies. Commanding Officer's vehicle inspections became a fruitful money spinner for the less scrupulous purveyors of spare rubies.

Companies named their vehicles on a system derived from the 2nd Battalion's tanks, a custom which continues.

TRAINING IN GERMANY

Bren shoot *L-R:* Gdan O'Reilly; L/Cpl Deegaa; Gdsm Lawless; L/Sgt Megaw; Lt Robert Corbett.

THE GUARDS DEPOT

With the end of National Service in 1960, it became necessary to consolidate the training arrangements of the Foot Guards. The Guards Depot had been in the grim barracks at Caterham since the previous century. Mecca of military standards, it contained a company from each regiment. Rivalry was friendly, but acute. No 5 Company Irish Guards occupied Roberts and Alexander blocks, and had their own cook house. The company was fully staffed by Irish Guards NCOs and Trained Soldiers (who wore a brass Brigade Staron the right arm to distinguish them from recruits). Training (drill, weapon training and physical training) took 24 weeks. Thereafter recruits became Trainee Guardsmen and moved to Pirbright to the Guards Training Battalion. This was run on similar lines to Caterham, but the emphasis was on field training. No 7 Company Irish Guards undertook all continuation and tactical training for the Regiment. There was a Battle camp in Pickering in Yorkshire.

In 1960 the Guards Depot closed at Caterham and moved to Pirbright. The tactical types from the Training Battalion said it would be all drill and no tactics. The drill people thought standards would never be the same again. The Training Battalion vanished for ever. And the Guards Depot became a stronger, more all-round, magnificently equipped organisation, fulfilling the most demanding training needs to perfection.

ennelager 1961.

This period saw the re-introduction of the wartime policy of cross postings of companies and platoons of the Household Division, just as X Company Scots Guards had been so special to the 3rd Battalion Irish Guards during the Normandy Campaign so the exchanges began anew.

No 3 Company. No 3 Company was detached to join 2nd Battalion Scots Guards in Kenya. It departed from Sennelager and marched past the Commanding Officer, Lt-Col Stephen Langton MVO, MC.

Army Athletics Championships, 1965. After a gap of 44 years, the Battalion won the Army Athletics Championship as well as being London District Athletic and Cross Country Champions, Eastern Command Athletic and Cross Country Champions, Lawson Cup and Prince of Wales Relay Race winners.
Back row: Gdsm Doyle; Gdsm Raley; Musn Ashford; Gdsm Hayden; Gdsm Fearon; Gdsm McManus; Gdsm Herriott; Gdsm Wishart; L/Cpl McDonagh; Gdsm Little; L/Cpl Gilpin; L/Cpl Lockhart; Gdsm Hickey.
Centre row: Gdsm O'Sullivan; Gdsm Parry; Gdsm Mooney; Gdsm Harper; L/Cpl Turner; Gdsm Graham; Gdsm MacDonald; L/Cpl Byrne; Gdsm Hanlon; Gdsm Stone; Gdsm Kewley; L/Sgt Smith; Gdsm Keane; L/Sgt McKinty.
Front row: Sgt Dent, A.P.T.C.; Lt R.C. Wolverson; Sgt MacDermot; Capt The Viscount Cole; L/Sgt Murphy; Lt-Col C.W.D. Harvey-Kelly; L/Sgt Cleary; Major G.A. Allan; L/Sgt Green; 2/Lt A.N. Foster; RSM Stuart.

Above: **Borneo,** February 1965. Returning from patrol, Padawan, Sarawak. *L-R:* Gdsm Donley, Sgt Johnston; Gdsm Fleming.

Above: **Borneo, 1965.** L/Sgt Carvill briefs his patrol. *L-R:* Gdsm Johnson; Gdsm Maxwell. *Rear Row:* Gdsm Butterworth (later Capt Colin Butterworth); Gdsm Connolly 36. (After active service in the Congo with the Irish Army he was one of several soldiers who later served in the Irish Guards and wore the UN Congo Medal. Needless to say he was universally known as 'Congo Joe').

Above: **Borneo,** 1965. Building a helicopter pad in the jungle. *L-R:* Gdsm Millar, Mackrell, Spencer, Johnson, Montgomery, L/Sgt Moore and Mitchell. This was at the height of the Vietnam War when helicopter tactics tried by the US Army revolutionised rapid reaction in jungle warfare.

No 4 Company was re-numbered as No 9 and joined 1st Battalion Scots Guards as part of the Commonwealth Brigade in Terendak, Malacca, Malaysia. After jungle training in Johore Bahru the Battalion deployed on the first of two roulement tours to Borneo, by then part of Malaysia. Operations consisted of setting up company bases in the jungle and undertaking long active service patrols in defence of the Malaysian border which was being 'confronted' by frequent raids by the Indonesian Army.

Right: **Pingat Jasa Malaysia Medal.** In 2004 the Malaysian Government offered the Pingat Jasa Malaysia medal to commemorate those who had served to uphold the sovereignty of Malaysia during the Malayan Emergency and Confrontation. Those who served in No 9 Company with the 1st Battalion Scots Guards in Borneo qualified.

Campaign Service Medal. Clasps Malay Peninsula, Borneo.

Padawan Camp, Sarawak. Gun pits in the company lines. The guns are 105mm Pack Howitzers of 6 (Light) Regiment Royal Artillery based at Terendak.

LIBYA, 1965

1st Battalion Irish Guards based in Chelsea Barracks found itself, somewhat improbably, offered a break from public duties in the form of a Battalion exercise in the Libyan desert. The Battalion's transport had an adventurous trip by road via Italy and thence by sea to Tobruk.

The remainder of the Battalion flew by RAF Transport Command to El Adem, a huge RAF base not far from the Egyptian border. Surprisingly all went more or less according to plan.

On arrival each company was driven for some distance along the coast road towards Derna, to an unlovely spot called Timimi. There, in widely spaced out locations, training went on, ending with several days of what were known as Battalion stunts.

It was proper, rough old 8th Army desert, and minefields and the odd unexploded grenade were still in evidence. So were occasional locals who appeared out of nowhere to sell miserable, small eggs to voracious Guardsmen who were not impressed, and said so, in the time honoured fashion … 'IMSHI!' Desert navigation was at best hazardous for a public duties Battalion, whether in transport, or on foot, but somehow supplies always reached the companies.

A 1965 nominal roll of the Battalion for emplaning purposes reveals over 85 per cent Irish addresses for the next of kin.

Three scenes in Libya. No 1 Company Base Camp.

Company base camp.

L/Sgt Cushion erects a bivouac.

Drummer Deane (later Drum Major Dixie Deane BEM) and Gdsm Jimmy Hayden, heavyweight boxer, with members of No. 1 Company. At this stage battle dress (BD) had been replaced by Combat dress, but puttees had not yet replaced 1938 pattern web anklets. New Boots DMS (Directly Moulded Sole) had just been introduced, but some still wore Boots CWW (Cold Wet Weather, known as 'Boots Cobbly Wobbly'). Berets remained dark blue, except in the case of one or two senior officers who had served in the 3rd Battalion during the war, who wore brown berets.

Early morning cordon and search operation, (Aden 1967).

Chapter Six

1966–1985
END OF EMPIRE

This period covers the end of residual imperial responsibilities. The Regiment, at its peacetime establishment of a single Battalion, deployed more frequently and to more different theatres than ever before.

In the Far East, No 9 company continued to serve in East and West Malaysia with 1st Bn Scots Guards until 1967, while the Battalion itself was in Hong Kong for two and a half years from late 1971. In 1965 an affiliation was cemented with 4th Battalion The Royal Australian Regiment which led to several excellent Australian officers later serving with the 1st Battalion Irish Guards, especially in British Army of the Rhine.

In the Middle East the Battalion was involved in the uncomfortable and scrappy Aden wind down (1966–1967).

In Africa the Battalion sent monitoring parties to Rhodesia in 1980, as well as a company exercise to Ghana (during 1975).

There were infantry exercises in Canada at Winnipeg and mechanised exercises in Alberta at British Army Training Unit Suffield. Operational tours also took place at intervals in the jungles of Belize.

In Europe the Cold War ebbed and flowed, with the Battalion taking its full mechanised part in BAOR, in 4th Guards Brigade at Munster (which, in what was perceived as a gesture to appease a 'high up', was re-named 4 Armoured Brigade in 1977).

At home public duties were still maintained at the usual immaculate level. Duties in aid of the Civil Power emerged in the form of OPERATION BURBERRY, firefighting in London during the national firemen's strike, using the venerable Green Goddess (elderly Civil Defence fire engines based on the petrol-powered Bedford three tonner), as well as standby duties for London flooding (OPERATION GIRAFFE) and Heathrow Airport emergencies.

Such were the balmy days of peace.

Presentation of Colours, 10 June 1966, Buckingham Palace.

March past with the new Colours.
L–R: Colour Point (marker) C/Sgt Allister. *On the steps:* Lt-Col Tony Aylmer, Commanding Officer; Field Marshal The Earl Alexander of Tunis (Colonel of the Regiment); Lt-Col The Lord Patrick Plunket (Irish Guards, Equerry to Her Majesty); Colonel William Harvey-Kelly (Regimental Lieutenant Colonel), and Her Majesty. The Colour Party *L–R:* 2/Lt Robin Bullock-Webster with the Queen's Colour (Crimson); C/Sgt George Fawcett, and 2/Lt Charles Aikenhead with the Regimental Colour.

ADEN

No sooner was the Birthday Parade over, and the new Colours were paraded for the first time, when training for Aden began in earnest. This included a Battalion exercise among the sheep at Sennybridge in Wales (a great setting for Arabian urban or mountain operations for which they were preparing!). Nowadays it seems astonishing that a public duties Battalion should be sent with minimal preparations to a place like Aden, where the operational situation was difficult and about to explode. It was a busy time.

The Battalion formed part of 24 Brigade (as it had been in Norway in 1940) and was based in Salerno Camp, Little Aden near the huge smelly BP refinery. Aden, once a crucial British coaling station on the route to India, had been struggling for independence. In 1966 the British government, keen to be rid of troublesome colonies, announced the date for independence to be late 1967. This was the signal for violence throughout the South Arabian Federation, as it had become. Power hungry rival armed groups, both of which hated the British, fought running battles with each other for power. They were FLOSY (Front for the Liberation of South Yemen), and the NLF (National Liberation Front). The Battalion, which relieved 1st Bn Welsh Guards, had an action packed tour.

No sooner had they arrived than they found themselves on OPERATION FATE, an amphibious landing down the coast of East Aden Protectorate at a guerilla training camp. This resulted in a number of suspects being detained and many illegal weapons confiscated.

Operation Fate. Suspects awaiting questioning are held in the compound erected by the Pioneer Platoon. In the background a landing craft from HMS *Fearless*.

Operation Fate. No 3 Company formed up, wearing life jackets, waiting to land at Hauf from HMS *Fearless*. At front right wearing a beret is 2/Lt Anthony Weldon and at the very back, on the left, Pipe Major Tom Ramsey's caubeen can be seen. He was the third Ramsey to be the Pipe Major.

The Battalion had its own air platoon under direct command for the first time. It consisted of three Sioux recce helicopters, one flown by Capt Garry Daintry (seen here over the Radfan), the others by Foot Guards officers on loan.

Patrolling and Internal Security duties in Aden occupied much of their time. Here 2/Lt David Carleton-Paget and Sgt Jim Driscoll with close support from a Land Rover are all alertness in Ma'alla, a notorious district in what was known as Big Aden.

Above: **Temple Hill Picquet, Dhala.** L/Cpls Jim Mooney and Stevenson.

Above: **L/Sgts Hoey and Noel Cullen** in a sangar up country with the unmistakable figure of Capt Shane Blewitt. In the foreground can be seen a wireless aerial of the fishing rod type.

Below: **Patrol near Habilayn.** Note the Commanding Officer, Lt-Col Tony Aylmer, nearest the camera, carries an Armalite rifle. He is followed by the Regimental Sergeant Major, Victor Sullivan.

There were also tours of duty up country at Habilayn, a sandbagged tented Battalion base and air strip astride the road to Dhala, which Royal Marine Commandos handed over to the Battalion several times … and the oil drums had once more to be re-painted blue-red-blue! A company was based at Dhala, near the border with Yemen.

During the early stages of the Battalion's tour, No 3 Company was in a detached company base in the Wadi Matlah, some miles from the bulk of the Battalion at Habilayn. In the temporary absence of the company commander, the second-in-command, Capt David Webb-Carter, was in charge. That evening and with no warning a determined attack was pressed home on the company camp under heavy fire from small arms and blindicide rockets. (Blindicide means armour killer, as in Insecticide!) Capt Webb-Carter put up stout defence, and astonishingly the only casualty was the company's fridge, grievously wounded. It was reported that one of the Battalion's characters, L/Sgt 'The Bat' Tighe, a shortsighted, Arabic-speaking mortar fire controller, issued a stream of Irish Arabic fire orders to the confused opposition. Capt Webb-Carter was awarded the Military Cross.

Below: **Replen.** Eggs, water and rations being delivered to a piquet. Land Rovers were adapted to carry a General Purpose Machine Gun even for street patrols, while an angle iron picquet was fitted to the front to counter the threat of piano wire stretched across the road.

Hearts and Minds patrols were undertaken in the mountains, and efforts were made to keep the wild Radfan countryside peaceful. Egyptian plastic antipersonnel mines were a worry up country, but seldom seen. There were numerous skirmishes and the Battalion set one hasty night ambush in which casualties were sustained from a volley of blindicides. Four died, amongst them the radio operator, so mortar fire could not be called down. L/Cpl Lewis won the Military Medal and Gdsm Bell was posthumously mentioned in dispatches.

History repeated itself when *The Harp*, a light-hearted Battalion newspaper was produced on a regular basis, echoing in style the levity and quality of its Great War trench predecessor, the *Morning Rire*.

During the Battalion's tour the 1967 Arab-Israeli war broke out. The locals, to a man, backed the Arabs with vigour and violence. There were taunting shouts from the urban rioters: 'Nasser Tamam', to which the Guardsmen boredly replied with the incomprehensible well worn Mick epithet 'Queen Victoria ... very good bloke'! The situation became much inflamed by the mutiny of the Armed Police in Crater, an almost inaccessible inner suburb and trouble spot where The Royal Northumberland Fusiliers suffered a number of casualties. Irish Guards companies were deployed to guard key points and patrolled the streets 24 hours a day. One night, communications with the platoon on duty at the oil refinery failed. Urgent investigation revealed a sporting young officer improvising with the long aerial of the C42 wireless set, fishing for king fish.

During these operations, which spoiled the Commanding Officer's planned drinks party to celebrate the Queen's Birthday, No 3 Company was withdrawn and hurriedly flown (exhausted) to RAF Riyan near Mukalla. The same evening, in the Regiment's first live helicopter assault, part of a platoon secured the town of Seiyun up country in the Hadhramaut, followed shortly after by further deployment of the remainder of the company to Ghuraf air strip and Shibam, the Queen of Sheba's wonderful city in the wadi.

As time in Aden began to run out, the local dockers went on strike and the Battalion found itself, in sizzling temperatures, loading valuable ammunition and stores which were to be evacuated by ships of the British India Line near Steamer Point.

Finally, the Barracks were handed over, less air conditioning, to the Russians!

History repeating itself. Not since the dock strike in 1949 had the Battalion loaded ships. This was another role as part of the Aden withdrawal.

About to go on patrol in Sheik Othman. L/Cpl 'Hovis' Brown (*left*) and L/Sgt Kelly closing the doors of a Bedford 3 Armoured 3 Ton Truck.

On 1 June 1967 No 3 Company was attached to 1st Bn The Parachute Regiment; this was the day (The Glorious First of June) on which there were more than one hundred 'incidents' before midday. Incidents had become blurred by continual skirmishing and fighting in the streets, and to everyone's surprise the animals were released from the rather moth-eaten zoo. There was also the Federal National Guard (a swarthy bunch with an eye to the future!) and the Federal Regular Army who were more reliable and still had some brave British Officers. Most Beau Geste of all were the Hadrahmi Bedouin Legion who, whilst nominally helping No 3 Company at Siyun, were regarded with some suspicion since they had murdered their British Commanding Officer the previous week.

Above: **No 3 Company briefing before a Hearts and Minds operation.** On left Sgt MacDermot and CSM Kelly.

Above: **L/Sgt 'The Bat' Tighe at Seiyun,** making the best use of his recently acquired Arabic in the hope of maintaining regular supplies.

GSM South Arabia.

Above: **A Hadrahmi Bedouin Legionnaire.**

Left: **An Aden policeman** accompanied each foot patrol. A very smart police force operated under difficult circumstances.

Visit to Aden by the Colonel of the Regiment, 1967. Field Marshal Alex visited the Battalion and distributed the Shamrock. The Field Marshal commented that, with the exception of the helicopter, the tactics being used up country in Aden were the same as he had known when he commanded the Nowshera Brigade on the North West Frontier. Indeed, the Mountain Warfare pamphlet used for training was a re-write of the pre-war pamphlet of the same name.

Officers of 1st Battalion Irish Guards, Aden, March 1967.
Back Row L–R: Major (QM) Paddy Mercer MBE, MM; Capt Sean O'Dwyer; Lt Colijn Thomson-Moore; Capt David Moore (Medical Officer); Major Bob Kennedy; Capt Simon Gordon Duff (SG Air Platoon); Major Peter Verney; Father Michael Holman; Capt John Lockwood; Major Brian Gilbart-Denham; Major (Rtd) Tony Mainwaring-Burton; Capt Patrick Grayson; Lt Mickey Barnes (WG Air Platoon); The Rev Frank Johnson; Capt (QM) Arthur Bell; Capt David Webb-Carter MC; Capt Shane Blewitt.
Middle Row L–R: Major John Hallmark (Paymaster); Capt Paul de Rémusat; Lt-Col Tony Aylmer (Commanding Officer); Field Marshal Alex; Major John Head; Capt Tom Brooke; Capt Christopher Wolverson.
Front Row L–R: 2/Lt David Carleton-Paget; 2/Lt Anthony Weldon; Lt Malcolm Ross (SG); Lt Savill Young; Lt Robin Bullock-Webster; 2/Lt Michael Chesterton.

The Field Marshal inspecting a newly introduced WOMBAT anti-tank gun. *L–R:* RSM Vic Sullivan; Major Peter Verney; the Field Marshal; Lt-Col Tony Aylmer, Commanding Officer; Capt John Lockwood, Adjutant. Just visible behind the commanding officer is the Trilby hat favoured by Assistant Regimental Adjutant Tony Mainwaring-Burton, always immaculately dressed even as a retired officer.

The Battalion returned from Aden to Elizabeth Barracks, Pirbright. Here Queen Elizabeth The Queen Mother presented her Shamrock on St Patrick's Day 1968. This was followed, interspersed with Spearhead (the standby Battalion) and public duties, by the first EXERCISE POND JUMP WEST to Canada.

Above: **Boxing.** The Regiment won the King's Trophy (the Army championship) in 1961, 1964 and 1966. Here the victorious 1966 team pose. Gdsm McKinty boxed for Ireland in the Commonwealth Games; the three O'Sullivan brothers (frequent 'visitors' to Commanding Officer's Orders) had a style all their own, and every man in the group was a character. The Regiment, following the tradition started by the first Quartermaster, Ginger Fowles, lived and breathed boxing and was intensely proud of these men.(Sadly Sergeant Fitzpatrick, back row extreme right, the trainer, was killed in Aden].

The Colonel in Chief, painted by Timothy Whidborne. The artist served in the Regiment between 1943 and 1948. This painting was presented to the Regiment by Capt Michael Boyle in 1969.

Exercise Pond Jump West, Canada, 1968.

Above: **Trekking.** L/Sgt John Simpson briefs his patrol before a trekking exercise.

Left: **The Quartermaster, Capt Arthur Bell,** entered into the spirit of things, although perhaps dressed for a few thousand miles to the south.

Better than walking. In 1968 the Battalion was flown en masse to Canada for training on the Camp Wainwright Training Grounds in Alberta. Also in attendance was Father Dolly Brookes from Downside who had been Adjutant in the First World War and Chaplain in North Africa.

CYPRUS 1969

Hurling Match. An exercise in Cyprus enabled a match between the Regiment and the Irish Army Battalion serving with the United Nations. Here the Commanding Officer, Lt-Col John Head welcomes the teams. Nearest the camera is L/Sgt Guerin and L/Cpl Fitzsimmons is also visible. The final score went unrecorded but the post match festivities in all messes were the stuff of legend. In fact, the Gaelic Athletic Association Rule 21 barred the British Army from playing Gaelic games until it was repealed in 2001 but as the Micks often stated 'rules are for others'. In 2015 it was agreed that an Irish Guards Gaelic football team could compete in a GAA London league.

A Battalion exercise in Cyprus gave an opportunity for the Micks to meet the Irish Army which was providing a United Nations Battalion. The two pipe bands play together at half time. The Battalion piper here is L/Cpl Johnston who later became Pipe Major.

Mini Micks. In the late 1960s it was decided that a good means of stimulating the Irish Guards numbers enlisting as Junior Guardsmen or Junior Leaders would be to institute Cadet Platoons in Northern Ireland. Here Field Marshal Alex performs one of his last duties with the Regiment, visiting the Cadet Platoon in Belfast. *Left:* L/Sgt McNickle (in No2 Dress); the Colonel of the Regiment; CSM Bill Allister, the Regiment's recruiter in Belfast.

Funeral of Field Marshal the Earl Alexander of Tunis, Colonel of the Regiment, 24 June 1969. As a Knight of the Garter the Field Marshal's funeral service was in St George's Chapel at Windsor. Here, the gun carriage turns off the High Street up towards the Henry VIII Gate of the Castle. Sergeant Irwin leads the charger with the boots reversed, while three Irish Guards Field Officers carry cushions bearing the Field Marshal's decorations. The Regiment was saddened that he had not lived long enough to name the new Guards Depot barracks at Pirbright, which his widow duly named Alexander Barracks.

Shooting Team with trophies, 1970. Winners of the London District Rifle Association (LDRA). This was the era of great shooting teams. Not all the names were recorded, but even thirty years later the following could be identified: *L–R Seated:* Sgt Shepherd; Sgt Chambers; D/Sgt Garner; Lt Philip O'Reilly; C/Sgt Roberts; Sgt Brown; L/Sgt Bittles. *Standing rows include:* Gdsm Byles and Lee; L/Sgt Leggatt; Gdsm Shanks; two Robinson brothers out of the four who eventually formed a strong family unit in the team, L/Cpl O'Neill and Furphy, as well as Gdsm Tobin at the top.

Ex Battle Royal. In August 1971, the Household Division organised a royal review in Aldershot to show the operational nature of the Household troops. The Irish Guards were deployed in the Far East so demonstrated their expertise in the jungle. The Quartermaster even obtained two pack mules named '*Capstar*' and '*St Patrick's Blue*'. Coincidentally, Her Majesty also has two race horses with the same names. Shown here is Lt Patrick Hungerford explaining the role to Her Majesty passing by L/Sgt John McKinty, who represented the UK and Ireland and won a silver medal in the Commonwealth Games that same year.

Recruit Mallet, tallest man in the Regiment, provided a challenge when he joined No 5 Company at the Guards Depot. Mallet, from Birmingham, stood 7ft 8 inches in a bearskin. Here Company Sergeant Major Tom Corcoran and L/Cpl Hanna from the tailor's shop pose for the photographer. Mallet was of course difficult to use for public duties, since he did not fit easily in a rank. However, he made a fine impression when opening the doors of visiting VIPs' cars.

HONG KONG 1970–1972

The Battalion flew to Hong Kong in late 1970. Battalion
Headquarters and two companies were at Stanley Fort
on the south side of Hong Kong Island while, because of
refurbishment, the remainder of the Battalion was based at Lye
Mun, some 25 minutes away on the north of the island.

The Battalion's role included border duties with the Royal
Hong Kong Police, and support of the Civil Power as necessary.
When carrying out tours of duty on the Chinese border, the
Battalion came under command of 48 Gurkha Infantry Brigade,
based at Sek Kong in the New Territories. Their unpleasant
task was to apprehend escapers, who had swum from China and
who were seeking freedom in Hong Kong. They were viewed
as illegal immigrants. The police would question them, and then
they were returned to China to an uncertain fate.

During the Battalion's tour in Hong Kong it experienced
several spectacular typhoons (the first of which removed the
paint from all the newly repainted Battalion signs). Another,
Typhoon 'Rose' was said to have been the most severe for
many years. Twelve ships were wrecked in Hong Kong
Harbour.

There were many exercises with the police
to provide reassurance as it was only three years
since there had been serious disturbances in the
Colony. Here Lt Michael Sharman, carrying
a Sub Machine Gun, liaises with his opposite
number in the HK Police.

Recruiting material used to increase the
Battalion's manpower before the tour.

Naval Support. The Battalion assemble on the deck of HMS *Intrepid* at the start of an exercise.

Left: **Marching through Kowloon.** Major Patrick Grayson leads No 2 Company down Nathan Road, Kowloon after the Queen's Birthday Parade, 21 April 1972. Keeping a supervisory eye from the roadside, D/Sgt Meredith. Their white No 3 Dress was known as Ice Cream Order. In Hong Kong the Queen's Birthday was celebrated on her actual birthday in April as it was too hot to do so on her Official Birthday in June.

Above: **Sixth Colonel of the Regiment.** On the death of Field Marshal the Earl Alexander of Tunis, Lieutenant General Sir Basil Eugster was appointed Colonel. Here he is seen in Hong Kong in 1970 (he was Commander British Forces) with other Irish Guardsmen serving in, or as part of, No 1 (Guards) Independent Company, The Parachute Regiment, visiting the Colony. *Standing, L–R:* Sgt Armstrong (Orderly); Sgt Sinclair; CSM Kelly; RSM Micky Moran MM (Garrison Sergeant Major); the Colonel of the Regiment; Capt Colijn Thomson-Moore; Capt Patrick Grayson (ADC); D/Sgt Murphy; CSM Stewart. *Front Row, L–R:* Gdsm Hughes; Gdsm Passant; Gdsm Moss; Gdsm McGormick; Gdsm O'Connor (killed in the Falklands War in 1982 serving with G Sqn 22 SAS); Gdsm Orrit; Gdsm Stevens.

Above: **Affectation?** The Commanding Officer, Lt-Col Tony Plummer, borrowed the Adjutant's tactical brolly during EXERCISE HARD NUT and the photographer won the Army Photographer of the Year prize. The Adjutant, Capt Willie Mahon, just got drenched! 'It is,' the Duke of Wellington had said some time before, 'a needless affectation for officers of the Foot Guards to carry an umbrella upon the battlefield.' Major Savill Young was known to have done so at Anzio, so it is almost a regimental custom, despite the Iron Duke's exhortation.

Kotewall Road Disaster. No 2 Company helping with search and rescue after freak monsoon rains had caused two high-rise residential buildings in a steep part of the Peak area to collapse in the middle of the night. Deep under the rubble, in a precarious cavity which was in danger of imminent collapse and which was filling with escaping gas, 2/Lt Johnny Gorman (son of John Gorman of King Tiger Tank, Normandy 1944) managed to undertake several hair-raising rescues for which he was awarded the George Medal. Gdsm Kennedy received the Queen's Commendation.

The George Medal.

Chinese Army guard post where trucks were stopped

Route taken by British Army trucks

8 Irish Guards held, then freed by PLA

By KEVIN SINCLAIR

CHINESE troops applauded and cheered early today as they escorted eight Irish soldiers back to the Hongkong border.

Earlier, the Chinese hosted the British soldiers at a fish and crab dinner on the other side of the wire at the divided border village of Shataukok.

The border "incident" began at 2.15 pm yesterday when a group of Irish Guards soldiers drove towards British Army positions near the China border – and kept on driving.

They ended up well inside Chinese territory.

The truck and landrover in the convoy were both carrying provisions for British troops.

When the Quarter Master Sergeant J. Skates realised he was in Chinese territory, the two vehicles stopped.

A Hongkong policeman, who reacted much faster than the soldiers, quickly grabbed an electronic microphone and yelled: "You are in Chinese territory. Don't move."

Curious Chinese troops

The troops stayed in their trucks. Peoples Liberation Army men quickly surrounded them, more curious than dangerous.

Then, under PLA foot guard, the two vehicles moved around the corner and out of view of the anxious Hongkong police watchers.

Early today, it was found the troops were ordered out of the trucks by Chinese troops soon after they were out of the sight of our border watchers.

Then they went into a police station where their identities were checked.

Finally, the British troops asked the Irishmen to go to a dinner party, where fish, crabs and prawns were served.

The personnel involved in the incident were: C.Q.M.S. J. Skates, L/Cpl. K. Gillen, Guardsmen B. Donnelly, N. Egan, C. Lavery, C. McMenamin, T. Meyler, A. Cullen.

The Famous Border Incident. The Battalion set off for yet another border tour on 18 May 1971. The easternmost company base was Shataukok, in which No 2 Company deployed. CQMS 'Joe' Skates, fully aware of the importance of not straying across the border, was in the lead Land Rover, delivering supplies and stragglers to the company outlying positions. He turned round to ensure that the 3 tonner was following, only to find that his driver had crossed the border. Frantically trying to reverse, he now found his way blocked by the 3 tonner. They were instantly apprehended by the People's Liberation Army. At once the incident hit the world's headlines. The untold truth was that the Battalion thought it knew who was in the convoy. However, the Chinese announced they held eight, not seven, British soldiers. Unbeknown to all, one Guardsman had been late for the main convoy to the border that morning. To avoid being reported absent, he quietly 'stowed away' in the back of the CQMS's truck, the last to leave Stanley. His plan was working well until the navigation problem, when instead of quietly taking up his position in his platoon, he ended up in China. Imagine the confusion!

1972–3

The Battalion returned from Hong Kong to Caterham in late 1972. While it was in Hong Kong the Army introduced the new Disruptive Pattern Material combat dress (initially christened 'Flower Power'), in place of the former plain green combat dress. After Hong Kong there followed a short tour, under Lt-Col Giles Allan, to Belize. This was the Battalion's first of many visits to the former British Honduras, countering external threats to the former colony.

Below: **Guards Parachute Company.** Mick members of No 1 (Guards) Independent Parachute Company, equipped with non standard Armalite rifles exercising in Malaysia in October 1973. From left to right they are LSgt Bobby Dunlop, LSgt Charlie Orritt, CSM Gerry Crymble, Captain Brian O'Gorman, Gdsm Chris Rimmer and Gdsm Tom Desmond. The Company were the pathfinder force with 16 Para Bde. It was a role they carried out for 27 years, based at Pirbright until disbanded in 1975 when the Brigade was dismantled as no future role could be envisaged for Airborne Forces. Unsurprisingly perhaps, the decision was reversed after the Falklands War in 1982 but a proposal to reform a Guards Pathfinder Platoon floundered in 1991. More recently a Guards Platoon has been established in 3rd Battalion The Parachute Regiment.

Above: **The Regimental Band, visiting the Battalion in Belize**, out of tunics!

Below: **Escort to the Colour**, June 1973. Subaltern, Capt Barry Gubbins, Ensign 2/Lt Jonathan Coe, Regimental Sergeant Major Frank Groves (the only Regimental Sergeant Major to have been Pipe Major). In the background is the Guards Memorial, a subscription to which was made by Rudyard Kipling, in memory of his son, John, from the proceeds of the sale of the regimental history, *The Irish Guards in the Great War.*

In 1975 the Battalion
moved to Buller Barracks,
Münster to be part of the
4th Guards Brigade.

Right: **Germany,** 1976. Lt-Col
Dick Hume, the Commanding
Officer, debriefs No 1 Company
during an exercise on the Haltern
training area.

Army Inter-Unit Cookery Champions, 1976 (previously won
in 1913!). One means of keeping morale high was the Commanding
Officer's insistence on good food. The Regimental Cooks, for the last
time, since they were rebadging to the Army Catering Corps, under
Sgt Clavin, won the 2nd Armoured Division, BAOR and Army
championships. As the Regimental *Journal* reported with delight:
'The competition required them to set up a field kitchen properly
camouflaged, and for two of them to cook a three course meal for
twenty men on a Number One burner, while the rest did the same in
the kitchen … Nobody knew until the day who would be selected to
cook what.' The menus never varied, much to the regret of certain
inhabitants of the Guardroom who were required to eat fish liberally
covered in white sauce every day for three months. But as the Messing
Officer so kindly put it: 'Some actually grew to like it.'

Chieftain tanks supporting the Irish Guards Battle Group
on training at Sennelager.

Belize, 1977. Summer 1977 was sunny and Silver Jubilee Year, and 1st Battalion Irish Guards was at Munster. The day after the Queen's Jubilee Review at Sennelager, No 2 Company under Major Sean O'Dwyer was flown on a six-month, emergency tour to Belize, where mounting security problems necessitated reinforcement.

HMS *Boxer*, a Type 42 guided missile destroyer. Throughout its history, the Regiment has enjoyed close ties with the Royal Navy. Boxer became the affiliated ship in 1984. She was decommissioned on 4 August 1999. Numerous groups from the Regiment visited the ship, and the strong friendship and admiration for the Royal Navy flourished.

Queen Elizabeth Silver Jubilee Medal, 1977. Only 30,000 medals were distributed in Britain and the Battalion's allocation was a mere six. 'Influence at Court' increased the number to be able to give it to the senior person serving in each rank on the day.

Firefighting. Recruits from the Guards Depot deployed on OPERATION BURBERRY.

OPERATION BURBERRY. In late 1977 the Fire Brigades Union called a nation-wide strike over pay. The Armed Services were equipped with venerable Green Goddess fire appliances, originally designed for the Auxiliary Fire Service, and which had been in store since the 1950s. All Regimental Headquarters deployed to sectors of London. The Irish Guards, under Colonel Giles Allan, went to Hounslow and controlled the Southwest sector of London. 1st Battalion Irish Guards took its place in the roster during the strike, and so did recruits from the Guards Depot. Several daring rescues were made. The greatest difficulty was preventing Guardsmen with no breathing apparatus or protective clothing risking their own lives for others. Here L/Sgt D. McDonnell rescues a child from a burning building. (Courtesy Daily Mail)

The Robinson Brothers. Just as there were O'Sullivan brothers in the boxing team, so the family factor was evident in the shooting team. All four Robinson brothers were members of the Household Division shooting team. Three brothers shot for the Army, and three brothers shot for Ireland. This is the only time in Bisley's history that four brothers shot for the same regiment at the same time. *L–R:* John, David, Kenneth and Stephen. They are pictured standing on the Green in front of the Officers' Mess at Victoria Barracks, Windsor.

New Colours, Windsor, 1978. The Colonel in Chief presented new Colours on the East Terrace at Windsor. Lt-Col James Baker, Commanding Officer, accompanies Her Majesty during the inspection. In her speech The Queen referred to the Colours of the disbanded Irish Regiments which are in safekeeping in Windsor Castle.

Laying up the Old Colours, Windsor, 1978. These Colours, presented by The Queen in 1966, were laid up at the Garrison Church, Windsor in October 1978. Here the Colonel of the Regiment takes the Colours from Colonel Giles Allan (Regimental Lieutenant Colonel) and Lt-Col James Baker, Commanding Officer.

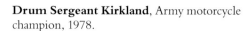

Drum Sergeant Kirkland, Army motorcycle champion, 1978.

Overseas Training in Ghana, July 1978. Major Robin Bullock–Webster took No 4 Company to Ghana, where Piper Stranix (later Pipe Major and Metropolitan Police Royal Protection officer) proved an instant attraction.

ST PATRICK'S DAY 1980

Two smiling Queens on St Patrick's Day, the weather notwithstanding.

Clement Weather? This is one of those famous occasions which nobody who was there will ever forget. It rained, the forecast said it would lift, but it just got worse. The Battalion, about to enter the public duties season after Belize, was wearing tunics for the first time, and The Queen and The Queen Mother were attending. Miraculously the tunics survived. However, the guests' canvas chairs filled with water when they stood for the National Anthem … so there was a curious reluctance to sit down.

The Rhodesia Medal.

Rhodesia, 1980. The Commonwealth Monitoring Force was assembled in Rhodesia to enable the 'Freedom Fighters' to hand in their weapons and to allow free elections to take place. Major Tim Purdon and Sergeant Jimmy Hagan are seen here discussing matters with new arrivals. Their Assembly Area, FOXTROT, eventually housed several thousand Communist trained ZANU and ZAPU freedom fighters who retained their weapons until the last moment. Football was one magic ingredient in keeping all happy. So was the fact that the Africans were pleased to be hosted by soldiers whom they mistakenly supposed to be Irish freedom fighters! Nobody discussed politics, and they were never disabused. A special medal was struck for this unusual operation. Major Tim Purdon was awarded the MBE for his work at Assembly Area FOXTROT.

Irish Guards Monitors in Rhodesia, 1980. *L–R:* Capt The Hon Jeremy Stopford; Sgt L. Templeton with pipes; Sgt J Knowles; Sgt B McMahon; Sgt A. McCrum; L/Sgt Dom Kearney – who has contributed greatly to this book – L/Sgt A. Mahon; L/Sgt L. Liddy; Sgt D. Cullen; L/Sgt J. Fitzpatrick; Capt Sebastian Roberts; Major Tim Purdon; L/Sgt M. Doherty; Sgt T. McGran.

Army Athletics Champions 1981. The Micks first became Army Athletics Champions in 1920. That feat was not repeated until 1965 (see p.141). Some 16 years later they were champions of the Army again and for the next 5 years were winners or runners-up to 50 Missile Regiment RA. It was a remarkable achievement given the Royal Artillery packed all their athletes into one unit, twice the size of the Battalion. After winning, a congratulatory signal was received from the 2nd Battalion Coldstream Guards in Fallingbostel. *"Many congratulations. Overheard in the Orderly Room 'What shall we send them? Anything but a trumpet as they appear to have one already!'"*
Not shown: Sgt Templeton; Sgt Rimmer; L/Sgt Leyland; L/Cpl Benn; Gdsm Hughes; Gdsm Foley; Gdsm McKay; Gdsm Brotherston. *Back row, L–R:* L/Sgt Collister; Gdsm McCallion; L/Cpl Farrell; L/Cpl Frazer; Gdsm Redmonds; Gdsm Dunn; L/Sgt Railton; Pte Kay, ACC.
Centre row, L–R: L/Sgt Horrigan; Gdsm Steed; Gdsm Walsh; Gdsm Bailey; L/Cpl Meadows; Gdsm Gregg; L/Cpl Grundie; Gdsm Gavin; L/Sgt Hemphill; L/Cpl Dunn; Gdsm Roach.
Front row, L–R: Cpl Shields, ACC; L/Sgt Veness; Major J.B. O'Gorman; C/Sgt Mooney; Lt-Col D.B.W. Webb-Carter MC; CSM Lowe; RSM McLean; Sgt Welsh; L/Sgt Dawson.
Trophies: Prince of Wales Relay Cup; Eastern Area Cup; Lawson Cup; Major Unit Challenge Shield; Field Events Cup; Carrington Cup; Sir Maurice Deane Trophy; London District Cup.

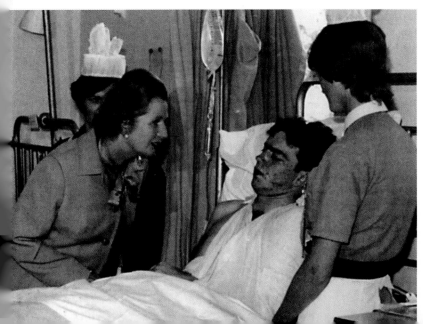

Chelsea Bus Bomb, 10 October 1981. The dismounting Tower Guard was approaching Chelsea Barracks when an IRA bomb made with heavy coach bolts was exploded at close range to their bus. Twenty-three NCOs and Guardsmen were injured. The following day Prime Minister Margaret Thatcher inspected the bus and then visited the injured in hospital. She is seen here talking to Gdsm Jones. Sgt Cullen and Gdsm Trafford were each awarded the British Empire Medal for their work on that occasion, the latter for performing a life saving improvised tracheotomy on a casualty on the pavement. In a truly touching gesture, a Dutch family living in Nijmegen who remembered the 3rd Battalion in the war, sent a letter of sympathy, saying '*you did so much for us, now let us do some small thing for you*', and included a donation for the welfare of the casualties.

Above: **Training on the Dorbaum training area, Münster,** 1983. The Armoured Fighting Vehicles (AFV 432) pictured here have the commander's turret with a pintle mounted machine gun. L/Cpl Morgan plays the heroic role as they clear the woods.

Right: **Brigade Commander's Visit to Oxford Barracks, Münster,** 1982. Brigadier Charles Guthrie, late Guards, Commander 4th Armoured Brigade (later Chief of Defence Staff) visits No 4 Company. *L–R:* RSM V. McLean, Capt Patrick Johns, Major Henry Wilson. Partly obscured: Lt-Col Robert Corbett, Lt Gavin Robinson, CSM 'Hovis' Brown, Capt David Hurley (The Royal Australian Regiment), Brigadier Charles Guthrie, Major Brian O'Gorman, OC 4 Coy.

Sennelager, May 1984. Sennelager, a huge training area in Germany originally used by the Wehrmacht, became in the 1960s one of NATO's finest range complexes, under British Army management. Here GPMG teams from No 4 Company are field firing. *L–R:* Sgt Collister, Gdsm McMullen, Woods and Swift.

The sixth Colonel of the Regiment, General Sir Basil Eugster KCVO, KCB, CBE, DSO, MC, died on 5 April 1984. At the request of the Regiment, Her Majesty the Queen invited HRH The Grand Duke of Luxembourg KG, who had served as a young officer in 3rd Battalion Irish Guards during the Second World War, to take on the role. He was appointed on 21 August 1984. Colonel John, as he became known at once, endeared himself to everybody by stating in the Messroom during a visit to the Battalion that he was thrilled by the appointment, and breaking into that familiar barrack room intonation used when stating your kit for an inspection, the new colonel ringingly announced that he was here 'at the service of the Regiment'. The Messroom roof nearly lifted with the cheering.

Above: **Statue of Field Marshal The Earl Alexander of Tunis.** On 8 May 1985 The Queen unveiled a statue of Field Marshal Alex outside the Guards Chapel. This was one of the new Colonel, HRH The Grand Duke's first public appearances in London. *L–R:* L/Cpl J. Mateer; in morning coat The 2nd Earl Alexander of Tunis, HRH the Colonel, HM The Queen (almost invisible) and Lt Col Sean O'Dwyer, Commanding Officer 1st Battalion Irish Guards.

Below: **The Field Marshal's cap decorated for St Patrick's Day, 1998.** This photograph may be out of sequence, but it is placed here to illustrate something indefinable about the Mick character. Somehow, the Regiment likes to convince itself that this sort of gesture of affectionate irreverence would never 'rub' in some of our more stately sister regiments! Decorating FM Alex's cap with shamrock on St Patrick's Day has since evolved into a fully recognized regimental custom.

Left: **Academy Sergeant Major Dennis Cleary** at the Royal Military Academy Sandhurst. This is the senior Warrant Officer's appointment in the Army and the first time held by an Irish Guardsman. He was awarded the MBE for his outstanding service in this appointment. He was followed by RSMs Simon Nichols in 2005 and Ross Martin in 2010.

Annual Review of a Unit (ARU), Newcastle Barracks, Hamm, 18 April 1985. Unlike the old Major General's Inspections, the ARU involved a serious tactical element with role play coupled with a rigorous administrative 'dig out'. A captured senior 'enemy officer', Capt Sebastian Roberts, is being questioned by the acting commanding officer, Major Brian Holt, while CQMS T.Lee keeps a smart watch on proceedings. All this is under observation by Divisional Staff, including a future Inspector of Prisons, General David Ramsbotham.

Battlefield Tour. Alwyn Charleton reads the citation for the Victoria Cross awarded to his brother, Eddie, in 1945, at the very scene of the action. (For full citation see p.288).

Winners of the Langton Trophy, 1985, The Corps of Drums. Drum Major 'Dixie' Dean BEM receives the trophy from the Divisional Commander watched by the Commanding Officer, Lt-Col Robert Corbett at Woodlands Camp, Sennelager.

The Langton Trophy. The Langton Trophy is an annual inter-platoon competition started in 1964 by the Commanding Officer, Lt-Col Stephen Langton MVO, MC. The trophy itself is a representation of the Armoured Humber 1 Ton APC (known not very affectionately as the 'Pig') with which the Battalion manouevred round Germany (in the 1960s).

Pristina, 13 June 1999. After months of terror, the surviving ethnic Albanians slowly emerge to greet No 4 Company, Irish Guards. It was more than an hour before the Albanians felt safe enough to gather on the streets. The atmosphere was still extremely volatile – even as the up-armoured Warriors drove in, defiant Serbs streamed past them, firing wildly.

Chapter Seven

1986–1999
END OF
THE CENTURY

This period saw the role of the Army changing rapidly from its Cold War concentration on the defence of West Germany, to a smaller force that was increasingly deployed worldwide, on peace support operations. The Battalion started and ended this era based in Munster, Westfalia. In 1986 it was a mechanised Battalion, part of the 1st British Corps (part of the 50,000 strong British Army of the Rhine), but by 1999 it was an armoured Battalion, part of the one British Division remaining on the European mainland for deployment worldwide.

During these hectic years the Irish Guards had six main moves. They were in Berlin in 1990 when the Wall came down. There were operational tours, twice to Northern Ireland, to Belize and to the Balkans. Companies also deployed operationally to the Falkland Islands, to Northern Ireland, and to Hong Kong just before the handover to China. Detachments were sent to help the affiliated The Royal Montserrat Defence Force to cope with the effects of volcanic eruptions. There were training exercises in Kenya, Oman, Denmark, Canada and Cyprus.

When in England, the Battalion played its full part in public duties and new Colours were presented and trooped twice.

The major operational feature of this period was the Battalion's role in the relief of Kosovo in 1999. At the end of the Regiment's first 100 years, the 1st Battalion Irish Guards is stationed in Münster, Germany.

Major General's Inspection, Chelsea Barracks, 1986. Major-General Christopher Airy inspects the Corps of Drums and the Pipes accompanied by the Adjutant, Major Bernard Hornung. In the background can be seen the Commander Supply, London District, the only Lieutenant Colonel's Post in the then Royal Army Ordnance Corps still to be entitled to wear a frock coat.

Left: **EXERCISE BRITANNIA WAY/IBERIAN FOCUS,** 1986. In 1986 an exchange exercise took place with the Spanish Army. A platoon from the Spanish Infantry Regiment of Mallorca, No 13, based at Lorca, Murcia, came to England, and No 1 Company went to Lorca. Here L/Cpl Hughes instructs Spanish conscript soldiers on the 9mm Sterling Sub Machine Gun.

Below: **The Queen's Birthday at Windsor.** The Windsor Castle Guard, augmented for The Queen's Birthday, commanded by Major Brian Holt, 21 April 1986. Here Her Majesty passes the Guard on return from St George's Chapel.

Left: **EXERCISE POND JUMP WEST**, Canada, 1987. Lt-Col Henry Wilson, the Commanding Officer, with Pipe Major Fraser and the Pipes. Note the new helmet worn by the Commanding Officer made of a new composite material, lighter and stronger than steel.

Below: **The Old and Bold. Marching past Her Majesty on St Patrick's Day**, 1987. In this photograph some distinguished veterans are visible. Leading is Brigadier Michael Gordon-Watson, who won his first MC in Palestine, his second in Norway and his third at Anzio. Next to him is Major Sir Oliver Chesterton MC, who won his in 1943 for capturing the Bou feature. Next to him is Brigadier Mick O'Cock who won his MC commanding a squadron of 2nd Battalion in Normandy in 1944. Colonel Tony Aylmer who served in the 3rd Battalion and commanded the 1st Battalion in Aden follows him, followed in turn by Brigadier Savill Young DSO who was decorated for Anzio. Also featured on Parade is Major Hugh Ripman RAMC whose redoubtable efforts with Mick casualties in 1944/45 forever endeared him to the Regiment.

Preparations for a charity abseil from the roof of the then highest hotel in Europe, the Forum in Brompton Road, London, 8 November 1987. *L–R:* Capt James Stopford; Sgt Cardy and Capt Colin Butterworth.

Above: **Queen's Birthday Parade, 1**988. This was the first Birthday Parade with the new SA80 rifle. There were still eight guards on parade (later reduced to six, so only one 'round the corner'). The Queen travelled by open carriage to the parade for the second year, Burmese, her fine Canadian mount having retired after the 1986 Birthday Parade. The Ensign was 2/Lt Stephen Segrave, and the Regimental Sergeant Major Vince McEllin.

Below Right: **Tunisia Battlefield Tour,** 1987. A group of some sixty members of the Regiment and their wives visited Tunisia to follow the 1943 actions of the 1st Battalion. Here the veterans pose in the area of the Doll's House (Battalion Headquarters near Medjez el Bab). *L–R:* Major Sir Oliver Chesterton MC; Lt-Col Jack Pestell MBE; Major Owen McInerney (from Canada); Major Brian Synge; Ex L/Cpl John Kenneally VC; Ex Gdsm Bill Crawford (from Australia); Ex Sgt Jim Ryan MM; Lt-Col Jimmy Kelly OBE; EX Gdsm John Cooney (one of two Irish Guards survivors from Recce Ridge); Ex Company Sergeant Major Gerry Whelan; Capt Mungo Park MBE; Major Colin Kennard DSO; Major Charles Larking; Major Mike Rawlence; Ex Gdsm Richardson; and Major-General Drew Bethell (the Royal Artillery officer from Recce Ridge). The Colonel of the Regiment, HRH The Grand Duke of Luxembourg, attended semi-incognito under the guise of Colonel Connor. (Connor was the name of the wolfhound at the time.) All was fine until one day the coach grounded. The Arab driver, nicknamed Seamus, turned to the Colonel who was sitting in front, and with Arab-American informality said 'You'll have to push, Dook!' And he did.

Below: **Laying up of Colours,** Guards Chapel, 5 September 1988.

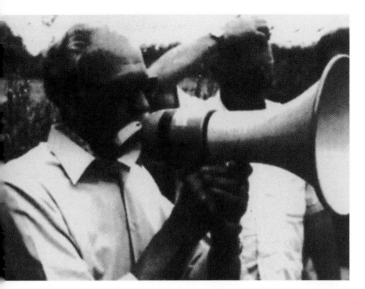

Normandy Battlefield Tour, 1988. Ex Guardsman Dick Russell, a stretcher-bearer speaks about the 3rd Battalion at Sourdeval, watched by Colonel William Harvey-Kelly, a platoon commander at the time. There were many who wanted to return to Normandy to hear from those who had been there what had happened to the 2nd and 3rd Battalions in 1944. So a tour was arranged, which included a representative of X Company Scots Guards. Seeing and hearing the veterans talk, and hearing their moving stories was a wonderful experience. Much of what they said was noted and a full photographic record placed in the Regimental Archives. Perhaps an unexpectedly vivid lesson to come from it was that the characters of the regiment in 1944 were so similar to those of 1988. Wit and wickedness, fun and fear, somehow that old spirit spanned the generations, unchanged by the passing of time.

Jungle exercise in Belize. The Battalion operated in the Northern Battle Group area for the 1988 exercises.

Regimental Band visits Paris and the Arc de Triomphe, June 1989. Sadly, this was the last appearance with the Band of the Director of Music, Lt-Col Mick Lane.

The Battalion took its turn in the continuing defence of Belize against external threat.

Right: **Distribution of Shamrock, Belize,** 1989. The Colonel of the Regiment visited Belize and distributed Queen Elizabeth's gift of Shamrock. The uniform is light weight combat dress, and officers' berets now carry an embroidered bullion star taken from the Mess jacket (hence without the date 1783 which signifies the year of foundation of The Order of St Patrick). *L–R:* The Commanding Officer, Lt-Col Brian Holt; RQMS Knowles; The Colonel, HRH The Grand Duke of Luxembourg; The Quartermaster, Major Bill Matthews MBE; Capt Hugh Howard-Allen.

Below: **Belize,** March 1989. A Scimitar recce vehicle, mounting the Rarden 30mm cannon follows the marching party.

Training in Belize.

Left: **A Special Pipe Banner.** HM Queen Elizabeth The Queen Mother's long and close friendship with the Regiment was marked in a personal way on St Patrick's Day in Berlin in 1990 when she presented her personal pipe banner, bearing her coat of arms, to be used by the Pipe Major. At this time this was the only pipe banner in the Regiment and bears a star of St Patrick on the reverse. Pipe Major Kevin Fraser was the first Irish Guards Piper to become the Senior Pipe Major in the Household Division.

The 1st Battalion found itself stationed in Berlin at the epic moment when the Wall was dismantled, and Germany had yet to be reunited. Owing to reorganisation within the Foot Guards, the Regimental Lieutenant Colonel's role became open to senior officers. In 1989 Major General Robert Corbett, the Regimental Lieutenant Colonel, was posted to Berlin, as was the Battalion. He can be seen in the photograph wearing the Foot Guards pattern frock coat (in the rank of Colonel) which would not have been appropriate under any other circumstances for the GOC Berlin.

Shillelagh: the Battalion's Ceiledh band looking for an audience at the Brandenburg Gate, Berlin. *L–R:* RSM Knowles; Stephanie Shields; C/Sgt Shields; L/Cpl Trainor; D/Sgt Lavery and L/Sgt McCarthy.

Gdsm 'Big Red' McCloskey talking to Major-General Robert Corbett during his farewell visit to the Battalion, Berlin, October 1990.

Milan firing. The Milan anti-tank missile system replaced the 120mm recoilless guns of the BAT series.

Feu de Joie. No 2 Company, commanded by Major Bernard Hornung, fires a *feu de joie* during The Queen's Birthday Parade in the Olympic Stadium Berlin, 1990.

Irish Guards Football Team, winners of the Infantry Cup, 1991. *Back:* L/Sgt Leinster, L/Cpl Fagin; Gdsm Dillon; L/Cpl Withers; Gdsm Campbell; D/Sgt Cloney; Gdsm Mooney; L/Sgt Parkins; C/Sgt Wynne; Lt-Col Christopher Langton; RSM Knowles. *Front Row:* L/Sgt Davies; L/Cpl Doyle; L/Sgt McComb; Capt Robbie Kelly; Sgt Halliday; L/Sgt Halliday; L/Sgt Donaldson; L/Sgt Brennan; Capt Venning.

The London Branch of the Regimental Association on St Patrick's Day, 1991, at the Guards Depot, Pirbright. Major Tony Mainwaring-Burton, Chairman of the London Branch, and members give three cheers for Her Majesty Queen Elizabeth the Queen Mother.

Above: **Connor's Last Parade.** Connor, heading for retirement, leads the Band away on St Patrick's Day, 1992 at Wavell Barracks, Berlin. Connor's successor was Malachy.

Right: **Leaving for Schleswig-Holstein.** Members of No 1 Company, Capt James Campbell-Johnston, L/Sgt Burge and L/Sgt Leinster, preparing to leave Berlin by cattle truck to go training in Schleswig-Holstein, September 1991.

New Friends.
With the fall of the Berlin Wall visits were exchanged between the Allies (British, Americans and French) and the Soviet Forces. Here Pipe Major Stranix explains the Irish secret weapon to the Russians.

Training in Berlin.
House clearing skills
being practised at
Rhuleben Fighting City.
A grenade having just
been thrown through the
window, the entrymen
follow.

Left: **Another Mick, another camel.** Capt David Hannah served as an observer on the
United Nations Mission for the Referendum in Western Sahara (MINURSO). It was for
a disputed Sahara territory claimed by both the Moroccans and Polisario guerrillas. The
mission started in 1991 and the problem was still not resolved by 2016.

Below: **EXERCISE MEDICINE MAN,** Alberta, Canada. Lt Sean Taylor's Platoon
Headquarters resting from the heat and dust.

Tango 30 Alfa. No 6 Platoon, 2 (Operations) Company on the helipad at St Angelo security force base in Fermanagh, before deploying to patrol the Beleek Triangle. *Back row L–R:* Gdsm Dillon; Gdsm Cartwright; Gdsm Dawes; Gdsm Doyle 36; Lance Corporal Ruddock; L/Sgt Taylor; Gdsm Holmes; L/Cpl Martin. *Front Row L–R:* Gdsm Wyse; Gdsm Woodham; 2/Lt Gavin Lloyd-Thomas; Gdsm Irwin; Gdsm Preuss.

GSM Northern Ireland.

Operational Tour in Northern Ireland, OPERATION BANNER: November 1992–May 1993. The Battalion undertook its first operational tour in Fermanagh. In the picture Malachy is seen with members of No 2 Company at Devenish Island. (*Photo courtesy of* Soldier *Magazine*).

Above: **Winter in Fermanagh.** Patrolling continued in all weathers. This 'multiple' is heading off in snow, but the abiding memory of winter 1993 is of rain, rain, and yet more rain.

Below: **Grosvenor Barracks, Enniskillen,** St Patrick's Day, 1993. Major General Robert Corbett, by now the Major General Commanding the Household Division, watches the march past. He is flanked by Drummer Coates with Malachy, and by L/Sgt Tumelty.

Above: **Malachy and Drummer Coates.** Malachy died suddenly in October 1993 following a visit to the dentist. A magnificent and much loved mascot. *(Photo* Mike Hollist)

50th Anniversary of the Liberation of Luxembourg. In September 1994 the Regimental Lieutenant Colonel, the Commanding Officer, Lt-Col Sebastian Roberts, the Regimental Band, the Pipes and No 1 Company travelled to Luxembourg for the celebrations. They were kindly entertained at Chateau Colmar Berg by the Colonel of the Regiment and the Grand Duchess.

The Colonel's Dinner, State Apartments, The Royal Hospital Chelsea, 10 September 1993. The Colonel of the Regiment was entertained to dinner by the Regimental Lieutenant Colonel, Brigadier David Webb-Carter OBE, MC and his predecessors after the Colonel's portrait by Theodore Ramos had been unveiled. *Front Row, L–R:* Brigadier M.J.P. O'Cock CBE, MC; Colonel P.F.I. Reid OBE; Brigadier DH. FitzGerald DSO; The Colonel of the Regiment HRH The Grand Duke of Luxembourg; Brigadier D.M.L. Gordon-Watson OBE, MC★★; Brigadier H.L.S. Young DSO; Colonel C.W.D. Harvey-Kelly. *Back Row L–R:* Colonel Sir William Mahon Bt; Brigadier J.N. Ghika CBE; Colonel J.A. Aylmer; Colonel G.A. Allan OBE; Brigadier R.T.P. Hume; Brigadier D.B.W. Webb-Carter OBE, MC.

Arnhem Cemetery. Commemoration of the 50th Anniversary of OPERATION MARKET GARDEN 1944 in which the Regiment played such a prominent part. Veterans from all Regiments returned to Holland and attended ceremonies in their honour.

Above: **RSM Brennan and Cuchulain** comparing moustaches. Sadly the mascot died within 5 years of heart failure.

Right: **St Patrick's Day, 1995, Chelsea Barracks.** Always the same, yet always different and for ever special. Her Majesty The Queen with Queen Elizabeth The Queen Mother and the Colonel (who had just been appointed honorary General) as the Regiment gives three cheers for the Queen Mother. This was the first parade for the new young wolfhound, Cuchulain.

Right: **VE Day 50th Anniversary Parade** and service at Newtownards Co. Down, 1995. The Regimental Band in Conway Square. The Irish Guards Association members are on the front right of the parade.

Right: **A Family Regiment,** 6 February 1996. The Roberts Family is inspected by their mother on mounting Queen's Guard. At the end of his time in command Lt Col Sebastian Roberts *(right)* mounted Queen's Guard as Captain, with his brother Major Cassian Roberts *(left)* as the Subaltern, and his younger brother, Fabian *(centre)* as the Ensign.

Below: **OPERATION BANNER, East Tyrone,** June–December 1995. Members of No 1 Company move forward to be deployed by Chinook helicopter from Dungannon, East Tyrone.

The annual Mick training team to Montserrat led by Major T. MacMullen changed roles at short notice to help with a non-combatant evacuation operation (NEO), OPERATION HARLECH, when volcanic activity in the Soufriere Hills started to erupt in July 1995.

Above: **The Irish Guards Training Team** with the gently steaming volcano in the background. *L–R:* Lt John Skerrit MDF; Major John Lynch OC MDF; Sgt Buckley; Lt Rupert Lockwood.

Above: **The Montserrat Defence Force (MDF) being briefed in the presence of the Mick team** on the left and the Royal Marines on the right at the main cricket ground, Plymouth. The Lynx is from HMS *Southampton,* the West Indies Guard Ship, whose Captain was commanding the NEO. Plymouth the capital was later abandoned forever.

Below: **The tented city for** evacuees in the north of the island at Gerald's Bottom.

The first large eruption of the volcano on 20 August.

Below: **Sgt McCarthy supervising the offloading of stores from an RAF Hercules** at Montserrat International Airport, 25 August.

Above: **East Tyrone,** 1995. L/Cpl McCool and Gdsm Finegan on patrol.

Below: **President of Ireland's Inspection**, June 1996. The President, Mrs Mary Robinson, visited The Queen at Buckingham Palace. A Guard of Honour, found by No 1 Company commanded by Major James Stopford, Subaltern; Capt Christopher Ghika; Ensign, Lt Fabian Roberts, was inspected.

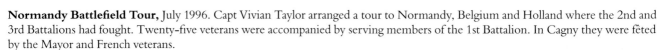

Left: **Mini Micks**. Irish Guards Cadet detachments took part in a competition arranged by No 2 Company during a recruiting tour of Northern Ireland. The winners were the Liverpool Detachment who are seen with the trophy they have just received from the Commanding Officer Lt-Col James Pollock.

Normandy Battlefield Tour, July 1996. Capt Vivian Taylor arranged a tour to Normandy, Belgium and Holland where the 2nd and 3rd Battalions had fought. Twenty-five veterans were accompanied by serving members of the 1st Battalion. In Cagny they were fêted by the Mayor and French veterans.

Left: **Oman,** EXERCISE ROCKY LANCE I. Lt John Webb inspecting the food… goat… during No 2 Company's joint training with the Omani Army at Sur, March 1996.

Below: **EXERCISE ROCKY LANCE** II. L/Sgt Clarke and L/Cpl Woodham apparently enjoying a meal of mutton during the exercise in the Wahiba Sands, September 1996.

Oman, September 1996. No 4 Company. The deployment which lasted for a month followed No 2 Company's similar exercise in March the same year.

Falkland Islands, October 1996–March 1997. No 1 Company provided the Falkland Islands Reinforced Infantry Company. L/Sgt Nicholson leads his patrol off from an outlying settlement.

Above: **Patrol in the Falklands,** 1997. A No 1 Company patrol with locals. *(Photo* PA News).

Left: **Kenya. EXERCISE MONOPRIX**, April 1997. No 2 Company commanded by Major James Patrick spent a month training in Kenya near Nanyuki. Lt Cahal O'Reilly, Sgt Moffett and L/Sgt Martin decide the best course of action as 5 Platoon prepares to attack.

Below: **Kenya, EXERCISE MONOPRIX**, April 1997. 5 Platoon training at Impala Farm.

Below: **New Colours, Windsor,** 22 May 1997. The Battalion commanded by Lt Colonel James Pollock MBE, formed up in the Quadrangle prior to the presentation of Colours by Her Majesty The Queen.

Above: **Presentation of Colours,** May 1997. The Queen addresses the Battalion.

Above: **The Field Of Remembrance,** November 1997, The Chairman of the London Branch of the Irish Guards Association, Colonel Giles Allan, at the Regimental Plot, with Association Members attending the annual ceremony of dedication and remembrance at Westminster Abbey.

Right: **St Patrick's Day Celebrations,** London, 15 March 1998. With the Battalion abroad once again in Münster, and no Guards Depot any longer at Pirbright to host St Patrick's Day, the Annual March to the Guards Memorial, which was celebrated on the Sunday nearest St Patrick's Day, was combined with the distribution of Shamrock at Wellington Barracks. Queen Elizabeth's gift of Shamrock was distributed by Mr John Kenneally vc. *L–R:* RQMS D. Ryan; Mr John Kenneally VC; Brigadier Christopher Wolverson OBE, Regimental Lieutenant Colonel; Major Mick Henderson, Director of Music; Colonel Giles Allan OBE, Chairman London Branch Irish Guards Association; Capt Edward Boanas. In Germany the Grand Duchess distributed the Shamrock on behalf of The Queen Mother.

Left: **12 Platoon 4 Company tactics at Haltern.**

Below: **The Island of Ireland Peace Park at Messines** commemorates all those who fought and died in the First World War. It was unveiled by The Queen and the President of Ireland, in the presence of King Albert of the Belgians, 11 November 1998.

Above: **Warriors in Germany,** February 1998. The Battalion converted to the Armoured Infantry role, equipped with Warrior Armoured Infantry Fighting Vehicles. The local training area for much of the initial manoeuvring was at Haltern. During 1998 the Battalion was constantly training, including undertaking simulated Virtual Reality Armoured Training with the United States Army at Grafenwohr and deploying to Canada for EXERCISE MEDICINE MAN.

Below: **Warriors of Nos 1 and 4 Companies advance to** contact during company training at Haltern.

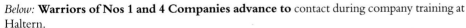

KOSOVO – OPERATION AGRICOLA

The Kosovo War was an armed conflict in the Balkans that lasted from 28 February 1998 until 11 June 1999. It was fought by the Serb forces of the Federal Republic of Yugoslavia, which controlled Kosovo before the war, and a Kosovo Albanian ethnic rebel group known as the Kosovo Liberation Army (KLA). The KLA attacks against the Yugoslav authorities increased leading to a more violent reaction by Serb paramilitaries and Regular Forces. The Serb authorities began a campaign of retribution targeting the KLA, leaving many dead and huge numbers of refugees. NATO intervened with air support for the KLA, calling the campaign an 'humanitarian war'.

After eleven weeks of aerial bombing by NATO and perhaps the attitude of Russia, President Milosevic agreed to withdraw Yugoslav Serb forces on 9th June allowing the deployment of NATO troops to oversee it.

Preparatory training had begun in Germany in February 1989. No 1 Company, under Major E.J.F.V. Melotte, with Support Company elements, formed part of the King's Royal Hussars Battle Group.

Above: **Recce Platoon Scimitar.** 'Cloughroe' with L/Sgt Fletcher and his section patrolling close to the Macedonia/Kosovo border, May 1999.

Below: **Pre K-Day Training.** Members of No 1 Company serving with the King's Royal Hussars Battle Group in Petrovac, Macedonia, debus as they train for operations in Kosovo.

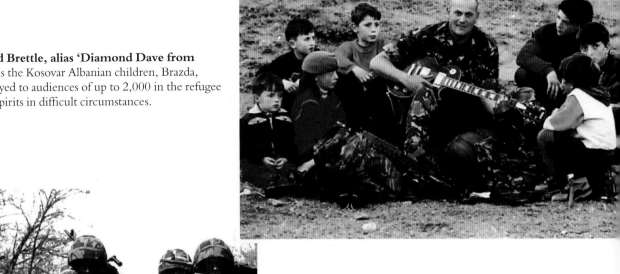

Right: **L/Sgt David Brettle, alias 'Diamond Dave from Dudley'**, entertains the Kosovar Albanian children, Brazda, Macedonia. He played to audiences of up to 2,000 in the refugee camp, helping lift spirits in difficult circumstances.

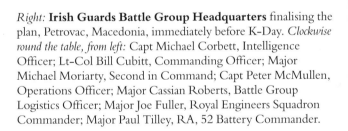

Left: **Even though mechanised, the Battalion still had to train on foot.** No 1 Company preparing for operations in Kosovo at Petrovac, Macedonia.

Right: **Irish Guards Battle Group Headquarters** finalising the plan, Petrovac, Macedonia, immediately before K-Day. *Clockwise round the table, from left:* Capt Michael Corbett, Intelligence Officer; Lt-Col Bill Cubitt, Commanding Officer; Major Michael Moriarty, Second in Command; Capt Peter McMullen, Operations Officer; Major Cassian Roberts, Battle Group Logistics Officer; Major Joe Fuller, Royal Engineers Squadron Commander; Major Paul Tilley, RA, 52 Battery Commander.

Left: **A final rendition of St Patrick's Day** by the Drums and Pipes on the morning of departure. L/Sgt Teague (flute); L/Cpl Gilfillan (Pipes); Drummer Partington; Drummer McLoughlin (sitting on top); Gdsm Hughes (leaning on door).

Above: **Maj B.C. Farrell, Liaison Officer with 4 Armoured Brigade** and Maj C.A. Craig-Harvey, Commanding No 4 Company, two hours after the Battle Group entered Pristina and following an ambush of a Yugoslav soldier by the Kosovar Albanians.

Above: **Gdsm Ben Noble establishing good relations.**

Right: **A Warrior from No 1 Company**, on K-Day + 3 is greeted as it drives for the first time into Podujevo, Kosovo.

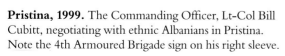

Pristina, 1999. The Commanding Officer, Lt-Col Bill Cubitt, negotiating with ethnic Albanians in Pristina. Note the 4th Armoured Brigade sign on his right sleeve.

In April, the Irish Guards Battle Group commanded by Lt Col Bill Cubitt, which included 'D' Squadron King's Royal Hussars, 'A' (King Harald's) Company Green Howards, 52 Battery Royal Artillery and 26 Armoured Engineer Squadron, deployed to Macedonia in order to train before moving north to become the High-Readiness Battle Group on the border.

On 12 June 1999 both Battle Groups entered Kosovo passing through the Kacanik gorge in the largest armoured operation in Europe since the Second World War. The Micks of No 4 Company had the key role of securing the Kosovan capital, Pristina.

The King's Royal Hussars despatched No 1 Company to secure Pristina Airport. On arrival, they found the Russians had arrived before them. They then waited in a high profile stand-off until Pristina was secured and were sent further north to Podujevo which they ran until their return to Münster in August.

The Irish Guards Battle Group set about the task of maintaining law-and-order as the Serbs withdrew, keeping a lid on inter-ethnic violence while coercing both sides to sit down and talk about the future. The Battle Group's areas of responsibility expanded to a 600 sq km area around Pristina.

The Albanian community returned rapidly in large numbers from Macedonia and Albania.

At various times the UK Brigade included British, Canadian, Finnish, Czech and Norwegian troops. Also for a time there was a distinct Irish flavour manifested in the co-operation between the Micks, the Royal Irish Regiment, an Irish Defence Force Transport Company and a Royal Ulster Constabulary recce party on the ground.

The operation was considered a huge success but the uncertainties and potential dangers amounted to considerable stress at home in Münster, for the Battalion, especially No 1 Company who had deployed at short notice on an open-ended operation. The Battalion returned to Munster in September after handing over to two Battalions of Scandinavians.

Regimental Band. It was over 50 years since the Regimental Band served in the same theatre of operations as the Battalion, the last time being Palestine. By chance it was their turn to reinforce an Army Medical Service unit on operations, this time 2 Armoured Field Ambulance. Apart from carrying out their medical and security duties, they raised everyone's morale by organising popular impromptu concerts, and even leading No 1 Company on a farewell parade through Podujevo.

Lance Corporal Shaw confiscating a pistol from a Serb civilian in Kosovo.

Above: **Fergus Greer, on the left, a renowned photographer** and former Irish Guards Officer, was attached to the Irish Guards Battle Group for three months as an officially accredited war artist and published a unique record of the operation.

On their return the Battalion produced a 50 page booklet of pictures to explain their part in the operation.

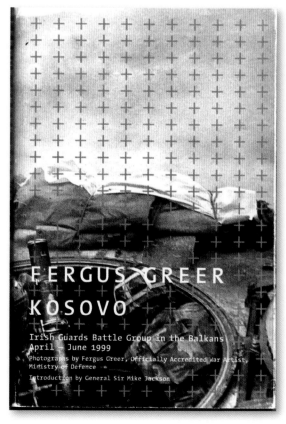

Above: **The Battle Group are cheered** as they cross the border into Kosovo.

Left: **The Kacanik Gorge.** A painting by David Rowlands, commissioned by the Battalion, of the Battle Group entering Kosovo through the Kacanik Gorge. Standing in the front of the Land Rover, Maj Ben Farrell (Brigade Liaison Officer) and C/Sgt Haines watch them pass.

Below: **Securing Prestina.** Another painting from David Rowlands of No 4 Company as it entered and secured the capital, Pristina, on 13th June.

Left: **Awards.** The Commanding Officer, Lt Col W G Cubitt, presents the 'Mention-in-Dispatches' to Sgt Meadows, and Commander British Forces Commendation to LSgt Dyer at the Battalion's Kosovo medal parade in Münster on 12th January 2000.

NATO Service Medal with 'Kosovo' clasp awarded to NATO Alliance forces in the Balkans.

Awards for OP AGRICOLA

Order of the British Empire (OBE)
  Lt Col W G Cubitt
Member of the British Empire (MBE)
  Maj B C Farrell
  Maj M A P Carleton-Smith (detached)
Mention in Despatches (MiD)
  Sgt J P Gribben
  Sgt T A Meadows
Queen's Commendation for Bravery (QCB)
  (RSM) A Gardner
Queen's Commendation for Valuable Service (QCBC)
  Maj C A Craig-Harvey
Joint Commanders' Commendation
  WO2 Bonner
  Gdsm Bradford
  LSgt Purtell
Commander British Forces Commendation
  LSgt Brettle
  LSgt Dyer
  CSgt Haines

Irish Guards Centennial Painting

Unveiled by the Colonel of the Regiment HRH The Grand Duke of Luxembourg KG on St. Patrick's Day, ANNO DOMINI MM

Painted by Theodore Ramos

Centennial Painting. This large picture commemorates the centenary of the formation of the regiment. Painted by Theodore de P Ramos, whose son Julian served in the Regiment. It portrays those Officers serving between October 1996 and 1st April 2000, together with Her Majesty Queen Elizabeth the Queen Mother.

The setting of the Duke of York's Steps recognises that Queen Elizabeth was the Duchess of York when she first presented shamrock to the 1st Battalion in 1928. Behind the Officers stand Colour Sergeants holding the 23 Company Colours. The uniforms of the Regiment throughout the century are shown from left to right in the foreground.

Major J R H Stopford proposed the concept of the painting at a mess meeting in Pirbright on 3rd September 1996. He was inspired to pursue it further when Major S P Owen wagered that if it was realised by the anniversary of the formation he would eat his forage cap. The wager was duly paid. The painting shows Major Owen holding his forage cap on a silver salver waiting to eat it.

Chapter Eight

2000–2007
INTO THE NEW MILLENNIUM

This period started with a series of events in the United Kingdom and Ireland to commemorate the Regiment's Centenary. The Battalion changed role from 'armoured' Infantry to 'light' and leave Germany for the last time but not before being deployed on operations in Iraq. In preparation they exercised in Poland, Canada and even Oman.

HRH The Grand Duke of Luxembourg relinquished his appointment as Colonel of the Regiment after sixteen years and was succeeded by the Duke of Abercorn.

Although 2002 was cause for celebration, being The Queen's Golden Jubilee, it was tinged with sadness at the death of Queen Elizabeth, The Queen Mother. The Regiment, naturally played a major part in her funeral in April.

2003 was dominated by the deployment from Germany to Iraq on Op TELIC for which they were later awarded a Battle Honour. Sadly, they suffered a number of battle casualties on the operation. Their return to Public Duties from Münster in Germany had been delayed because of Iraq so their stay in Wellington Barracks, London was only to be two and a half years before another move to Mons Barracks, Aldershot.

They undertook their third and final operational tour of Northern Ireland, this time to South Armagh. The Princess Royal distributed the Shamrock at Bessbrook Mill, Co. Armagh on St Patrick's Day 2004 for the first time following the death of her grandmother.

The Battalion's last deployment to Iraq was in 2007, but individuals and a small group had deployed with the Coldstream Guards two years earlier.

When not preparing for or recovering from operations, sport and training exercises dominated their lives and with considerable success. Converting to the Army's new digital radio system and exercising in Warcop, Otterburn, Kenya and Belize kept them operationally sharp. The Drums and Pipes played in the USA and South Korea and the Regimental Band toured Australia.

Presentation of shamrock. The Irish Guards Association, serving Micks and Irish Guards Cadets give an 'eyes right' to the Queen Mother on the Mall on St Patrick's Day 2000. Her Majesty had earlier presented the shamrock in the garden of Lancaster House for the first and only time. It was to be the last year she presented the shamrock, having done so for over 30 years.

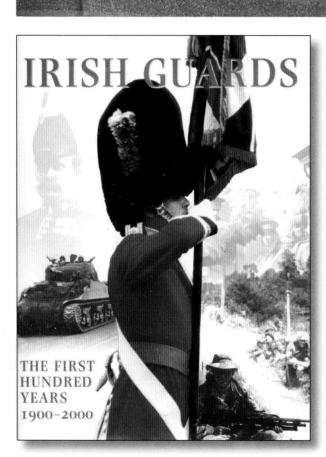

Centenary Book. Every serving Irish Guardsman was given a copy of this book, which was specially produced to commemorate the first 100 years of the Regiment. The project, universally praised, was led by Colonel Sir William Mahon.

Cutting the birthday cake. Her Majesty The Queen cut a centenary birthday cake at the all ranks reception in the State Apartments at St James's Palace on 7 June. The Colonel of the Regiment was unwell but was represented by the HRH The Grand Duchess of Luxembourg. Brigadier Sebastian Roberts, as Regimental Lt-Col, was the host. The Royal Colonels were invited and Her Majesty Queen Elizabeth The Queen Mother, of course attended, never one to miss a party.

Battalion celebrates the centenary. On 1st April 2000, in Münster, Germany, the Battalion held a Drumhead Service in the barracks and an all-ranks party in a huge marquee. Entertainment was provided by Shillelagh (CSM McCarthy and Sgt Trainor). Everyone enjoyed the strong family atmosphere of the day, which was a fitting celebration of the centenary.

Daughters of the Regiment. The Tara Troupe Dancers, all children of the Regiment, performed at the Battalion's Centenary Party at Oxford Barracks, Münster, then pose with the wolfhound, Cuchulain and his handler Drummer Rooney.

Freedom of Liverpool. The Battalion marched through Liverpool with bayonets fixed, drums beating and Colours flying after being given the Freedom of the City of Liverpool. The Micks wear 'Irish Guards' designations on the shoulders of No 2 Dress, a hark-back to The Great War and 2nd World War. They were re-introduced, replacing the metal IG and Star on the epaulettes which were being damaged when carrying the SA80 rifle.

The Regimental Band in Dublin. The band made an historic four day visit to Dublin in June 2000. It was the first time a British Army Band had performed in the city since 1921. In a charity concert in the National Concert Hall in Dublin, the band joined forces with the Irish Defence Forces' No 1 Band whose conductor, Commandant Joe Ryan, declared "The programme was a celebration of music which reflected both our traditions." They also played in St Patrick's Cathedral, home of the Order of St Patrick, and Beat Retreat at Dublin Castle and Leopardstown Hospital. They met again five years later at the Concert for Peace in Belfast.

Commemorative plaque. During a tour to South Africa in 2000, a plaque was unveiled in St Patrick's Church, Bergville, to honour the formation of the Regiment, which was a tribute to the bravery of the Irish Regiments who fought there, especially in the operations to relieve the Siege of Ladysmith.

New Colonel. In place of Colonel John, The Grand Duke of Luxembourg, The Queen appointed James Hamilton, 5th Duke of Abercorn, KG, as the 8th Colonel of the Regiment. He was an ideal choice with his impeccable Irish connections and, having served in the Foot Guards, understood the ethos of the Household Division. Although he served in the Grenadier Guards, he had strong Mick connections as his brother and nephew both served in the Regiment.

7th Colonel retires. After the Centenary celebrations in 2000, the Grand Duke of Luxembourg notified The Queen of his wish to stand down as Colonel of the Regiment. Colonel John, as he was called, was a hugely popular member of the Regiment who gave so much in his 16 years as the Colonel. He would undoubtedly have been proud that within 10 years three of his grandsons would follow him into his Regiment.

Below: **Ex Saif Sareea II.** This exercise took place in Oman in September and October 2001 and was the largest military deployment since the First Gulf War in 1990. The Battalion participated as an armoured Battalion from Germany. It tested the effectiveness of the Joint Rapid Reaction Force and was effective in highlighting the shortcomings and practices, of such a deployment, including inadequate footwear and the SA80A1 rifle which suffered stoppages and jamming due to the sand. Some of these problems were resolved in time for the invasion of Iraq in 2003.

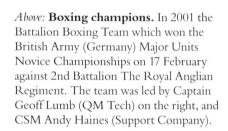

Above: **Boxing champions.** In 2001 the Battalion Boxing Team which won the British Army (Germany) Major Units Novice Championships on 17 February against 2nd Battalion The Royal Anglian Regiment. The team was led by Captain Geoff Lumb (QM Tech) on the right, and CSM Andy Haines (Support Company).

Below: **Naval Affiliation.** The Regiment has traditionally been affiliated with a Royal Navy ship. Sporting and social links benefit both organisations and the opportunity to go to sea is appreciated by the Micks. Staff from Regimental Headquarters visited *HMS Portland* in Plymouth to attend the commissioning service in 2001. A Type 23 frigate, she was the penultimate ship of the 'Duke' class of frigates. From left: Lt Cdr Miller, RQMS Gannaway-Pitts, Gdsm Wilson, Capt M.P.M. Grayson, L/Cpl Hewitt, Cdr J.M. Handley and Sgt Browne.

Below: **Show dog.** Aengus had an unusual outing in May 2001 – down an elaborate grouse moor catwalk, whilst modelling summer guard order at the Game Conservancy Ball in London. He was escorting Charlotte Stockdale who was wearing a summer ball dress, with an appropriate saffron coloured fringe. The event raised funds for research of the ecolog of game species.

THE QUEEN MOTHER'S FUNERAL

Sadly, HM Queen Elizabeth, The Queen Mother, died peacefully on the 30 March 2002 aged 101. State Funerals are not put together over a weekend so it was already known that 'My Micks', as she referred to the Regiment, would be involved in the funeral.

She had no official association with the Regiment until her friend Field Marshal Alexander asked her over lunch to consider presenting the Shamrock to the Regiment on St Patrick's Day. She graciously agreed to do so for the next 35 years. It was no surprise, therefore, that she indicated that the Regiment should be involved in her funeral. We were honoured to provide the Bearer Party, Pipe Band, and Officers for the Vigil during her lying-in-state in Westminster Hall and funeral in Westminster Abbey on Tuesday 9 April 2002.

A last wave. As we all remember her. Queen Elizabeth, The Queen Mother on the last occasion she presented the shamrock at Lancaster House on 17th March 2000. She made a point of always wearing St Patrick's blue on Irish Guards occasions.

Bearer Party. The Bearer Party prepare the coffin in Westminster Hall for the processions to Westminster Abbey for the funeral service. The bearer party was made up of Captain Fabian Roberts, CSM C Oswald, Guardsmen S Campbell, T Major, G O'Neill, P Hewitt, J Organ, M Wall, R Sampat and A Azad. All were personally rewarded by The Queen by being appointed Members of the Royal Victorian Order. Captain Roberts and CSM Oswald were appointed MVO and the remainder were all awarded the Royal Victorian Medal.

The Battalion, which was in Münster, Germany, was on standby at the time to deploy as the lead armoured battle group. It was five years since the battalion had done public duties, so there was the need to find smart men available at short notice who could be fitted with tunics in time.

The Bearer Party reflected the main regimental recruiting areas – Republic of Ireland, Northern Ireland, Merseyside, Birmingham and London. Those chosen certainly rose to the challenge, and made everyone proud to be associated with the Regiment.

Procession in the Mall. Queen Elizabeth's Procession moves from the Queen's Chapel down the Mall towards Westminster Hall on 5th April.

The Last Watch. 35 Irish Guards Officers were involved in the vigil in Westminster Hall as Queen Elizabeth, The Queen Mother lay-in-state. In total, 144 Officers from the Household Division participated. When her husband King George VI lay-in-state in 1952, 21 Regimental Officers were involved.

Statue of Queen Elizabeth, The Queen Mother. In 2009, seven years after her death, a national memorial to the Queen Mother was unveiled on the Mall and, appropriately, the Regimental Band was involved in the ceremony. The 9ft 6in monument depicts her aged 51, which was her age when her husband died. Looking towards Buckingham Palace, there is a hint of a smile.

Processing to Westminster Abbey. After lying in state for three days Her Majesty was taken to Westminster Abbey for the funeral. At her request the Pipe Band led the gun carriage with other military pipers.

MVOs awarded. The Bearer party were made members of the Royal Victorian Order (MVO) or received the Royal Victorian Medal (RVM), a personal award from Her Majesty.

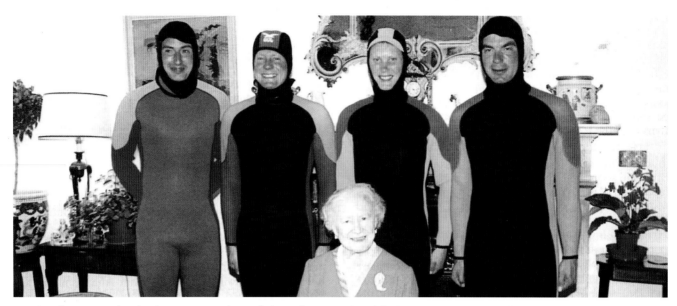

Castle of Mey, Scotland. The Queen Mother will always be remembered for her vitality and sense of fun, as shown in this picture taken at the Castle of Mey in Scotland. Every summer she would invite her former equerries to stay, to enjoy Scotland and provide entertainment. From the left; Captains Jamie Lowther-Pinkerton, Giles Basset, Edward Dawson-Damer, and Charlie McGrath pose with Her Majesty before going surfing in the chilly waters of Caithness.

Right: **Gift from the Household Division.** To mark The Queen's Golden Jubilee in 2002, the Household Division presented Her Majesty with a stained glass window for Her newly refurbished private chapel in Buckingham Palace. The design, by Mr Alfred Fisher, measures 7ft 5in by 4ft 8in and was paid for by donations from all regiments.

Left: **Queen's Golden Jubilee.** Not only was 2002 The Queen's Golden Jubilee year, but it also marked 1000 years of the monarchy in Britain. Guardsmen serving on Accession Day, 2 February, and who had served for five years, qualified to receive the medal, and some 93,000 throughout the Army qualified. It was a much more generous allocation than for her Silver Jubilee in 1997.

Drums and Pipes in South Korea. In October 2002 the Drums and Pipes were invited to participate in the Gangwon Military Tattoo in South Korea. Their performance led by Drum Major Teague and Pipe Major Allan was hugely well received to the extent that they were mobbed for their autographs. They are pictured teaching girls the pipes at the Buk Won Senior High School. Piper Muzvuru from Zimbabwe, pictured in the centre, was killed in action in Iraq the following year.

Presentation of Shamrock. In 2002 the Duchess of Abercorn presented the Shamrock in Wellington Barracks. She is accompanied by the Regimental Adjutant, Lt Col Robin Bullock-Webster.

MILITARY TRAINING

Since 1887 the training of Foot Guards recruits has evolved as outlined on page 140. More recently, the Army has downsized and the training base has been centralised. In 1993, after 33 years, the Guards Depot at Pirbright closed and became the Army Training Regiment, Pirbright, taking in Guardsmen but also non teeth–arm recruits as well. Guardsmen continued to train there for Phase 1, the initial 12 weeks, covering the Army-wide Common Military Syllabus before transferring to the Infantry Training Centre at Catterick, Yorkshire, for Phase 2, the Combat Infantryman's Course.

Being the lone Infantry trainees at Pirbright was not very successful, and apart from anything else there was a lack of competitive sport. In 2001 trials began to combine the two phases of training at Catterick, North Yorkshire. The last Foot Guards recruits at Pirbright passed out in June 2002. With new accommodation built at Catterick to take all Infantry trainees, the Foot Guards now completed 26 weeks training, including an extra two weeks for drill, in the Guards Training Company part of the 2nd Infantry Training Battalion.

Field Training.

Field Training.

Football Tour to Australia. With the assistance of the Guards Association of New South Wales and many others, the Battalion Football team went on a successful tour to Sydney, Australia in 2003.

Sport has always been encouraged in the Regiment and individuals supported to achieve success.

Successful Oarsman. In 2003 LCpl Pete Wilson rowed for the Household Division, the Army and Combined Services with considerable success. He was also a member of the elite Thames Rowing Club and competed in the fours for them in the Head of the River Race

London Marathon. Sgt M Johnson, the Master Tailor at Regimental Headquarters completes the London Marathon in a personal best time of 3.45 hours and raises money for military charities.

World Cycling Championships. In 2002 LCpl Peter Rice was placed 13th in the ICF World Cyclocross Championships in Belgium. It is one of the toughest sports to train for; it combines cross country cycling and running. He has also competed in road racing with the Army team.

Channel Swim. In 1875, the famous Captain Webb became the first man to swim the Channel… while in August 2003, the not so-famous Irish Guards Captains Gordon Simpson and Nick Gay became equal 668th to swim the Channel. Although they set off at the same time and from the same beach, they had separate support boats and after a few hours there was a significant distance between them. They landed two miles apart in France, both on 15 hours and 51 minutes. They later posed in Victorian Channel Swimming Order.

Rock Climbing in Canada. Guardsman Cook successfully climbed Mount Laurete in the Rocky Mountains during the summer of 2002.

OPERATION TELIC 1 – IRAQ – MARCH–MAY 2003

Op TELIC was the British contribution to the coalition effort in Spring 2003 and was the largest operation since the 1990-91 Gulf War, forcing Iraq to comply with UN Security Council Resolutions. The Battalion at that time was stationed in Munster, Germany as armoured infantry as part of 4 Armoured Brigade but formed part of an expanded 7 Armoured Brigade in Iraq.

In late 2002 there were several imponderables affecting the Battalion. They were on standby as the leading armoured Battle Group. The political commitment to the Iraq operation had not been declared. At the same time the plan was for the Battalion to handover in Münster to the Scots Guards in early 2003, and to return to England after five years abroad. They were also preparing for

Right: **Prayer before battle.** A pensive Commanding Officer in Kuwait, Lt Col James Stopford kneels with his Battalion to receive the blessing after being presented with Shamrock. It was his last event before handing over command to Lt Col Charles Knaggs later that day.

Left: **Final Briefing.** A final briefing is given to No 2 Company by Lt John Plummer at Shaibah airfield, 7km west of Basra for the attack on the university.

Stand-down. Members of No 2 Company shelter from the sun in Kuwait.

the Firemen's strike in England. Preparing for operations and organising a handover and unit move concurrently was not ideal but eventually the move was delayed for 6 months and the Battalion was committed wholeheartedly to the operation, to everyone's delight.

The Battalion's contribution was settled at 530 Irish Guardsmen across the 7 Armoured Brigade. Nos 1 and 2 Companies under Majors Peter MacMullen and Ben Farrell respectively, were brought up to strength of 160 each and became the armoured infantry element of the Royal Scots Dragoon Guards Battlegroup. No 4 Company

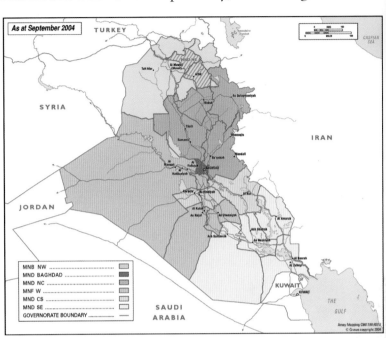

Personal Admin. Personal admin never goes away. Stringing a line between two vehicles makes an effective clothes line. The red animal painted on the vehicle indicates it is part of 7 Armoured Brigade, the so called 'Desert Rats'. In fact, it is a gerboa taken from the 7 Armoured Division's sign, deployed in the North African desert in World War 2.

Divisional Responsibility. A map of Iraq showing the area of responsibility of the Multi National Division-South East (MND SE) and Kuwait from where 7 Armoured Brigade launched its assault.

Briefing. No 2 Company attend an orders group in Kuwait. With limited time to prepare for the operation not everyone could be equipped with desert uniform.

In support. The Drums Platoon attached to No 1 Company on the outskirts of Basra.

and Support Company were split-up. No 10 Platoon, with Mortar and Milan sections reinforced the Royal Regiment of Fusiliers Battlegroup. No 11 Platoon, (actually the Scots Guards exchange platoon) with support elements reinforced the Black Watch Battle Group. Another Platoon, comprised mainly of HQ Company personnel, formed a Divisional HQ Defence Platoon. The uncommitted members of the Officers' and Sergeants' Messes were deployed across the Brigade as Liaison Officers and Watchkeepers.

Above: **'Captain Courageous'** It always helps to have the media present to report on your efforts. Initiating raids into the city, Captain J Moulton found himself, much to his embarrassment, dubbed 'Captain Courageous' by both the *Daily Mail* and *Time Magazine* for his coolness under fire. He was awarded a Joint Commanders' Commendation.

THE FINAL ASSAULT

Royal Regiment of Fusiliers

10P1+ IG

al-Ma'gil

B A S R A

Black Watch and 1st Royal Tank Regiment

11(SG)P1

Old Town

Manawi al-Basha district

Main concentration of Fedayin and Ba'ath party loyalists

Two miles

Desert Rats and Royal Scots Dragoon Guards

No1 & 2 Coys IG

Royal Marine Commandos

Above: **Entry into Basra.** Map of the final assault on Basra city involving Irish Guardsmen with the three Battle Groups on the left.

Left: **Sniper position.** LSgt C Briggs in an overwatch position for the Company assaults into Basra. This picture was used by the media worldwide.

Below: **Infantry carrying vehicle.** The Warrior Infantry Fighting Vehicle (IFV) provided essential firepower and protection for raids into the city of Basra. This combat vehicle had been trialled by No 1 Company in Munster back in 1982 before being deployed across the Army. Then it was called the Military Infantry Combat Vehicle – MIC(K)-V for short.

New Year 2003 saw intensive training and live firing at Sennelager and Hohne in Germany and Numbers 1 and 2 Companies deployed to Kuwait in early March. Four days before crossing the line of departure, all Irish Guardsmen came together for St Patrick's Day. From then on, all elements were fully involved in events that led to the securing of Basra on 6th April.

An initial relief-in-place of the US 7th Marines to the southwest of Basra left the Brigade encircling the town of Az Zubayr and blocking the bridges over the Shatt al-Arab river. As the situation became clearer the Brigade reconfigured to deal with the stabilisation of Az Zubayr, and

Left: **No 1 Company assault.** To commemorate No 1 Company successfully attacking the Fedayeen stronghold at the Basra College of Literature, the Sergeants, Mess commissioned a painting from the artist David Rowlands.

Below: **No 2 Company assault.** A second painting was commissioned from David Rowland showing the clearing of the enemy positions on the outskirts of the college. Gdsm A.L. Branchflower was subsequently awarded the Military Cross for actions during this operation.

Overwatch. Gdsm Cardwell overlooking the Shatt al-Arab waterway with oil installations on fire in the distance.

IRAQ 2003

to prevent enemy interference with Basra from the south. Enemy activity during this 10 day period ranged from armoured forays from what was left of the Iraqi Regular Army in T55 tanks, with artillery in support, to isolated activity of small teams of Irregulars armed with AK-47s and RPGs.

The Micks were involved at every stage. On the bridges leading into Basra, the Mortars and MILAN with the Fusilier Battle Group were kept busy keeping the block in place. No 11 (SG) Platoon with the Black Watch Regiment took part in the gradual, and at times bloody, eradication of the regime in Az Zubayr. To the north of Basra, the two rifle companies were placed in a blocking position early on, and then undertook various clearances, conducted with considerable bravery for which a number of awards were subsequently given.

Above: **Escorting suspects.** Maintaining law and order in Basra after the assault was difficult and not dissimilar to Kosovo, four years previously. Sadly the outcome was not as successful.

As the Iraqi Regular Army units became less effective the Battlegroups were able to conduct more ambitious raids into Basra. The Royal Scots Dragoon Guards in the south and the Black Watch in the centre were each given responsibility for the routes into Basra, while the Fusiliers maintained their dispositions in the north. This left No 1 and 2 Companies with the responsibility for the road up to the 'Gates of Basra' – a known Fedayeen stronghold and of huge symbolic significance locally.

Like winning the lottery. Guardsman Saint, No 5 Platoon, guarding thousands of newly minted banknotes, needed for the recovery of Basra and a return to normality.

Keeping in touch. Colour Sergeant M Swift posting a 'bluey' home.

"The Micks were here…" It was too much of a temptation for No 2 Company not to remind Saddam the Micks had been there in Basra.

As the Iraqi command and control weakened, raids into the city became bolder. The Black Watch Battle Group with No 11 Platoon made rapid early progress to punch into the eastern side of the city. Further north, the Fusiliers with 12 Platoon seized Basra University. The Irish Guards Rifle Companies probably experienced the hardest fighting as their route in was the best defended. In attacking to seize the College of Literature, No 1 Company passed through No 2 Company to confront successfully up to 400 Fedayeen and militia. It was as they consolidated their position on the night of 6th April that LCpl Ian Malone and Ppr Chris Muzvuru were killed by enemy small arms fire.

The taking of Basra brought a host of new problems, starting with the re-establishment of basic law and order, as one might expect in a city with no public servants, no respect for property and criminal behaviour rife. There was an air of relief among the local population at the end of 20 years of Saddam Hussein's regime, although many of the problems had not been resolved before the Battalion returned on Op TELIC 10 four years later.

The Battalion returned complete to Münster in the early hours of 17 May 2003 to a rapturous welcome.

Above: **LCpl Logue** with a policeman directing traffic in Basra.

Left: **L/Sgt P Clifford** directing locals in Basra.

Above: **A thank you message.** '*Tank Allied for Thier help get rid of Saddam*' (sic). Major Ben Farrell and Lt Tom Orde-Powlett beside a banner showing that someone appreciated their efforts

Campaign Medal. The operational service medal for Iraq bears a portrait of the Queen on one side and on the other the Lamussa, a sculpture from the Assyrian period which is symbolic of the region

Above: **Queen's Gallantry Medals.** LSgt Simon Campbell and Gdsm Lee Wheeler were both awarded the Queen's Gallantry medal for their bravery in Basra in April 2003. As their section came under heavy machine gun fire, they crossed open ground to save their Section Commander who had been critically injured by sniper fire. Their swift actions, bravery and professionalism helped save their section commander's life. In 2001 LSgt Campbell had also been awarded the Royal Victorian Medal when he was a member of the bearer party at the funeral of Queen Elizabeth, the Queen Mother.

Above: **Funeral in the Republic of Ireland.** LCpl Ian Malone was killed by an Iraqi sniper in Basra. His funeral in Dublin was the first occasion that British soldiers have been seen in uniform in the Republic of Ireland since the creation of the Free State in 1922. The funeral was an important occasion, moreover, in terms of the tacit recognition of Irishmen serving previously and currently in the British Army.

Awards Op TELIC 1 – 2003
Order of the British Empire (OBE)
    Lt Col M A P Carleton-Smith (detached)
Member of the British Empire (MBE)
    Maj P C A MacMullen
    Maj E J F V Melotte (detached)
Military Cross (MC)
    Lt D C M O'Connell
    Lt Hon T P A Orde-Powlett
    Gdsm A L Branchflower
Queen's Gallantry Medal
    LSgt S D Campbell
    Gdsm L Wheeler
Joint Commanders' Commendation
    Capt J D Moulton

New Battle Honour. The Battle Honour 'Iraq 2003' relates to operations between 19th March and 30th April 2003. It was approved by HM The Queen and formerly announced to Parliament on 9th June 2005 which enabled it to be displayed during the Trooping the Colour on 11th June.

Bravery awards. Collecting their awards at Buckingham Palace, from the left: Lt Hon T P A Orde-Powlett MC; Maj P C A MacMullen MBE; Gdsm A L Branchflower MC; Lt D C M O'Connell MC.

Girdlers' Livery Company

A new affiliation was formed in 2004 with the Girdlers' Company, one of the ancient Livery Companies of the City of London. The Livery Company traces its origins back to the 12th Century and was involved in the making of girdles (sword belts). Although the craft is no longer practised it still has the honour of presenting the girdle and stole worn by the Sovereign at the coronation.

The affiliation was proposed by their recent Past Master and wartime Irish Guardsman, John Udal. The Girdlers visit the Battalion on training exercises and regularly attend Regimental functions to develop a common understanding. The association has been mutually beneficial and they have been very generous to the regiment. Each year they present prizes to those judged to be the best Best Young Officer, Best Section Commander and Outstanding Guardsman on the Lance Corporals Course.

Right: **Section Commander's Award.** In 2006 a silver obelisk, similar to the one commemorating the Freedom of Ladysmith in South Africa, was presented by the Girdlers' Company to be awarded as a prize to be known as a Section Commander's Prize.

Girdlers' Hall. The Girdlers have had their own hall and garden in the City of London since 1431. It is looked down upon with envy from the high rise developments which surround it. This is their third hall, the first destroyed in the Great Fire in 1666, the second by the Luftwaffe in 1940.

Prize Giving. Each spring an awards lunch is hosted in the Hall to acknowledge the recipients, to which family and friends are also invited. In 2011 the Master, Lord Strathalmond, hosted the event for the winners, Capt Nick Gaggero, LSgt Nigel Scargill and Gdsm Michael McMurtry and their families.

Sergeant Major's Pace Stick. Also in 2006 the Girdlers' Company presented a pace stick for use by the Regimental Sergeant Major of the Battalion and a belt for use with home service clothing. The supporters of the belt locket union are of Royal Dublin Fusiliers' pattern.

OPERATION BANNER – SOUTH ARMAGH – NOVEMBER 2003–APRIL 2004

Op BANNER was the Army's longest continuous operational deployment. The 'Troubles' in Northern Ireland lasted almost 38 years from a vicious insurgency in the early 1970s (171 military personnel were killed in 1972 alone) through a terrorist campaign of some 25 years before the desired end state was achieved to allow a political process to be established.

Although the policy was that Irish Regiments would not deploy there as formed bodies, many Irish Guardsmen volunteered to serve, often with other Foot Guards Battalions. Even the Regimental Band had accumulated enough time for a Northern Ireland clasp to their General Service Medals after numerous musical tours to the Province.

The only serving Irish Guardsman killed in the Province attributed to Irish terrorism was Gdsm Sam Murphy, aged 21, who was shot on 15th November 1977, near his mother's home in Andersonstown in Belfast. He was on terminal leave, finishing his military career.

As the political climate improved, the Battalion deployed to Fermanagh in 1992/3 and to East Tyrone in 1995. In December 2003, only eight months after they returned from operations in Iraq, they deployed to South Armagh. Although the situation had undoubtedly improved in the notorious

Above: **Awaiting resupply.** Gdsm Sheehy providing security at the helicopter landing site, awaiting resupply in South Armagh, which even in 2004 was still carried out by air rather than road.

Left: **Previous units.** Nearly every Infantry Battalion in the Army was based in South Armagh for a four month tour at some time and left their Battalion signs in Bessbrook Mill, Newry, often commemorating personnel killed by snipers and bombers. It was by far the most dangerous area in which to operate.

'bandit country' along the border with the Republic, there was still no vehicle movement south of their base at Bessbrook Mill even four years after the Anglo-Irish Agreement came into force in December 1999. The observation towers along the border were not dismantled for another two and a half years after the Battalion's tour in response to the Provisional IRA's declaration that their campaign was over.

As devolution returned and the police assumed full responsibility, without the need of Army support, the 'Troubles' were finally declared over in July 2007, with neither fanfare nor celebration.

Left: **Royal visit to Bessbrook.** The Princess Royal, who presented the Shamrock for the first time in 2004, with outgoing RSM K T D Fox and incoming RSM S M Nichols on St Patrick's Day. The 17th March is often the traditional day for handing over key Regimental appointments. RSM Fox was then commissioned and RSM Nichols went on to be Academy Sergeant Major at Sandhurst and was later commissioned.

Patrolling. Piper McGing being reminded he is in so-called 'bandit country' and that the IRA had not gone away.

Above: **Supporting the police.** By 2004 the police had primacy but still needed military escorts when conducting vehicle check points in the border area, which had always been considered lawless.

Manning the permanent OPs. Sgt Parke's multiple from No 2 Company in front of the R12 surveillance tower on the border in South Armagh. Ten years later he became Regimental Sergeant Major of the Battalion.

Right: **Commanding Officer.** Lt Col Charlie Knaggs commanded the Battalion from 2003-2006. Pictured here with a Zulu Guard of Honour.

Above: **Order of St Patrick.** A sash of the Order, from which the cap badge is taken, is on loan to Regimental Headquarters. The Order has not been awarded since the partition of Ireland in 1922.

Right: **New Battle Honour trooped.** Lt Ben Pennington, the Ensign marching on the Mall with the Queen's Colour after the 2005 Queen's Birthday Parade when the Battalion displayed its new battle honour 'Iraq 2003' for the first time.

Left: **Three Brothers.** The family side of the Regiment was demonstrated again on the 2005 Queen's Birthday Parade, when the Irish Guards Colour Party comprised three brothers, the Hogans from Liverpool.

Below: **Troop.** Despite only two pipers having previous experience of Horse Guards and established for a strength of only nine pipers, the Pipe Band turned out a record 22 pipers for the Queen's Birthday Parade in 2005. Afterwards, HM The Queen was a little surprised but delighted to learn that one piper in the rank was in fact an Officer masquerading. The officer, the much liked Captain Matt Collins, was killed on active service in Afghanistan.

Training in Kenya. A Battalion exercise in Kenya should have been a relief for troops carrying out Public Duties in London, but Exercise Grand Prix in 2005 was confined to the arid and uncompromising area of Archer's Post in the north of the country. This tested the Q side responsible for supplying the rifle companies with food, water and ammunition. Seen here is CQMS Eccles with Guardsmen Birnie, Reed and Richardson of No 2 Company.

Ladysmith. Although a plaque had been placed in Bergville Church in 2000 to commemorate the formation of the Regiment, on 1st April 2005, the Regiment was given the Freedom of the City of Ladysmith in KwaZulu-Natal, South Africa. A plinth was also placed outside the Siege Museum in the town bearing the inscription: *"Dedicated to those whom Queen Victoria called 'My Brave Irish Soldiers' whose courage and sacrifice in the fighting that led to the relief of Ladysmith on 28th February 1900 inspired the formation of the Irish Guards by Royal Command on 1 April 1900. 'Quis Separabit'."* The badges of the brave Irish regiments are shown at the base of the memorial.

Winning Golf Team. In 2006 a Regimental team of former Micks won the Colonel-in-Chief's Cup, the Household Division Inter Regimental competition, for the first time at Worplesdon Golf Club. The team, from the left, were Bobby Nason, John Dempster, Mark Cannon Brookes, Robin McN Boyd, Sean Shields and David Porteous. The regiment successfully defended their title for the next three years.

Left: **Regimental hero.** Capt (Retd) Vince McEllin, the Assistant Regimental Adjutant and gifted horseman from Co. Mayo, represents the Regiment in South Africa in 2005.

Irish Guards Singers. The Irish Guards Singers began in Merseyside in 1982 as a small group of six former Micks, led by John Hyland, the then Secretary of the North of England Branch of the Irish Guards Association. They continued to grow, and although John Hyland died in 2012, they are still thriving and a credit to the Regiment. They have raised huge amounts of money for Regimental benevolent funds and other charities, even touring the Republic of Ireland. They are pictured in Lancashire with Canon Alf Hayes, a much loved Catholic Padre in the Battalion.

Para Micks. Former Mick members of the No 1 Guards (Independent) Parachute Company attend the Cenotaph Parade in November 2005. The Pathfinder Company had disbanded 30 years earlier but still forms up and marches on Remembrance Day. By custom, the Regiment does not parade on Remembrance Day, but has its own parade at the Guards Memorial towards the end of November following the Association's London Branch Dinner.

Right: **Queen's Birthday Parade.** In early June 2006 The Major General Commanding the Household Division, Major General Sebastian Roberts, carries out the inspection during his review of the Queen's Birthday Parade from a phaeton. The Queen gave him permission to do so, instead of being mounted, because a leg injury meant he was unable to ride that day.

Left: **Colonel William at Sandhurst.** In early January 2006 Prince William, the future Colonel, started his 44 week course at Sandhurst. He is pictured on Day 1 under the watchful eye of Academy Sergeant Major Nichols, Irish Guards. In April he visited the Battalion training at Otterburn, as a potential Mick Officer, together with Officer Cadet Orlando Roberts, son of General Sebastian, the then Regimental Lieutenant Colonel. Being driven in a Land Rover, escorted by a NCO from Support Company, the driver hit a bump on the rough track. The driver was quickly admonished by the escort: *"For goodness sake, be careful. Don't you realise we have the Lieutenant Colonel's son in the back?"* No mention of the future King!

Autumn training. Gdsm Cathcart of No 2 Company on field training at Otterburn in October 2006.

Langton trophy. Captain Patrick Lance and 2Lt Chris Lambe and the Support Platoons relax after completing the March & Shoot element of the Langton Trophy, which was won by the Drums Platoon, on Salisbury Plain in July 2006.

Below Left: **Battalion Warrant Officers.** The 1st Battalion Warrant Officers at the Guards Chapel in March 2006. Rear from left: Pipe Major D Rogers, Regimental Signals Warrant Officer D Crawford, Company Sergeant Majors T Watling, T Eccles, K Mayne, S Brettle, Master Tailor M Johnson, Drum Major T Farrelly. Front: Drill Sergeant R Martin, Regimental Quartermaster Sergeant P Lally, Regimental Sergeant Major J Donaldson, Regimental Quartermaster Sergeant P Fagin, Drill Sergeant I McNaughton.

Above: **State Opening of Parliament.** The General Officer Commanding, London District, Major General Sebastian Roberts checks the route before the State Opening of Parliament in November 2006, accompanied by two Irish Guards Officers, his ADC Captain John Plummer and the Brigade Major, Lieutenant Colonel Edward Melotte.

Milan Platoon Training. LCpl Harte questions the 'man pack-ability' of the Milan weapon system at Otterburn in October 2006. It was to be the last course and live firing of the Milan weapon, (24 hits, 2 misses and one rogue) before being replaced by the Javelin, a much more potent weapon. It ceased to be called the Anti–Tank Platoon as its capabilities made it more of a 'bunker buster' in combat.

Realistic Training. The village of Copehill Down on Salisbury Plain was modelled on a village in Northern Germany. It became redundant at the end of the Cold War but was still very useful as a training facility for a Middle East scenario.

Jungle Training. The jungle of Belize is always a testing environment in which to train and in 2006 it was the first opportunity to try the new Bowman radio system at Battle group level. The training culminated with a Battle Group level test exercise set by Brigade Headquarters.

Machine Gun Platoon. The Corps of Drums, which is also the General Purpose Machine Gun (Sustained Fire) (GPMG(SF)) Platoon fire their weapons on Warcop ranges in November 2006, the culmination of a course at Aldershot and Northumberland.

Commanding Officer. Lt Col Michael O'Dwyer who commanded the Battalion 2006–2008 being interviewed for RTE 6 O'Clock News. His father commanded the Battalion from 1984–1986.

Tactical Training. LCpl Lomas moves fire position with his GPMG on pre-deployment training.

Realistic training. Almost a year of mission specific training in different part of the country is carried out before an operational deployment. On Salisbury Plain, Gurkhas impersonating Arabs enjoyed being aggressive and provoking the Micks.

Heading Home. The Battalion returns home in convoy on a frosty spring morning from Thetford in Norfolk. They had been training over St Patrick's Day but the Princess Royal still distributed the shamrock.

Framework operations. LCpl Orr of Support Company leads a patrol through the mock village of Copehill Down on Salisbury Plain.

OPERATION TELIC 10 – IRAQ – MAY–NOVEMBER 2007

In the Spring of 2003 the Battalion crossed the border, as armoured infantry, from Kuwait into Iraq on the initial Op TELIC at only 10 weeks notice. It was a considerable military success achieving the main military objectives within four weeks.

In 2007, four years and nine Brigade roulements later, they returned to Southern Iraq with the 1st Mechanised Brigade. Winning in 2003 had been easy but the nature and size of the post-conflict tasks had been extremely difficult to predict and plan for. Initial euphoria at removing Saddam and the Ba'thist regime passed and efforts to return to normality were soon hindered by a very violent, mainly Shia, insurgency.

The Brigade's main effort in 2007 was to concentrate on developing the Iraqi Army by Monitoring, Mentoring and Training (M2T). In May, the Battalion, entering again via Kuwait, was split-up to undertake a number of tasks in different locations. During the tour, the Iraqi Army had formed a new Division and it was the Battle Group's task to form it into a fighting force.

The Contingency Operating Base (COB) was established at the International Airport where the Battlegroup HQ was also located. Initially, No 1 Company was attached to 4 RIFLES operating from Basra Palace. They were under constant barrage from indirect fire and rockets which only diminished when an 'accommodation' was reached with the Militia and the Palace was handed back to the Iraqi Government. It was on August 9th that LSgt Christopher Casey and LCpl Kirk Redpath were killed when hit by a roadside bomb in a vehicle providing protection to one of the long resupply convoys between Kuwait and Basra.

Pre-deployment church service. Fergal, still a puppy, leads the Battalion to church in Aldershot for a pre-deployment service. It was the first time the Guardsmen paraded in desert combat kit.

Black Bag. No 4 Company pleased to receive the 'black bag' containing their new Op TELIC issue of kit.

No 1 Company started in Basra Palace before changing with No 2 Company in Baghdad as the Force Protection Company. Both Companies left behind a Platoon with Badger Sqn, RTR, to surge into Basra City.

No 4 Company ran a Divisional Training Centre (DTC) in Shaibah, an Iraqi logistics base some 10km from the COB, for the collective training of Iraqi Army Companies. Two four-man Military Transition Teams (MiTTs) were formed to help the Battalions with low level tactical skills.

Other troops were deployed to the 'Green Zone' in Baghdad with the role of Force Protection covering the Baghdad Support Unit and VIP protection. They also provided protection between the Green Zone and the Airport down the notoriously dangerous 'Route Irish'.

As the Commanding Officer said, 'It was a tour of two halves', the first a story of unprecedented violence until Basra Palace was vacated, then an important mentoring role for the fledgling Iraqi Army. Lt Col Michael O'Dwyer, the Commanding Officer commented on their return; *'The journey had its ups and downs, it has been frustrating, comical, boring, exasperating, exciting, tragic and more, but the junior leadership, courage and initiative shown was extraordinary.'*

Basra Palace. The view from Basra Palace and the car park after indirect fire has hit the city.

Mobile patrol. On patrol in the International Zone in the infamous Snatch vehicle, developed for operations in Northern Ireland, but provided inadequate protection in Iraq.

Above: **Platoon Photograph.** Lt James Gaggero's 6 Platoon of No 2 Company on a popular, if overused, location for group photographs. It is a parade ground used by Saddam Hussein to review his troops.

Right: **Force Protection.** On guard at Maude House, the residence of the British commander.

Above: **Take cover.** No 2 Company take cover in a 'duck & cover' in Baghdad. They were under constant threat from Indirect Fire and drills were established to mitigate the risks. They were forced to retreat to the 'Bagdad coffins' at least 10 times a day.

Heavy protection.
LSgts Kavanagh and
Jackson man a Mastiff
vehicle brought in
to replace the lighter
Landrovers.

Repatriation. The
Regimental Sergeant
Major P Lally preparing
the Battle Group for the
repatriation of a soldier
killed on duty.

Awards Op TELIC 10
Member of the British Empire (MBE)
   Capt J A E Palmer
Queen's Gallantry Medal (QGM)
   WO2 B J Campbell RVM
   LSgt K W Thompson
Mention in Despatches (MiD)
   LSgt G P O'Neill
Joint Commanders' Commendation
   LSgt W J Lyttle
   LSgt F M Whelan
General Officer Commanding's Commendation
   Cpl Hogan
   Gdsm Brierley
   Gdsm Sinnott

Killed in Action in Iraq 1994–2007	
Captain Harry Shapland	14 April 1994
Piper Christopher Muzvuru	6 April 2003
Lance Corporal Ian Malone	6 April 2003
Lance Sergeant Christopher Casey	9 August 2007
Lance Corporal Kirk Redpath	9 August 2007

Above: **Queen's Gallantry Medals.** WO2 BJ Campbell and LSgt K W Tomlinson receive their Queen's Gallantry Medals at Buckingham Palace.

Right: **Mention-in-Despatches.** LSgt G P O'Neill receives his award from the Commanding Officer, Lt Col Ben Farrell.

The Ensigns prepare to return to the Guards with the New Colours which had been blessed earlier in the proceedings.

Chapter Nine

2008–2016
BEARSKINS AND BAYONETS

During this period the Battalion moved from Aldershot to Windsor and back to Aldershot with much involvement in state ceremonial.

The Army's main effort during this period was Operation HERRICK in Afghanistan. The Battalion deployed in 2011 on Op HERRICK 13 as part of 16 Air Assault Brigade, but also contributed individuals and slam detachments with other Foot Guards Battalions on previous rotations.

HM The Queen presented New Colours at Windsor Castle in 2009 and the new Queen's Colour was trooped on her Birthday Parade weeks later. A successful Appeal was launched to increase Regimental Benevolent Funds and everyone was delighted that HRH Prince William, Duke of Cambridge, became the new Colonel of the Regiment in 2011 and wore the uniform of the Irish Guards at his wedding the following year. A fine statue of an Irish Guardsman, dressed for operations in Iraq, was unveiled in Windsor.

During the 2012 Olympics, the Battalion had responsibility for security at the rowing venue at Dorney Lake near Windsor. The Queen's Diamond Jubilee year was celebrated, and the Irish Guards fired a 'feu de joie' at Buckingham Palace. Alongside extensive ceremonial duties, operational and training commitments continued apace. The Irish Guards found the United Kingdom Standby Battalion in 2012 and 2015. In April 2013 the Irish Guards concurrently deployed No 1 Company to Bosnia (Op ELGIN), No 2 Company to Afghanistan as the Task Force Helmand Brigade Operations Company (Op HERRICK 18), and No 4 Company and Support Company to the Falklands (FIRIC), with the remainder finding the Windsor Castle Guard! In 2014, the Irish Guards Battle Group deployed to Cyprus in blue berets as the UN Peacekeeping Force in Cyprus, on the 50th anniversary of this mission. Multinational training commitments also offered variety during this period, French and Omani troops were grouped with the Micks for its field test exercises in 2013 and No 4 Company deployed a Company Group to Oman in 2015.

Above: **Fathers and Sons.** In 2008 there were 12 sons of former and current officers serving in the Regiment. Here are 10 of the fathers with their sons behind, named in brackets, on St Patrick's Day in Mons Barracks Aldershot. From left: Capt P C C Solly 73–83 (Nick), Col C R Langton 69–01 (Johnny), Maj J D Kennard 69–86 (Adam), Maj R A Wilson 62–77 (Edmund), Lt Col J B O'Gorman 69–02 (Sam), Maj Gen Sir Sebastian Roberts 77–10 (Julian), Lt Col S G O'Dwyer 59–87 (Michael), Brig R A C Plummer 48–85 (John), Lt Col R J S Bullock-Webster 65–93 (James), Lt J P G Gaggero 79–82 (Nicholas).

Above: **Family links at RMA Sandhurst.** A picture taken at Sandhurst illustrating the family connections within the regiment with four Officer Cadets and three Academy staff. From left: OCdt P S G O'Gorman, son of Lt Col J B O'Gorman (1968–2002), WO1 F Howell, son of Gdsm F Howell (1958–1961), OCdt N J Gaggero, son of Lt J P G Gaggero (1979–1982), Capt R J Plummer, son of Brig R A C Plummer (1949–1985), OCdt A D S Kennard, son of Maj J D Kennard (1969–1986), and grandson of Maj C D Kennard DSO (1940–1946), WO2 W Buckley, nephew of Sgt V Buckley (1970–1992), OCdt O T A L Roberts, son of Maj Gen Sir Sebastian Roberts KCVO OBE (1976–2010).

Above: **Band of Brothers.** Siblings in the Regimental Band are not uncommon. On the left L/Cpl Owen and Musn Ryan Duffield; C/Sgt Paul Hooper and Sgt John Hooper on the right and C/Sgt Andy Grimwood in the centre stands in front of his brother Sgt Neal Grimwood, a tuba player with the Scots Guards who hopefully might be persuaded to transfer to the Micks. Not included in the photograph is Musn Nick Wakely, who followed his father, Steve, into the band. He was a noted trombone player in the 1970s.

Above: **Remembering a VC.** Every year on the anniversary of the death of Michael O'Leary VC, representatives from the London Branch of the Association lay a wreath on his grave in Mill Hill, London. Here, LCpl Dunbar, of the Pipes, plays a lament attended by Arnold Gregory, Bill Green and Tom Barry. O'Leary was the first Irishman to be awarded the VC in the Great War for an action on 1st February 1915.

Left: **The Colonel Retires.** The Duke of Abercorn, the 8th Colonel of the Regiment, retired in 2008 after eight very successful years, but continued to show a real interest in all Mick matters including the forthcoming Appeal.

Below: **Garden of Remembrance in Co Mayo.** On 7 October 2008, The President of the Republic of Ireland, Mrs Mary McAleese opened the Mayo Peace Park – Garden of Remembrance in Castlebar, Co Mayo. A small detachment of pipers participated in the ceremony and our Dublin Branch standard was also present. Over 1000 names feature on the memorial of which ten per cent are Irish Guardsmen who died in the Boer and Great Wars. One of the smaller stones is dedicated to the regiment.

Right: **New Colonel of the Regiment.** On St Patrick's Day 2008 Major General Sebastian Roberts, who was the Regimental Lieutenant Colonel, assumed the appointment as our 9th Colonel from the Duke of Abercorn who stood down after eight years.

Right: **Rugby tour to South Africa.** In the summer of 2009, 27 members of the Battalion Rugby Club went on a very successful tour of South Africa, which just happened to coincide with the British and Irish Lions tour. They played three games, won two and just lost the third and played hard on and off the rugby field. They are pictured in Cape Town with Table Mountain in the background.

Left: **Exercise 'I'm a Mini Mick – Get me out of here…'.** In June 2009, 30 children from Irish Guards families deployed on a 24 hour survival exercise just for fun, in a special jungle school built in Hampshire by the Gurkhas. Without fear, they all handled tropical insects, reptiles and a huge python called Slitheron. After a well deserved barbecue, they cooked marshmallows over the camp fire before retiring to their camp beds. All lived to tell tales of fun and daring do and received prizes and Mini Mick tee shirts.

Right: **A suitable affiliation.** The Regiment has had an official affiliation with the Royal Montserrat Defence Force for many years, and when possible, a team is sent from the Battalion to assist with their training. In 2008 Capt Tim Rogers led such a team, which included Gdsm Weekes from the Island who was serving in the Battalion. The 'Irishness' of this island near Antigua goes back centuries, and many of the local population now have Irish surnames. Passports are stamped with a shamrock on entry, and a national holiday is declared on St Patrick's Day.

PRESENTATION OF NEW COLOURS

On 6 May 2009, HM The Queen presented New Colours to the 1st Battalion in the Quadrangle at Windsor Castle. Due to wear and tear the Colours are replaced after 8 to 12 years and this was the fifth occasion HM The Queen has done so in her reign. The old colours were presented at the same place twelve years before, but the five years spent away from public duties prolonged their use. It was a solemn yet festive occasion and was followed by an All Ranks garden party in Victoria Barracks attended by HM The Queen and Prince Philip.

Above: **Conmeal** leads the Regimental Band into the Quadrangle at Windsor Castle.

Above: **Royal Salute**. The Queen, as the Colonel in Chief, addressed those on parade, and the Commanding Officer, Lt Col B C Farrell, replied. A Royal Salute was given before the Colours were marched off.

Above: **HM The Queen** passes the new Regimental Colour to the Ensign, 2/Lt C W J Gair, assisted by the Field Officer, Major R J Plummer.

Left: **New Colours.** The new Colours with the Queen's Colour on the right. In the centre of the Regimental Colour on the left is a six pointed star with a red hand in it, taken from the Arms of Ulster, which is the emblem of No 10 Company. The twenty-three Company badges are borne in rotation on the Regimental Colour.

TROOPING THE COLOUR

On Saturday 13 June 2009, some six weeks after receiving new Colours from The Queen at Windsor, the Battalion trooped the new Queen's Colour on Her Birthday Parade on Horse Guards. It was five years since they had last done so. The Battalion were so well recruited at the time, that on this occasion they managed to provide four Guards, making a total of seven on parade. The last time this happened was 1967. Her Majesty, who wore her striking St Patrick's blue outfit, declared afterwards that it had been an excellent parade.

Right: **Colour Point.** C/Sgt Grimes, one of the markers behind the Officers about to be called onto parade by the Field Officer. The SNCO markers have the unenviable job of being the first and last to leave the parade with little movement in between.

Left: **RSM draws his sword.** Regimental Sergeant Major R A Martin about to take hold of the Queen's Colour from its escort before handing it to the Ensign. This is the only occasion the RSM draws his sword. The escort was provided by the three Hogan brothers; James, Michael and Peter, came from Merseyside.

New saddlecloths. The Field Officer in Brigade Waiting, Lt Col B C Farrell, riding Wellesley, is dressed with a new Regimental shabraque or saddle cloth for the first time. Six were made using bullion thread, with the St Patrick's star, shamrocks and harps. They are only used on State Occasions when a member of the Royal Family is present.

The Inspection. The Queen inspecting her Guards from a carriage passed the Guards Memorial. Note her horses are wearing the new State saddlecloths.

Harry Robertshaw Bequest.
A bottle of beer was distributed
to every soldier on parade.

Above: **Marching Past.** The Ensign, 2Lt
Andrew Campbell and the Subaltern, Lt Sam
O'Gorman on the right, 'recover arms' after
saluting the Sovereign.

Left: **Escort salutes The Queen.** The
Escort to the Colour gives an 'Eyes Right'
to the Queen as the Ensign, 2nd Lieutenant
Campbell, lowers the Queen's Colour in
tribute. The Escort had practised the march-
past 82 times at Pirbright and on Horse
Guards Parade to reach perfection on the
day.

Marching off. At the end of the parade, the
Divisions march off parade with the Queen's
Guard behind Her Majesty's carriage. The
Major General Commanding the Household
Division and General Officer Commanding
London District, Major General W G
Cubitt leads the Foot Guards. Although he
was also Regimental Lieutenant Colonel
Irish Guards, on this occasion he wore
the tunic of his appointment as the Major
General Commanding the Household
Division.

© Tempest Photography

IRISH GUARDS OFFICERS & WARRANT OFFICERS
PRESENTATION OF NEW COLOURS
WINDSOR – 6TH MAY 2009

Back row L to R: 2/Lt CWJ Gair; 2nd Lt BF Leonard; WO2(CSM) MI Butler; Maj RJ Plummer; Padre ARF Battey; 2ndLt GC Sprake; 2ndLt ACS Campbell; Lt Col CA Craig-Harvey; Capt TDH Oakley; Capt NS Solly; WO2(CSM) I Pickford; Lt PSG O'Gorman; Capt HJN Collis; Capt OTAL Roberts

Third row: WO2(CSM) TA Hobbs; Lt ADS Kennard; Capt JJJL Roberts; Capt DT Evans; Capt PA Fagin; Capt CA Allman-Brown; WO1(BM) M Walters; WO1(BSM) S Forgie; Lt Col CJ Ghika; Capt WR Maunder-Taylor; Capt CGG Howard; Capt GT Murphy; Capt CEV Williams; WO2(CSM) BR Taylor; Maj(DOM) PD Shannon MBE

Second Row: DMaj C Patterson; WO2(DSgt) NA Perry; MTlr C Sheehan; Capt PW Lally; WO2(DSgt) JDW Dyer; Lt GESD de Stacpoole; WO2(CSM) DD Johnstone; Lt Col DM Hannah MBE; WO2(CSM) JG Parke; Lt MK Dooher; Sgt SR Sharples; Capt AJL Prior; WO2(CSM) K Fletcher; Maj MJ Collins; Capt SGHC Wolseley; WO2(RQMS) T Eccles; Capt BJ Irwin-Clark; Maj JS Langton; Capt FW Howell; PMaj DH Rogers

Front Row: Maj PF Shields; WO2(RQMS(M)) SA McMichael; Maj MRN Stewart; Maj AJ Wills; Capt JRHL Bullock-Webster; WO1(RSM) RA Martin; HRH The Duke of Edinburgh; Lt Col BC Farrell (Comd Offr); HM The Queen; Maj Gen WG Cubitt CBE (RLC); Maj FADL Roberts MVO; Lt Col J B O'Gorman (Regt Adj); Maj ET Boanas; Maj IAJ Turner; Capt RP Money; WO2(RQMS(T)) BJ Campbell QGM; Capt KTD Fox

LAYING UP THE OLD COLOURS

The stand of Colours presented by HM The Queen on 22 May 1997, and placed in suspension at Windsor Castle on 6 May 2009, were 'laid up' in the Guards Chapel (Royal Military Chapel), Wellington Barracks on Friday 4 December 2009. The Regimental Council decides where the old Colours should be laid up. They could be placed in affiliated Town Halls, Livery Companies, Churches or Schools associated with the Regiment. The regiment retains an interest in all laid up colours, so that were a church containing colours to be closed, the regiment should be consulted as to their disposal. Wherever they go, they cease to be the property of the Regiment. The Guards Chapel has received most of the former colours, so it was appropriate that the eighth stand should reside there.

Left: **Old Colours marched in.** The old Colours are marched into the Chapel. The Queen's Colour on the left is carried by 2nd Lieutenant C W J Gair and 2nd Lieutenant G C Sprake carries the Regimental Colour.

Above: **Company Colours.** Senior Non-Commissioned Officers of the Battalion carrying the Company Colours line the steps of the Guards Chapel supervised by RSM R A Martin in anticipation of the arrival of the old Colours.

Below: **Handing Over.** The Regimental Colour in the foreground is handed to the Commanding Officer Lt Col B C Farrell by 2nd Lieutenant G C Sprake and behind, 2nd Lieutenant C W J Gair has handed the Queen's Colour to the Regimental Lieutenant Colonel, Major General W G Cubitt.

Below: **Colours handed over.** The Colonel of the Regiment, Major General Sir Sebastian Roberts KCVO OBE hands the Queens's Colour to Padre Paul Wright of the Guards Chapel for safekeeping.

Above: **Warrant Officers' Club.** Former and serving Warrant Officers of the regiment meet annually for dinner to maintain the friendships built up over many years service in the Micks. They are an important part of the family and continue to support the serving and retired Irish Guardsmen. In 2008 they assembled in the Guards Chapel, dressed in their distinctive St Patrick's Blue ties, for a photograph with the Regimental Lieutenant Colonel, Major General Sebastian Roberts.

Above: **Treasuring the moment.** David Beckham, footballer and national icon, on a flight back from Afghanistan, visiting the troops, treasures the opportunity of being able to hold RSM Mayne's Mick beret.

Above: **Military Cross.** LSgt J S Cooke at RHQ after receiving his MC at Buckingham Palace. He was serving in Afghanistan with the Guards Parachute Platoon in 3rd Battalion The Parachute Regiment in 2008 and the citation read '…*despite the obvious threat to his own life, Cook's immediate intervention, disregard for his own safety, and unflinching courage, undoubtedly saved the life of a comrade who was in mortal danger.*' In 2009 13 Micks passed Parachute Selection, so the platoon in 3 PARA was largely composed of Irish Guardsmen.

Right: **Commanding Officer.** Lt Col Ben Farrell who commanded the Battalion 2008–2010.

ARMY CADET UNITS

There are some 15 Army Cadet Force units badged as Irish Guards in England and Northern Ireland. They are a cherished part of the Regiment and are supported when possible by the Battalion. A few may join the Regiment later as adult soldiers, but the aim is to raise the profile of the Regiment and represent the Micks in our main recruiting areas. The cadets are proud to be in the regimental family, as we are to have them associated with us.

Left: **Mini Micks Competition.** Every year teams battle it out in Ballykinler, Co Down, for the honour of being called the Best Irish Guards Cadets in the UK. Military skills, including drill and shooting are tested. In 2012 the Ballygowan Detachment from the 2nd (NI) Battalion won and proudly pose with their trophies.

Right: **The Duchess of Cambridge** meeting cadets on St Patrick's Day in Aldershot in 2012. As a reward the winning team from the Mini Micks Competition in Northern Ireland is invited to parade with the Battalion on St Patrick's Day.

Left: **Best Cadet.** LCpl Jacob Draper of the Crosby Detachment of Merseyside ACF was judged Best Cadet in 2013.

Below: **Cadet Corps of Drums.** In 2009 a Corps of Drums was raised in the 1st (Northern Ireland) Battalion Army Cadet Force. It proved to be very popular and every month 70 cadets meet for practice at Ballymena. Their uniform may be unorthodox but their ability and enthusiasm is unquestioned.

KENYA

Ex Grand Prix was a Battalion level exercise in Kenya undertaken in early 2010 in preparation for deployment to Afghanistan. It offered an ideal insight into operations among the population in an austere environment. Commanding Officers changed shortly after the exercise but it was a seamless transition such was the professionalism of the Battalion.

Training was both arduous and realistic in preparing to deploy to Afghanistan later in 2010.

Below: **Grandfather's Pipe Banner.** Lieutenant Prince Josef of Liechtenstein, training in Kenya, beside the Pipe Major who carries the pipe banner of his grandfather, Colonel John, the Grand Duke of Luxembourg, and 6th Colonel of the Regiment. He was followed into the Regiment two years later by his two cousins, Prince Wenceslas of Nassau and Alexander of Habsburg, Archduke of Austria.

Major Alex Turner briefs No 2 Company on future tasks.

ST PATRICK'S DAY 2010

On 17 March, a break was taken from the intensive pre Afghanistan training to celebrate St Patrick's Day in the field at Archer's Post in Kenya. The shamrock was distributed by Lady Roberts, wife of the Colonel of the Regiment, Major General Sir Sebastian, who had travelled from England for the occasion.

Right: **Lady Roberts** hands a basket of shamrock to the Adjutant, Capt James Bullock-Webster, for the Drums and Pipes.

Above: **The Drums and Pipes** are not phased by the uneven, but only, parade ground available.

Left: **On Parade.** With the whole Battle Group formed up, the Commanding Officer declares the parade to the Colonel.

Above: **The Commanding Officer**, Lt Col Ben Farrell, leads his Battalion off parade saluting the Colonel on the dais.

Right: **One loyal Kenyan** Sumburu tribesman entered into the spirit of the day by wearing shamrock and an Irish Guards wristband.

Above: **Sergeant Major's Farewell.** Lt Col Ben Farrell bids farewell to Regimental Sergeant Major Ross Martin on the St Patrick's Day parade. The RSM immediately departed by helicopter to continue his career as a Commissioned Officer.

IRISH GUARDS APPEAL

In 2010, the Regimental Council launched an appeal to raise charitable funds for the Regiment, to sustain the increasingly high demand for welfare assistance. Much needed action has been taken nationally to improve support for the Armed Forces in recent conflicts, but a family regiment takes care to look after its wounded, their families and the families of the bereaved. Benevolent funds are also required to maintain the quality of life for serving Guardsmen.

Over the next three years over one million pounds was raised by a huge voluntary family effort. Among hundreds of imaginative fundraising ventures, the wives and girl-friends climbed Mount Snowdon and the Irish Guards singers performed in Widnes and Liverpool shopping centres.

A 'Row Home Challenge' was set up by Micks in Afghanistan, each rowing 300km on a dusty old Ergo rowing machine in a patrol base. Regimental wristbands were sold all over the world. An evening race meeting was held at the racecourse in Windsor, attended by the serving officers and Sergeants' Mess members in mess dress.

One sporting grandmother of a serving Mick made a sponsored sky-dive.

A spectacularly successful charity boxing night was held in the Banqueting House, Whitehall, through the energy and leadership of one dynamic individual. The imagination employed throughout the appeal was a delight.

The Irish Guards Appeal lasted for two years. Charitable fundraising continues. The generosity shown has been overwhelming, and of course the need will remain for years to come.

The Irish Guards Appeal

RHQ Irish Guards, Wellington Barracks, Birdcage Walk, London, SW1E 6HQ
Tel: 020 7414 3297   Mob: 07824557916   E-mail: igappealfund@gmail.com

Irish Guards Appeal. The appeal was launched in June 2010 by the Colonel of the Regiment, Major General Sir Sebastian Roberts, as the Battalion started OP HERRICK 13 in Afghanistan, and raised over £1million in two years.

The Irish Guards Appeal

www.irishguardsappeal.com

Above: **Irish Guards wristbands.** Military wristbands were fairly ubiquitous during recent conflicts, but they did show support, and raised a considerable amount of money for the Appeal.

Below: **Trustee walks for the Regiment.** In 2010 Peter Nutting, a former officer and Regimental trustee for over 35 years, walked the North Downs Way to raise over £20,000 for the appeal. The 141 mile route ended at Canterbury Cathedral where he was greeted by his family, Conmael and a piper.

Left: **Guardsman Beer.** The local brewery in Windsor produced a special beer, and local landlords generously contributed 15p for every pint sold to the Appeal.

Friends of the Irish Guards Gala Dinner in Belfast
2nd September 2010

The Colonel of the Regiment addresses the diners about the appeal.

Left: **Belfast Gala Dinner.** On 2 September 2010 the Friends of the Irish Guards in Northern Ireland organised a well supported dinner in Belfast City Hall.

Below: **Windsor Race Meeting.** On 4 July 2011, the entire Battalion was invited to an evening race meeting. There was an Irish Guards enclosure, the Drums and Pipes played (away from the horses) and the mascot attracted the crowds. There was even an Irish Guards race and the whole event raised £20,000 for the appeal.

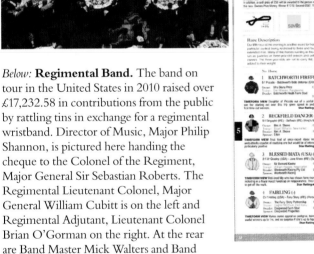

Below: **Regimental Band.** The band on tour in the United States in 2010 raised over £17,232.58 in contributions from the public by rattling tins in exchange for a regimental wristband. Director of Music, Major Philip Shannon, is pictured here handing the cheque to the Colonel of the Regiment, Major General Sir Sebastian Roberts. The Regimental Lieutenant Colonel, Major General William Cubitt is on the left and Regimental Adjutant, Lieutenant Colonel Brian O'Gorman on the right. At the rear are Band Master Mick Walters and Band Sergeant Major Stuart Forgie.

Above: **Beating Retreat.** In June 2012, a musical evening and reception was held at the home of Captain Patrick Hungerford, a former Irish Guards officer, and raised £50,000 for the appeal. He is pictured handing over a cheque to the Regimental Lieutenant Colonel, Major General Mark Carleton-Smith with Mr Justin Marking of Savill's Real Estate Company who generously sponsored the event.

Below: **Wives climb Mt Snowden.** Some of the Battalion wives climbed Mt Snowdon to raise money while their husbands were in Afghanistan. A selfless effort, and appreciated by everyone.

NEW COLONEL OF THE REGIMENT

As the Battalion approached the end of its tour in Afghanistan it was announced in February 2011 that HRH The Prince William was to become the 10th Colonel.

Above: **Colonel's sword.** Traditionally, the Colonel of the Regiment has carried a levee sword believed to be the first sword made for the regiment and indeed, he used it to cut the wedding cake. However, in 2011, Pooley & Son, swordmakers generously made a new one for the regiment, with a solid silver hilt, for use by the new Colonel.

ST JAMES'S PALACE

It is with very great pride that I take over as the 10th Colonel of the Irish Guards. It has long been a firm-held aspiration of mine to be associated with the Micks.

Ours is a unique regiment; a combination of the matchless traditions of the Foot Guards and that indefinable spark and spirit that marks out the Irish – all that distilled into one of the world's great fighting regiments. It is a supreme honour to be joining your ranks, in succession to Major General Sebastian Roberts, a great Mick.

For the remainder of the Battalion's tour to Afghanistan I send All Ranks my heartfelt best wishes. God speed your safe return.

Quis Separabit

Colonel William

10th February, 2011

Above: **Colonel's Handover.** Everyone was thrilled that the Duke of Cambridge was to become Colonel of the Regiment. The 9th Colonel, General Sebastian Roberts, who stepped down to make way for the Duke had done a splendid job and had been very closely involved since he joined 34 years before. Hugely popular and well known in the Regiment, in accordance with the *Quis Separabit* motto, it was understood at once that nothing would separate him from the Micks. And nothing has. He is pictured here in Kenya on his last St Patrick's Day as Colonel.

Above: **New Colonel.** On 10 February 2011, while the Battalion was on operations in Afghanistan, it was announced that HRH The Prince William would become the 10th Colonel of the Irish Guards. The Regiment had been very pleased that, whilst at Sandhurst in 2006, he had considered commissioning into the Regiment and visited the Battalion on training as a Potential Officer. He was commissioned into the Household Cavalry, but from that time onwards there flickered an unspoken hope in the regiment that someday he would have an official link. He refers, charmingly, to his 'firm-held aspiration' in his letter to the regiment on appointment as Colonel.

Left: **Colonel's First Queen's Birthday Parade.** 2011 was the first time Colonel William rode on the Queen's Birthday parade as Colonel of the Regiment. The magnificent Irish themed bridle (officially called horse furniture) designed by Regimental Headquarters was first used in 1996. It came about through a conversation between the Colonels of the Coldstream and Irish Guards on St Patrick's Day. The Colonel of the Coldstream boasted that his regiment had designed and procured a new set for state occasions.

ROYAL WEDDING APRIL 2011

On 16 November 2010 it was announced, to everyone's delight, that the new Colonel was to marry Miss Catherine Middleton. The wedding took place the following Spring. There was much speculation in the press as to what the groom would wear on the day, with most predicting RAF uniform, as his current employment was as an Air Sea Rescue pilot. The Regiment was delighted that Prince William chose to wear his Irish Guards uniform which had been made by the official regimental tailors in great secrecy. The Prince William and Miss Catherine Middleton Charitable Gift Fund was established as an alternative to receiving wedding presents and the Irish Guards Appeal was nominated as a designated charity and later benefited from a generous donation.

The Commanding Officer, Lieutenant Colonel Christopher Ghika, commanded the Queen's Guard on the day of the wedding, an appointment he would traditionally only fill on the first or last guard mount of a period of public duties.

Below: **Pageboy:** The pageboy on the right wears a form of Irish Guards tailcoat with four buttons and shamrocks in the style of the 18th century. Billy Lowther-Pinkerton is the son of Major Jamie Lowther-Pinkerton, Private Secretary to the Colonel, who served in the Regiment from 1980 to 1998. Billy has generously loaned his uniform to the Regiment for display in the Guards Museum.

Left: **Path liners.** Twenty-four personnel from the three Armed Services, with whom Prince William has an association, were selected to line the path from the Abbey to the carriage at the end of the wedding service. The Regiment was asked to provide four path liners and the Colonel specifically requested RQMS Jimmy Parke who had been his Platoon Colour Sergeant at Sandhurst. He and his wife were also personal guests at the wedding. The two Officers in view are the Regimental Adjutant, Lt Col Brian O'Gorman and Capt Max Dooher. Purists commented that the Colonel did not wear a sword in Home Service clothing. It had been wisely decided, after advice, with the agreement of the Colonel-in-Chief, that on this occasion it would be sensible to dispense with a sword, which would not be not conducive to kneeling in the Abbey under world-wide television scrutiny.

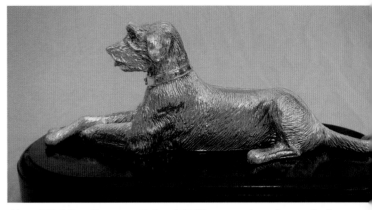

Above: **Wedding Present.** Colonel William was given the standard wedding present of a silver wolfhound from his fellow officers.

Below: **The newly created** Duke and Duchess of Cambridge wave to the crowds on the carriage drive back to Buckingham Palace.

Above: **The Regimental Band** was involved on the day and here Conmael, a favourite with the spectators, is shown leading them into position on the Mall.

Right: **There were rumours** that Colonel William would have liked to have married wearing a frockcoat but his grandmother had pointed out it that it was not a 'dress' uniform and therefore unacceptable. However, he did wear it leaving the reception after the wedding, driving his new bride in his father's Aston Martin car.

OPERATION HERRICK – AFGHANISTAN

Operation HERRICK was the name given for the deployment of British troops into Afghanistan. In October 2001 Britain and the United States launched air strikes on Afghanistan after the Taliban refused to hand over Osama bin Laden for his role in the September 11th attacks on the World Trade Centre in New York.

However, it was not until 2006 that NATO announced that Britain would lead the International Security Assistance Force (ISAF) in Helmand Province.

The aim was to prevent international terrorists from using Afghanistan as a base, and to create the conditions for a brighter, more secure and more stable future for the country.

During the first thee years, 2006-2008, the insurgent activity increased in Helmand Province, and as it grew more violent, only then did resources begin to meet ambitions. 2009 was the most difficult year but the introduction of additional troops and more heavily defended vehicles put the insurgency back on the defensive. At its peak the British military force strength was of 9,500 in 137 bases.

Above: **Attached to the Royal Marines.** In September 2006, Captain Rob Money deployed Op HERRICK 5 to the lower Sangin Valley as second-in-command of W Company, 45 Commando, part of 3 Commando Brigade. As the tour progressed, so did the expertise of the Taliban and for over three months they were under daily attack from 102mm mortar and 107mm Chinese made rockets. In return they fired over 20 Javelin missiles, dropped 140,000lb of bombs and were calling in 55 and 70 HE 105mm rounds per day. He is shown here under fire on Op SLATE as they attempt to put in place three Permanent Vehicle Check Points in Gereshk. Spartan conditions and shortage of water meant shaving was not a priority to CSM Jones and Capt Rob Money in W Company.

Right: **A Mick among the Argylls.** On Op HERRICK 8 Captain George Aitken commanded 3 Platoon, A Company of A Coy, 5 SCOTS. It was largely made up of augmentees, Reservists and non-infantrymen based around Argyll NCOs. It proved that with strong leadership, correct attitude from the receiving regular battalion and a pragmatic approach, non-Regulars in the ranks can work very successfully.

From 2010–2014 the Afghanistan National Security Forces (ANSF) developed and expanded to a force of 350,000 with support, enabling the NATO Allies to withdraw by 2014.

The Regiment played its full part in the operation. Although the Battalion went there in September 2010 on HERRICK 13, many Irish Guardsmen had already served there, in Kabul or Helmand in Headquarters, with Special Forces, or attached to other Foot Guards Battalions and the Parachute Regiment for a six month tour. The last Micks to deploy there were No 2 Company, in 2013, as the independent Brigade Operations Company with 1 Mechanised Brigade on Op HERRICK 18.

In all, 454 British Servicemen were killed in Afghanistan by 2014, including three Irish Guardsmen, but more than 36 other Irish Guardsmen were wounded, many of them serious and life changing.

Above: **Last Patrol.** A dusty Major Matt Collins, delighted to have finished his last patrol in a Jackal vehicle in November 2009, completing the training organised for 11 Brigade at the start of Op HERRICK 11. He was killed in action on Op HERRICK 13.

Above: **Three Micks in Helmand.** 16 Air Assault Brigade deployed for 6 months in April 2008 on Op HERRICK 8. It was commanded by Brigadier Mark Carleton-Smith (centre formerly Irish Guards). His ADC for the tour was Captain Julian Roberts on the left. They arranged to visit another Mick, Captain James Bullock-Webster, manning an outpost outside Musa Qaleh.

Above: **Bluey in Kajaki.** Captain Sam O'Gorman, deployed in September 2009 on Op HERRICK 11 to Forward Operating Base (FOB) Zeebrugge at the Kajak Dam in northern Helmand, leading a team to assist the Afghan Security Forces. He is reading an e-bluey from home. E-blueys are airmail letters which can be sent to personnel on operations at no cost. It arrives at its destination almost as quickly as an email. An integrated mail printer at the BFPO prints it out in letter form and a machine seals it automatically so no-one can read it at any stage. It was very popular, especially in isolated outposts of Afghanistan with limited access to computers and wi-fi. On Op HERRICK 11 two multiples were also attached to 1 GREN GDS. T Battalion was under command of Lt Col C R V Walker, a former Mick Officer.

Above: **Helmand Training Package.** While the main effort of the Battalion in 2009 was Public Duties, between August and November 55 members of the Battalion provided the Regulatory Headquarters and in-theatre training for the Relief in Place (RiP) of 19 and 11 Light Brigades. They delivered training to over 1100 troops on 10 separate training programmes on any given day. A vast array of new weapons, vehicles and equipment are made available in-theatre which must be mastered before deploying. It was a useful experience before the Battalion's deployed the following year.

Above: **Operational Mentoring Liaison Team (OMLT).** On HERRICK 10 in April 2010 Captain Tim Rogers with Sergeant Kirkham providing the Mick element of a composite OMLT under 2 MERCIAN. Intense fighting had dominated the Garmsir area for three years. But in July some relief was provided by the arrival of a hugely well supported US Marine Expeditionary Force who launched a ground/air assault named Op RIVER LIBERTY in the Garmsir and Nawa area. Shown here is Sgt Kirkham observing the break-in point on the operation.

IRISH GUARDS BATTLE GROUP DEPLOYMENT: OPERATION HERRICK 13 – SEPTEMBER 2010–APRIL 2011

Based at Camp Tombstone, adjacent to Camp Bastion, Battalion HQ led the Brigade Advisory Group with most of the Battlegroup deployed on the Mission of developing 3rd Brigade of 215 Corps of the Afghanistan National Army.

No 2 and 4 Companies, though, were allocated to the Danish Battlegroup as ground holding Companies in the Upper Gereshk Valley and No 1 Company was responsible for the security of 79 km of Highway 1 as it passed through the UK area of operations. Four infantry Kandak Advisory Teams, were based around infantry companies – Nos 1, 3, 11 and 12. The latter two Irish Guards companies were reformed for the task having been placed in suspended animation in 1945.

Sign for Camp Tombstone. The Battle Group was advising 3rd Brigade of 215 Corps.

No 3 Company Orders during Op OMID CHAR. L to R Maj Matt Collins, CSM Sixmith, Capt Charles Howard, Capt Chris Lambe, Capt Hough, Capt Ben Irwin-Clarke, Sgt Bull-Edwards and Lt Nick Gaggero.

An O Group in Compound 2 on Op OMID CHAR in 2010. It took two weeks to secure and build Patrol Base Hazrat on a high feature east of Gereshk. It was later occupied by 5 Platoon, 2 Company and is where Gdsm Davies was killed-in action.

Passing Time. Gdsm Griffiths, and LCpls Kettle, Cousins and Carson of 5 Platoon, 2 Company pass the time playing Monopoly in PB HASRAT in 2010 HERRICK 13.

Left: A Battalion O Group at MOB PRICE on Op HERRICK 13. L to R: The Commanding Officer, Lt Col Christopher Ghika; Maj Micky Stewart; Capt Ed Paul, London Regt; Maj Alexander Turner; Maj Matt Collins; Capt Hugh Dickinson.

Below: A member of No 4 Company is not impressed at having to carry a GPMG and mine detector.

Above: Capt Ben Irwin-Clarke on Op OMID CHAR.

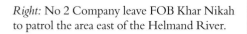

Right: No 2 Company leave FOB Khar Nikah to patrol the area east of the Helmand River.

Left: **Personal Role Radio.** LSgt Roberts providing security for a shura (the Arabic word for a consultation with the locals) in Tor Gai during Op HERRICK 13. Every Guardsman in a section is issued with a small transmitter-receiver that allows them to communicate over small distances and is effective through thick cover and walls of buildings. It enhances combat effectiveness by providing all-informed communications to front-line soldiers, replacing traditional methods based on shouting and hand signals.

Below: **Latest Equipment.** LSgt Reeves on Patrol in Nad e Ali, Helmand in 2010. Personal equipment improved considerably over the campaign, funded by an Urgent Operational Requirement, enabling quick implementation. The enhanced 'black bag' contained items such as anti-microbial underpants, designed to be worn for days at a time. It included flame resistant clothing, sleeping systems, 'Osprey' body armour and Personal Load Carrying Equipment with everything needed for 48 hours.

Above: **Op HERRICK 16.** In April 2012 a Mick group of 14 volunteers, made up of relatively experienced NCOs and junior Guardsmen, deployed under the command of a new Ensign, 2/Lt Freddy Simpson, forming a composite platoon attached to Inkerman Company of the Grenadiers. They operated some 10km north-east of Gereshk. The picture includes Micks, Lt Simpson, Sgt Hill, LSgt Payne, LCpls Harris, Hanna, Bridgeman and Gdsm Weir, Wright, Downie. Not shown are LCpl Phillips and Gdsm Nichols, who were wounded in action.

Below: **New Combat uniform.** LSgt Roberts on patrol in Nad-e-Ali. By this tour the Combat Dress - Desert DPM (Disruptive Pattern Material) which had been issued since the 1990s was replaced by a MTP (Multi Terrain Pattern). Buttons were replaced by velcro fastenings. It is a tougher, more comfortable and efficient combat uniform but still generated much discussion back in the UK. Are sleeves rolled up and shirts tucked in or not?

Below: **Presentation of Awards, and Awards Op HERRICK.**
The Regimental Lieutenant Colonel presented some of the awards in Aldershot on behalf of the Colonel. Back row: Capt CWJ Gair (MiD), Gdsm JT Rainey (JCC), Third row: Lt RStJE Gore (MiD), LCpl AJ Morgan, (JCC) Gdsm SJ McCormack (JCC). Second Row: Gdsm MWH McMurtry (QCB), Gdsm CM Tobin (MiD), Maj MRN Stewart (JCC), WO1 (RSM) JG Parke. Front Row: Lt Col CJ Ghika OBE (Commanding Officer), Major General Bill Cubitt (Regimental Lieutenant Colonel), Capt GT Murphy (Adjutant)

Op HERRICK 18 – Last Tour. No 2 Coy deploying on operations in Helmand using an American Osprey aircraft as the Task Force Helmand Brigade Operations Company (BOC) in the summer of 2013. No 2 Coy commanded by Maj Jono Palmer deployed between April–October 2013 as the BOC. This was a prestigious role that saw them able to conduct intelligence-led operations to interdict the Taliban's supply of weapons and bomb-making equipment at a time when the majority of British troops had been pulled back into their bases in preparation for the UK withdrawal. Their operations employed helicopters, aircraft and 'warthog' tracked armoured vehicles.

Killed in Action

Guardsman Christopher Davies	18 November 2010
Major Matt Collins	23 March 2011
Lance Sergeant Mark Burgan	23 March 2011

Awards - Op HERRICK

Distinguished Service Order (DSO)
Col H A B Holt OBE (Detached)
Lt Col R W E Walker (Gren Gds)
Maj I A J Turner

Commander of the British Empire (CBE)
Brig M A P Carleton-Smith OBE (Detached)

Order of the British Empire (OBE)
Lt Col C J Ghika

Military Cross (MC)
LSgt J S Cooke (Detached)
LSgt M P Turrell

Mention in Dispatches (MiD)
Capt C W J Gair
Lt R StJ E Gore
Gdsm C M Tobin
Lt A E Floyd
Gdsm G Boyce

Queen's Commendation for Bravery (QCB)
Gdsm M W H McMurtry

Queen's Commendation for Valuable Service (QCVS)
Col C P H Knaggs OBE (Detached)
Maj J A E Palmer MBE

Joint Commanders' Commendation
Maj M R N Stewart
LCpl A J Morgan
Gdsm S J McCormack
Gdsm J T Rainey
LSgt G Fitzgerald

Commander Task Force Helmand's Commendation
CSgt J J Gavin
LSgt Hobson
LCpl Quinlan

Estonian Army Silver Cross of Merit
Sergeant K Tomlinson

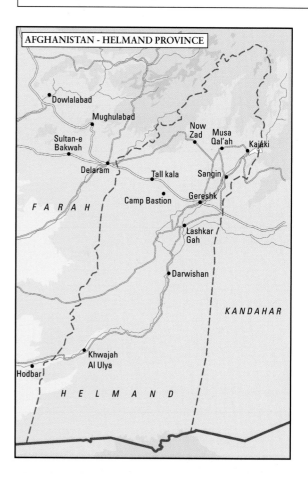

AFGHANISTAN - HELMAND PROVINCE

Dowlalabad
Mughulabad
Sultan-e Bakwah
Now Zad
Musa Qal'ah
Kajaki
Delaram
Tall kala
Sangin
F A R A H
Camp Bastion
Gereshk
Lashkar Gah
Darwishan
K A N D A H A R
Khwajah Al Ulya
Hodbar
H E L M A N D

UNVEILING A STATUE IN WINDSOR

On Friday 24 June 2011 a two metre bronze statue of an Irish Guardsman dressed for combat in Iraq, was unveiled in Windsor by the Mayor, Councillor Asghar Majeed and Major General Sir William Cubitt, the Regimental Lieutenant Colonel.

Above: **For years to come** Micks will debate the true identity of the bronze Guardsman, claiming themselves as the inspiration. In truth, a number of Micks modelled for Mark Jackson, but mainly Gdsm Mason, shown here beside a small clay model suggesting the pose.

Above: Bronze statues of Saddam's Generals pointing to Iran over the Shatt-al Arab waterway.

Above: **New Statue.** It was the idea of the Commanding Officer in 2008, Lt Col Ben Farrell, to create a statue as a tribute and celebration of all Irish Guardsmen, 'Past, Present and Future', rather than to commemorate those who lost their lives, and are remembered in the Guards Chapel. It took four months for the figure to be carved in clay, in a garage, in Victoria Barracks, before being moved to the foundry in Basingstoke to be cast in bronze.

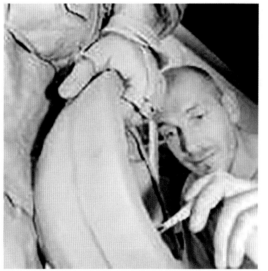

Above: **The Royal Borough of Windsor** and Maidenhead Council were very supportive with the planning process and provided civil engineers and contractors to clear a suitable site. Positioned by the castle looking down Sheet Street, everyone passes it on their right as they mount Windsor Castle Guard. 22 Engineer Regiment carried out the installation helping to reduce the overall cost by giving their time and expertise. Here, Lt Col Ben Farrell, on the left, looks on as the Mayor and the Regimental Lieutenant Colonel, Maj Gen Bill Cubitt, unveil the statue. Master Tailor Else, wearing the traditional Homberg hat and carrying a tailor's measuring stick, ensures his shroud is working.

Above: **A sculptor was selected** – Mark Jackson, a former Paratrooper who had been invalided out of the Army following a training accident. He had friends in the Regiment, but of more importance he was extremely talented, although he had never created anything on this scale before.

SERVICE OF THANKSGIVING AND MEDAL PRESENTATION 25 JUNE 2011

On 25 June 2011, after their return from Afghanistan, the Battalion marched through Windsor, with great public support, to St George's Chapel at Windsor Castle for a Service of Thanksgiving. This was followed by the presentation of campaign medals in the Barracks by the Colonel and the Duchess of Cambridge. It was their first public engagement since their wedding seven weeks earlier.

Above: **The Commanding Officer**, Lt Col Christopher Ghika, leads his Battalion and others who served in the Battlegroup, through Windsor to St George's Chapel in Windsor Castle.

Above: **The Corps of Drums** lead the troops past the new Irish Guards statue in Windsor which had only been unveiled the day before.

Above: **Colonel William** and the Duchess took the opportunity to speak to many of those on parade as they presented the medals for service in Afghanistan.

Below: **The Colonel** takes the salute as the Battalion march past and off parade having received their medals.

Left: **Operational Service Medal (OSM) – Afghanistan.** For service on operations within Afghanistan from 11 September 2001. The OSM replaced the General Service Medal (GSM) in 2000 and the clasp signifies service in a 'more dangerous area or period of conflict'.

Above: **Elizabeth Cross Presentation in Dublin.** On 30 September 2011, The Queen's Representative in Dublin, The British Ambassador, His Excellency Julian King CMG CVO, on the left, presented the Elizabeth Cross to the families of four Irish Guardsmen living in the Republic of Ireland. Three of them, Patsy Corry, Liam Coleman and Liam O'Reilly had been killed in Aden in 1967. Shown here with the Ambassador is Mrs May Malone and her family whose son, LCpl Ian Malone, was killed in Iraq in 2003.

Above: **Elizabeth Cross.** The Elizabeth Cross Brooch was granted to the next-of-kin of British Armed Forces personnel who have died on operations or as a result of terrorism since the Second World War in national recognition of the loss and sacrifice. It was instituted in 2009, not as a posthumous medal, but specifically to recognise the unique challenges that service personnel face and in particular the burden this places on their families.

Above: **Christmas Card.** Every year a regimental Christmas card is created for sale to the regimental family to generate welfare funds. In 2011 Sean Bolan painted a scene of the Drums playing outside Windsor Castle.

Right: **Elizabeth Cross Presentation in Aldershot.** When the Duke and Duchess of Cambridge presented campaign medals to the Battle Group on 24 June 2011, the Colonel also presented Elizabeth Crosses to the families of those killed in action. Here he presents the Elizabeth Cross to Leanne Burgan, wife of Lance Sergeant Mark Burgan, who died on 23 March 2011. Her father, on the left, is John O'Brien, a former Irish Guards Colour Sergeant.

ST PATRICK'S DAY 2012

The Colonel could not be with the Regiment on St Patrick's Day in 2012 because he was deployed with the RAF in the Falkland Islands, providing air support. The Duchess of Cambridge graciously agreed to distribute the shamrock in his place. The Princess Royal had presented it for six years until 2010 but when Prince William was appointed Colonel her pragmatic view was that, in future, it would make sense for the Colonel's wife to carry out this duty and stood aside.

Shamrock Brooch.
Commanding Officer, Lt Col C H Ghika, escorts the Duchess of Cambridge to the cookhouse after the parade. She is wearing the gold shamrock brooch that had been presented by the Regiment to Princess Mary, The Princess Royal in 1961. When she died suddenly in 1966 it was noticed that her personal jewellery was to be sold, so the Regiment bought it back at auction. It was used by The Queen Mother for 32 years and passed to Princess Anne, the Princess Royal for six years when presenting the shamrock on St Patrick's Day. How appropriate that the Duchess should continue the custom.

Queen Elizabeth The Queen Mother always wore the brooch.

The Princess Royal, wearing the brooch.

The brooch in its original box.

The Duchess presents the wolfhound, Conmael, with his shamrock for the last time before his retirement to Co. Tipperary for a well earned rest as the 16th mascot.

The Colonel's wife hands baskets of shamrock to the company and detachment commanders for distribution. The Commanding Officer, Lt Col Christopher Ghika, is behind, and the gentlemen in bowler hats are former officers, Major the Lord Bruntisfield collecting for the Quis Separabit Club, and Colonel Sir William Mahon for the Association.

Right: **Future Army Dress.** It was not until 2012 that the Battalion was issued with the new Service Dress. The aim was for a universal pattern to be adopted, although regimental identity was not ignored. The new colour was the same as the Officers' 'Guards Barathea' and the opportunity was taken to have the whole Battalion wearing buttons in fours. Here, Gdsm McNaughton, winner of the Girdlers' Prize, and RSM Parke model the new style.

Left: **No 2 Dress.** Khaki coloured No 2 Dress – Temperate Parade, otherwise known as Service Dress (SD) was introduced in the 1960s replacing pre-War Battle Dress. It was the standard issue for 50 years before Future Army Dress (FAD) was introduced in 2009.

Right: **A Mick Commanding Grenadiers.** Unusually, a Guard of Grenadiers on the Birthday Parade in 2010 was commanded by a Mick Officer. Major Ed Boanas was serving with the Grenadiers as a Company Commander and indeed commanded the Inkerman Company on operations in Afghanistan. A St Patrick's blue plume in a sea of black bearskins. The Grenadiers would have it no other way; the logic being if he can successfully commanded a Company of the First Foot Guards on operations, he can command them on parade.

Commanding Officer. Lt Col Christopher Ghika, who commanded the Battalion 2010–2012.

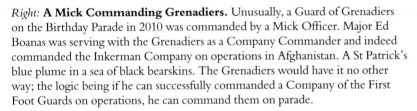

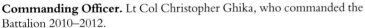

Diamond Jubilee Celebrations. 2012 was HM The Queen's Diamond Jubilee year. 60 years on the throne was a good reason for a series of special celebrations. It included a Guard of Honour in the forecourt of Buckingham Palace firing a 'Feu de Joie', and giving three cheers led by the Major General. All went well eventually, even though the Health and Safety enforcers pointed out that anyone within 100m of blank firing must wear serviceable ear defence but the bright yellow foam ear buds 'on issue' have a tendency to pop out when pressured by fast drill movements. Commonsense prevailed and a solution was found.

Right: **Olympic Games Opening Ceremony.** Sergeant Kyle Reains, on the right, was the Army representative in the tri-service group raising the union flag at the opening ceremony of the Olympic Games in August 2012. The Regimental Band was also involved. On the day they pretended to play as their music had been pre-recorded.

Above: **Olympic Games.** The Battalion was responsible for security at the rowing venue for the games at Dorney Lake near Windsor. Here are the civilian organisers, with Conmael in front of the Battalion assembled for a mass photograph at the venue.

Right: **Queen Elizabeth II Diamond Jubilee Medal 2012.** Officially called HM The Queen Elizabeth II Diamond Jubilee Medal, this commemorative medal was created in 2012 to mark the 60th anniversary of her accession to the throne. Recipients had to have completed five years service on 6 February 2012, the same criteria as the Golden Jubilee in 2002.

BOND
OF
FRIENDSHIP
DINNER
DÚN UÍ MHAOILÍOSA

19th September 2013

Right: **A Mick as the Sovereign's Piper.**
In 2012 Pipe Major Davy Rodgers received his Meritorious Service Medal for twenty years service from the Chief of the General Staff (CGS), General Sir Peter Wall. The Pipe Major is dressed as the Sovereign's Piper. He is the first Irish Guardsman, indeed first non-Scotsman to become the monarch's personal piper since the appointment started in 1842. The CGS is a particular friend of the Micks having been attached to the Battalion in Belize as a Captain.

Left: **Bond of Friendship Golf.** In 2006, at the suggestion of the then Colonel of the Regiment, The Duke of Abercorn, an annual golf match was instigated between the Irish Guards Golf Society, the Irish Defence Force, the Police Service of Northern Ireland and the Garda Siochana. It continues to be a great success as does a separate annual match for the Curragh Quaic between the Micks and the Irish Defence Forces.

Right: **Guards Museum.** The Guards Museum, beside the Guards Chapel in Wellington Barracks is a repository for the five Foot Guards regiments and is primarily intended as an educational aid to help young Guardsmen learn about their heritage.

Above: **New Regimental Lieutenant Colonel.** On St Patrick's Day 2012 Major General Mark Carleton-Smith succeeded Major General Sir William Cubitt as Regimental Lieutenant Colonel who retired after four years in the appointment.

Above: **Eton Field Game.** In February 2013 the Irish Guards fielded 11 Old Etonian Officers (wearing white) to challenge a team of boys put together by Max Carleton-Smith, son of the Regimental Lieutenant Colonel. Sadly, the Colonel of the Regiment was unable to make the team sheet and youth triumphed over experience on the day. The winning goal was scored by Lord Setttrington, the great, great grandson of one of the Regiment's founding Officers. (See page 20, Lt Lord Settrington in photo of the Officers at the Tower of London)

Right: **Australian Exchange Officer.** General David Hurley, Chief of the Australian Defence Force, and his wife Linda greet the Colonel and the Duchess of Cambridge at Brisbane in April 2014. General David later became Governor of New South Wales.

Above: **Commanding Officer.** Lt Col Ed Boanas commanded the Battalion 2012–2014.

Above: **Commanding Officer.** Major Alexander Turner after being invested with his DSO. As a Company Commander, he commanded FOB Khar Nikah in Helmand on Op HERRICK 13 for which he was awarded the DSO for his outstanding leadership. On promotion, he later became Commanding Officer of the Battalion in 2014.

Right: Micks fondly remember him as Captain David Hurley with the Battalion in the 1980s when he was an exchange officer with the Battalion and Second-in-Command of No 4 Company in Germany. He is pictured here on the prairie in Alberta, Canada during Ex Medicine Man either doing his ablutions or possibly panning for gold.

INTERNATIONAL OPERATIONS AND EXERCISES 2012–2015

This was a very international period for the Battalion. It deployed company groups on operations to Bosnia, Afghanistan, and the Falkland Islands (twice), as well as conducting training activities with French and Omani soldiers in Otterburn, Salisbury Plain and Oman. As a Battalion, it was twice rostered as the United Kingdom Standby Battalion. In 2014, it deployed as the UN Peacekeeping Battle Group responsible for the Nicosia Sector of the Cyprus Buffer Zone – the first Regular Infantry Battalion to do so for several decades.

Bosnia. No 1 Coy conducting riot training in Bosnia as part of the European Union Force (OP ELGIN) in April 2013. DSACEUR had requested that the UK should demonstrate its commitment to the mission in Bosnia by the deployment of troops to conduct operational rehearsals. No 1 Coy, commanded by Maj Tom Oakley was the first British sub-unit to conduct this task, deploying their Snatch vehicles in Russian made Antonov aircraft.

Mortar Firing with the French. French Alpine Troops experience an Irish Guards Church Parade before the Battle Group Live Firing (Exercise Border Storm) in Otterburn in November 2013. Afterwards a fully integrated mortar line conducted live firing as part of the exercise.

Training the Omanis. Irish Guards Short Term Training Team to Oman mentor an Omani Rifle Company in preparation for their participation in the Irish Guards Battle Group test exercise (Ex WESSEX STORM) on Salisbury Plain in November 2013.

Cyprus UN tour. In 2014 100 Micks and 50 Reservists deployed to Cyprus on Op TOSCA for a six month tour. Since 1974, UNFICYP has supervised ceasefire lines, maintained a buffer zone and undertaken humanitarian activities. They were awarded a UN medal for their efforts although those Micks left behind in Aldershot believed it was for water-skiing.

Armed overwatch. There were numerous visitors to the Battalion in Cyprus, including the US Vice President, as it was 50th anniversary of the UN mandate and 40th of the Turkish Forces intervention/invasion. This required an extra armed presence.

The first 15 years of the twenty-first century saw the Army continue to modernise in equipment, clothing and manpower levels. The strength of the Regular Army was 102,500 at the start of the period but by the end had reduced to 82,000 with an intended corresponding increase in the Territorial Army, now called Reservists. Of the 32 remaining Regular Army Battalions the Foot Guards provide five. The Regiment is now the fourth oldest in the Infantry with 115 years of unbroken service without amalgamation. Up the Micks!

COLOURS AND BATTLE HONOURS OF THE IRISH GUARDS

BACKGROUND

Flags were used as rallying points as long ago as the Kings of Babylon. In the Middle Ages, each Lord or Baron flew his banner as a sign by which his followers could distinguish him in battle. By the time of Elizabeth I a great number of 'low born captains in the Infantry' who had no Arms to bear on their standards, were obliged to trust in the distinction of colour only. Consequently, their flags assumed a great diversity of hues and gained the names 'Colours'.

During the Civil War 1642–1660 Colours came into use in individual Companies and a battalion would have had ten or more. Regulations of 1661 established some kind of order and at the time of Queen Anne in 1707, the number of Colours was reduced to two per Regiment.

Colours were last carried into action by the 58th Foot (later the 2nd Battalion The Northamptonshire Regiment) in South Africa in 1881. Up to that time they participated in all the varying fortunes of their Regiment; were often torn by enemy fire and acquired an almost religious significance. Uncased Colours are invariably carried by an officer and accompanied by an armed escort.

Battalion Colours

His Majesty King Edward VII approved designs for the Colours of the 1st Battalion and presented them to the 1st Battalion in June 1902.

The Queen's Colour, Gules (crimson). In the centre the Royal Cypher or (gold), within the Collar of the Order of St Patrick with badge appendant proper, ensigned with the Crown.

The Queen's Colour.

The Regimental Colour. The Union. The current Regimental Colour has: in the centre No X Company Badge depicting a six pointed star with a red hand from the Arms of Ulster. The 1st Battalion company badges are borne in rotation. 21 Battle Honours (shown in bold type on page 275) are borne upon the Queen's and Regimental Colour and on the Drums.

The dimensions of the Queen's and Regimental Colours are 3 feet 9 inches flying and 3 feet deep on the pike excluding the fringe, which is about 2 inches wide. The pikes are 8 feet 7½ inches long including the Royal Crest on top. The pikes are surmounted by the Imperial Crown surmounted by a lion crowned.

The occasions on which the Colours are to be carried and lowered are detailed in Queen's Regulations, Her Majesty's Regulations for the Household Division and Standing Orders of the Household Division.

When the Colours are not on parade they are hung in the Officers' Mess with the Queen's Colour on the left (as observed from the front) with its pike under that of the Regimental Colour.

When a Battalion parades to change quarters, the Colours are always carried cased and colour belts worn. The Colours are normally replaced every 10–15 years.

The Regimental Colour of 2IG in 1940.

BATTLE HONOURS

The Battle Honours, granted by Royal authority in commemoration of war service, are shown below. Battle Honours are emblazoned on the Queen's and Regimental Colours and are listed in bold below. Theatre Honours are not emblazoned on the Colours but are printed in the Army List alongside the Battle Honours as shown below. They are awarded for providing sterling service in a campaign but were not part of specific battles for which Battle Honours were awarded.

First World War

Mons
Retreat From Mons 1914
Marne 1914
Aisne 1914
Ypres 1914–17
Langemarck 1914
Gheluvelt
Nonne Bosschen
Festubert 1915
Loos 1915
Somme 1916–18
Fleurs Courcellette
Morval
Pilckem
Poelcappelle

Passchendale
Cambrai 1917, 18
St Quentin
Lys
Hazebrouck 1918
Albert 1918
Bapaume 1918
Arras 1918
Scarpe 1918
Drocourt-Queant
Hindenburg Line 1918
Canal Du Nord
Selle
Sambre
France And Flanders 1914–1918

Second World War

Pothus (1IG – Norway)
Norway 1940 (1IG)
Boulogne 1940 (2IG)
Cagny (2&3IG – Op GOODWOOD)
Mont Pincon (2&3IG – Normandy)
Neerpelt 1944 (2&3IG – Joe's Bridge)
Nijmegen (2&3IG)
Aalst (2&3IG – Escaut Canal)
Rhineland (2&3IG)
Hochwald (2&3IG)

Rhine (2&3IG)
Bentheim (2&3IG)
North West Europe 1944–45 (2&3IG)
Medjez Plain (1IG)
Djebel Bou Aoukaz 1943 (1IG)
North Africa 1943 (1IG)
Anzio (1IG)
Aprilia (1IG)
Carrocetto (1IG)
Italy 1943 – 1944 (1IG)

Post 1945

On 9 June 2005 HM The Queen approved the award of the Battle Honour **'Iraq 2003'** and Theatre Honour 'Al Basrah' for participating in Op TELIC during the period 19 March–30 April 2003. This was the first to be approved of any regiment for service in Iraq which allowed the Battalion to troop their Colour two days later with the new Theatre Honour emblazoned upon it. Other Regiments and Corps were awarded their Battle and Theatre Honours on 10 Nov 2005.

'DECKING' OF THE COLOURS

When on parade and uncased, the Colours are decked with a laurel wreath on the following anniversaries:

22 January	Anzio	12 May	North Africa 1943
8 February	Rhineland 1945	18 May	Festubert 1915
7 April	Iraq 2003	22 May	Boulogne 1940
13 April	Hazebrouck 1918	6 June	North West Europe 1944–45
21 April	Norway 1940	30 July	Mont Pincon 1944
27 April	Djebel Bou Aoukaz 1943	23 August	Retreat From Mons 1914

8 September	Marne 1914	27 September	Loos 1915
10 September	Neerpelt 1944	27 September	Hindenburg Line 1918
14 September	Aisne 1914	9 October	Ypres 1914–17
15 September	Somme 1916–18	27th November	Cambrai 1917–18
19 September	Nijmegen 1944		

REGIMENTAL COLOURS – 1ST BATTALION

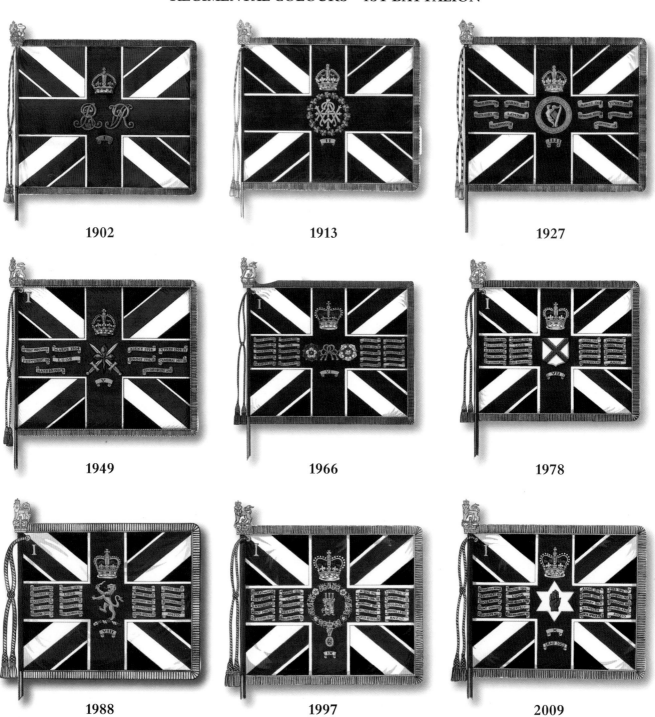

1902   1913   1927

1949   1966   1978

1988   1997   2009

The No 4 Company badge (see p. 278) does not feature above because it was borne on the 2nd Battalion's Regimental Colour from 1940 to 1947.

LAYING UP OF THE COLOURS

The Battalion Colours[1]. These were presented and laid-up as shown below:

Bn	Sovereign	Date	Location	Laid up[1]
1st	Edward VII	30 May 1902	Horse Guards	Guards Chapel[2]
1st	George V	28 Jul 1913	Buckingham Palace	Guards Chapel
2nd	Prince of Wales	14 Jan 1919	Cologne	RC Church, Caterham
1st	George V	27 May 1927	Buckingham Palace	Westminster Cathedral
2nd	George VI	14 Feb 1940	Wellington Barracks	Guards Depot Church, Caterham (transferred to Chapel, Pirbright)
1st	George VI	27 Jun 1949	Buckingham Palace	Guards Chapel
1st	Elizabeth II	10 Jun 1966	Buckingham Palace	Holy Trinity Church, Windsor
1st	Elizabeth II	11 May 1978	Windsor Castle	Guards Chapel
1st	Elizabeth II	24 May 1988	Buckingham Palace	Guards Chapel
1st	Elizabeth II	22 May 1997	Windsor Castle	Guards Chapel
1st	Elizabeth II	6 May 2009	Windsor Castle	

THE COMPANY BADGES OR COLOURS

It is unique to the Foot Guards that the Sovereign approves individual badges for Companies. They are normally made into flags mounted on a crimson background measuring twenty inches by eighteen inches. This does not apply to the Scots Guards, some of whose Company Flags are on a blue background. There are 24 and they are surmounted with the Imperial Crown and have the number indicative of the Company below.

In the Irish Guards they are called Company 'Colours', in the Coldstream 'Silks' and by the Scots Guards 'Flags'. The Welsh Guards have 'Company Colours' but in the shape of heraldic standards. They are not consecrated as are the Battalion Colours.

Company Colours are used as the Commanding Officer may direct. They are normally used for ceremonial purposes such as the marking of saluting bases and points on the square. On parade they are held on a six-foot pike by a Non-Commissioned Officer and used as marker flags. Only the Colours of those on parade are used. It would for example, be inappropriate for the Commanding Officer's Colour to be used on an Adjutant's Parade. The Colours of the Senior Officers on parade should be placed either side of the saluting dais.

The Company Colours are the property of the Regiment and are held on charge by the Officer Commanding the Company to whom they are issued. Repairs and replacements are arranged by Regimental Headquarters, who also decide how the cost will be borne.

Company Commanders may keep their Company Colours on completion of their Command so long as they provide a new one, at their own expense, of an acceptable standard, after application to Regimental Headquarters.

PIPE BANNERS

In 2011, the Regimental Council and Army Dress Committee agreed the use of pipe banners based on the badges on the Company Colours. The following guidelines for their use were agreed by the Council.

a. They are not to be used when the band is practising.
b. They are used on all formed parades when Home Service Clothing is worn.
c. Only the appropriate banners are to be used according to who is on parade. The Commanding Officer, Adjutant etc but not the Colonel's.
d. All playing pipers should carry one, so it is 'all or nothing' when on parade. This may require flexibility from the guidance above on which ones to use.
e. They should not be used when the pipes are competing in a civilian capacity.
f. They should not be taken into the field on Company training.

---

1. Colours once laid-up become the property of the Church and not the Regiment.
2. The first colours were presented during the Birthday Parade.

IRISH GUARDS COMPANY BADGES

1 I  The Royal Cyphers of King Edward VII and Queen Victoria.

 No 1 Company 1IG. Originally intended, imitating the Grenadier habit, of using the royal cypher for the senior company. When the original drawing was submitted showing the cypher of Queen Victoria, King Edward asked why his cypher, which was the Royal Cypher by then, was not included. So the two cyphers were approved, and the contemporary Royal cypher as originally intended, never happened.

2 II  The Cypher of the Duke of Connaught encircled by a wreath of shamrock.

 No 2 Company 1IG. A reminder of the rivalry between the Roberts ring and the Wolseley ring in the early 20th Century. Lord Roberts wished to earmark The Duke of Connaught as his successor as Colonel of the Irish Guards. He asked his leave, as a soldier Royal Duke with an Irish Dukedom to have his cypher as No 2 Company, after the Royal Cypher for No 1 Company. Lord Roberts outlived his plan, for by the time he died in 1914 the Duke of Connaught had become Colonel of the Scots Guards.

3 III  The Royal Badge of Ireland within a circle and the motto of the Order of St. Patrick.

 No 3 Company Support Company 1IG.

4 IV 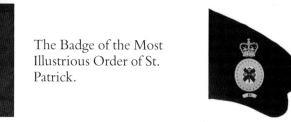 The Badge of the Most Illustrious Order of St. Patrick.

No 4 Company 1IG.

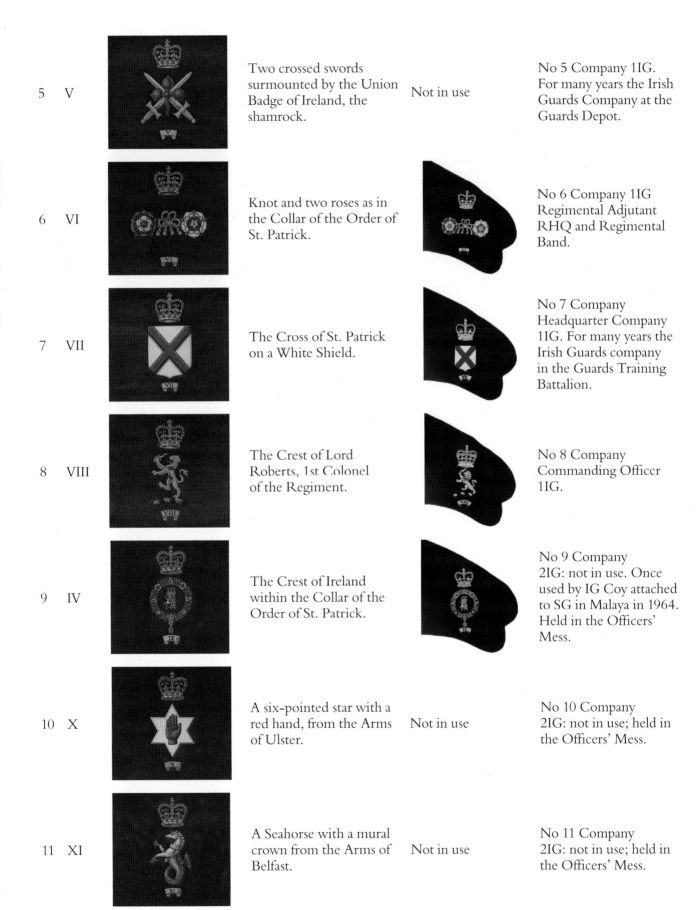

5	V		Two crossed swords surmounted by the Union Badge of Ireland, the shamrock.	Not in use	No 5 Company 1IG. For many years the Irish Guards Company at the Guards Depot.
6	VI		Knot and two roses as in the Collar of the Order of St. Patrick.		No 6 Company 1IG Regimental Adjutant RHQ and Regimental Band.
7	VII		The Cross of St. Patrick on a White Shield.		No 7 Company Headquarter Company 1IG. For many years the Irish Guards company in the Guards Training Battalion.
8	VIII		The Crest of Lord Roberts, 1st Colonel of the Regiment.		No 8 Company Commanding Officer 1IG.
9	IV		The Crest of Ireland within the Collar of the Order of St. Patrick.		No 9 Company 2IG: not in use. Once used by IG Coy attached to SG in Malaya in 1964. Held in the Officers' Mess.
10	X		A six-pointed star with a red hand, from the Arms of Ulster.	Not in use	No 10 Company 2IG: not in use; held in the Officers' Mess.
11	XI		A Seahorse with a mural crown from the Arms of Belfast.	Not in use	No 11 Company 2IG: not in use; held in the Officers' Mess.

12 XII		A Castle inflamed, from the Arms of Dublin.		No 12 Company 2IG: not in use; held in RHQ Used in Afghanistan by No 12 Coy in 2010/11.
13 XIII		An ancient Irish Crown, from the Arms of Munster.	Not in use	No 13 Company 2IG: not in use; held in the Officers' Mess.
14 XIV		An Irish Wolfhound.		No 14 Company 2IG: not in use; held in the Officers' Mess
15 XV		A halved eagle joined with an arm holding a sword, from the Arms of Connaught.	Not in use	No 15 Company 2IG: not in use; held in the Officers' Mess.
16 XVI		A pierced Narcissus, from the Arms of the Earl of Cavan, 4th Colonel of the Regiment	Not in use	No 16 Company 2IG: not in use; held in the Officers' Mess
17 XVII		An Irish Harp on a green ground.		No 17 Company 2IG: not in use; held in the Officers' Mess
18 XVII		The Crest of Earl Alexander, 5th Colonel of the Regiment.		No 18 Company Not in use; held in RHQ

19 XIX — The Crest of Earl Ypres, 3rd Colonel of the Regiment.

No 19 Company Adjutant 1IG. The crest of Sir John French, Earl of Ypres, 3rd Colonel of the Regiment.

20 XX — A bustard from the Arms of Lord Kitchener, 2nd Colonel of the Regiment

No 20 Company Regimental Lieutenant Colonel

21 XXI — A flax flower, alluding to the staple industry of Northern Ireland.

No 21 Company Not in use. Held in RHQ.

22 XXII — An Irish Bagpipe.

No 22 Company Colonel of the Regiment.

23 XXIII — The Armorial Bearings of HRH the Grand Duke of Luxembourg KG, 7th Colonel of the Regiment.

No 23 Company 7th Colonel of the Regiment, held in RHQ.

24 XXIV — Arms of James Hamilton, 5th Duke of Abercorn, KG, 8th Colonel of the Regiment.

No 24 Company Held by the Duke of Abercorn.

Crest of HM Queen Elizabeth, The Queen Mother.

Appendix B

IRISH GUARDS VICTORIA CROSSES

The Victoria Cross, introduced in 1856, is the highest military decoration awarded for *'....most conspicuous bravery, or some daring or pre-eminent act of valour or self sacrifice, or extreme devotion to duty in the presence of the enemy'* and may be awarded to any rank. It is extremely rare but the Regiment can lay claim to seven VCs worn by Irish Guardsmen although one was awarded before he transferred to the Regiment.

Of the regiment, one was the first given to an Irishman in the Great War, two were awarded to members of the same platoon, one of whom was court-marshalled for going absent in London after being presented with the medal by the King. Two of them were announced only after hostilities had ended. One was awarded with the recommendation of the enemy who had witnessed his bravery. It was also the last of the 2nd World War. Another was awarded to an Irish Guardsman with a false name.

Captain Charles FitzClarence

Capt Charles FitzClarence.

'On the 14th October , 1899, Captain FitzClarence went with his squadron of the Protectorate Regiment, consisting of only partially trained men, who had never been in action, to the assistance of an armoured train which had gone out from Mafeking. The enemy were in greatly superior numbers, and the squadron was for sometime surrounded, and it looked as if nothing could save them from being shot down. Captain FitzClarence, however, by his personal coolness and courage inspired the greatest confidence in his men, and, by his bold and efficient handling of them, not only succeeded in relieving the armoured train, but inflicting a heavy defeat on the Boers, who lost 50 killed and a large number wounded, his own losses being 2 killed and 15 wounded. The moral effect of this blow had a very important bearing on subsequent encounters with the Boers.

On the 27th October 1899, Captain FitzClarence led his squadron from Mafeking across the open, and made a night attack with the bayonet on one of the enemy's trenches. A hand-to-hand fight took place in the trench, while a heavy fire was concentrated on it from the rear. The enemy was driven out with heavy loss. Captain FitzClarence was the first man into the position and accounted for four of the enemy with his sword. The British lost 6 wounded. Captain FitzClarence was himself slightly wounded. With reference to these two actions, Major General Baden-Powell states that had this officer not shown such extraordinary spirit and fearlessness the attacks would have been failures, and we should have suffered heavy losses both in men and prestige.

On the 26th December 1899 during the action at Game Tree Fort, near Mafeking, Captain FitzClarence again distinguished himself by his coolness and courage, and was again wounded (severely through the hip).'

Although strictly speaking he was not a cap-badged Irish Guardsman when he displayed these acts of valour, nor was he serving with the Royal Fusiliers to whom he had transferred from the Militia three years earlier, he did, however, transfer to the Irish Guards on its formation in 1900 and wore the uniform at his VC investiture. So he is included in the distinguished group of Irish Guards VC holders.

He was born in 1885 at Bishopscourt, Co Kildare and was Grandson of George, 1st Earl of Munster eldest (illegitimate) son of King William IV and educated at Eton and Wellington College.

He commanded the 1st Battalion for four years in London before the Great War and was Regimental Lieutenant Colonel until the outbreak of the War. He was then appointed to command 1st Guards Brigade with the British Expeditionary Force in Belgium. In the First Battle of Ypres in late October 1914 he was credited with saving the day by holding the British line at Gheluvelt by ordering charge by the 2nd Worcesters. On 11 November the Prussian Guard attacked again and he counter-attacked the next day, this time leading the Irish Guards forward in

Menin Gate, Ypres.

Worcesters counterattack.

person as Brigade Commander. He was killed in action, aged 49, at Polygon Wood, Zonnebeke. He is the highest ranking officer inscribed on panel 3 of the Menin Gate in Ypres, commemorating those with no known grave.

His medals were sold at auction on 8 February 1990 for £38,000 and are now in the Ashcroft Collection at the Imperial War Museum.

Lance Corporal Michael O'Leary

LCpl Michael O'Leary.

'For conspicuous bravery at Cuinchy on 1 February 1915. When forming one of the storming party which advanced against the enemy's barricades, he rushed to the front and himself killed five Germans who were holding the first barricade, after which he attacked a second barricade, about 60 yards further on, which he captured after killing three of the enemy and making prisoners of three more. L/Cpl O'Leary thus practically captured the enemy's position by himself, and prevented the rest of the attacking party from being fired upon.'

In late January 1915 a large scale German attack succeeded in penetrating the Cuinchy sector, south of the La Bassee Canal, Northern France. On 1 February 4th (Guards) Brigade ordered a counter attack by 50 Coldstreamers supported by No 4 Company Irish Guards. The enemy attack was halted although all the officers of No 4 Company were killed. 2/Lt Innes of No 1 Coy was sent forward to take command and organise the withdrawal of the survivors. 2/Lt Innes and his Orderly, L/Cpl Michael O'Leary, remained forward in position as the Coldstreams counter-attacked. As this attack faltered, O'Leary took the initiative and rushed forward by himself, without support, capturing the enemy positions and seized two prisoners. For this action he was awarded the first Irish Guards VC of the Great War and 2/Lt Innes was awarded an immediate MC.

Michael O'Leary was the third of four children born in 1890 near Macroom, Co Cork. He worked on the small family farm before joining the Royal Navy in 1906. He was invalided out with rheumatism in his knees but enlisted in the Irish Guards in July 1910. He served for three years before leaving in August 1913 to join the Royal Northwest Mounted Police in Canada. When the First World War broke out in Europe the following year, he was rejoined the British Army as an active reservist. In November 1914 he joined the 1st Battalion in France. After a short time he was Mentioned-in-Despatches for gallantry and promoted to Lance Corporal. He was promoted in the field to Sergeant immediately after his VC action described above.

O'Leary's action caught the imagination of the public and he was feted in London and used as a figure to encourage recruiting from Ireland. One person who was not so impressed was his father, a strong Irish nationalist and fine sportsman, who when asked to comment about his son's bravery, replied *'I am surprised he didn't do more. I often laid out twenty men myself with a stick coming from the Macroom Fair, so it is a bad trial of Mick that he could kill only eight, and he having*

Relaxing at home.

O'Leary was feted in Hyde Park.

a rifle and bayonet.' Nevertheless, the authorities thought it would be a good idea to use his father to recruit more soldiers from his native Cork. On his first outing in Inchigeela District, Co Cork he urged young men to join the British Army. '*If you don't*', he told them, '*the Germans will come here and will do to you what the English have been doing for the last seven hundred years.*' He was not used again!

In 1915 George Bernard Shaw wrote a comic one act play – 'O'Flaherty VC – A Recruiting Pamphlet' based on the return to Ireland of Michael O'Leary VC. In it, the hero returns home on a recruiting drive, but had omitted to tell his mother, a firm Fenian, that he was fighting for the British. The play at the Abbey Theatre in Dublin was withdrawn just before its first performance because of its anti-establishment tone and was not performed until 1920.

In October 1915 he was commissioned into the Connaught Rangers and served in Salonika and Macedonia where he was again Mentioned-in-Despatches. He retired from the Army in 1921 and returned to the Police Service in Canada. In hindsight, making him a licence inspector for the enforcement of the prohibition of alcohol and later a Police Sergeant on the railway was not in his best interests. Although arrested on several occasions for corruption he was never convicted. He later told a newspaper… 'Unfortunately on the railway I came into contact with bootlegging and smuggling interests…. A detective has to take bribes to keep his mouth shut or else people are out to get him.' In 1926 his family returned to Ireland without him. He later returned to England, assisted by the British Legion, and worked as a Commissionaire at the Mayfair Hotel in London for seven years.

He was recalled from the Reserve of Officers in 1939 and went to France as a Captain in the Middlesex Regiment. He was invalided back to England before the evacuation of Dunkirk, transferred to the Pioneer Corps and placed in charge of a POW Camp in Southern England. In 1945 he was discharged on medical grounds and worked in the building trade until his retirement in 1954. He lived in London for 30 years and died in on 1 August 1961 after a long illness. His funeral was well attended by the Regiment and a lone piper played a lament. Six of his seven children attended his funeral including his twin boys who both won DFCs flying in Bomber Command in the Second World War. His grave at Mill Hill Cemetery is tended by the London Branch of the Irish Guards Association which lays a wreath each year.

In July 1962 his medals were presented to the Regiment and are on display at the Guards Museum.

Postcard of his action.

Private Thomas Woodcock

'For most conspicuous bravery and determination. He was one of a post commanded by L/Sgt Moyney which was surrounded. The post held out for ninety-six hours, but after that time was attacked from all sides in overwhelming numbers and was forced to retire.

Pte Woodcock covered the retirement with a Lewis Gun and only retired when the enemy had moved round and up to his post and were only a few yards away. He then crossed the river, but hearing cries for help behind him, retuned and waded into the stream amid a shower of bombs from the enemy and rescued another member of the party. The latter he then carried across the open ground in broad daylight towards our front line regardless of machine-gun fire that was opened on him.'

Pte Thomas Woodcock.

The Broembeck stream cut through the northern sector of the Ypres front. On the extreme left where the British and French lines met it went through a cluster of isolated posts within 100 yards of the enemy. It was a tactically weak position which 2 Company 2IG took over on 12 Sep 1917.

Within Ney Copse LSgt Jack Moyney (also awarded the VC) took over advanced posts with orders not to withdraw unless completely surrounded. Three hours later a barrage started leading to a Company sized attack by the Wurttemburg Sturmtruppen resulting in 80 members of No 2 Company being killed, wounded or missing. Authority for the remainder to withdraw was given but the message was not received by LSgt Moyney. He stood firm and his 'lost' platoon appeared 96 hours later 'tired, very hungry, but otherwise in perfect order' having fought off continual attacks.

When the opportunity arose, LSgt Moyney and Pte Woodcock personally covered the withdrawal of the platoon over the stream and Pte Woodcock even returned under fire to rescue a comrade as described in the citation above. A month later it was announced the two men from the same platoon had been awarded the VC.

Tom Woodcock was born in Wigan in 1888 and worked in the John Scowcroft Colliery before joining the Irish Guards on 26 May 1915. After five months training he proceeded to France with the 2nd Battalion. A married man with three children, he was feted on his homecoming on 27 February 1918. On 9 March 1918 he and his Platoon Sergeant Jack Moyney were presented with their VCs by King George.

His leave ended on 17 March and he was back with the Battalion for his 30th birthday. (LSgt Moyney, however, had gone absent.) In the days that followed the Guards Division suffered heavy losses as they attempted to stem the Germans' spring offensive. On 30 March, he was killed near Bullecourt and is buried in Douchy-les-Ayette British Cemetery.

His gravestone at Douchy-les-Ayette, France.

Lt (acting Lt Col) James Neville Marshall VC, MC★

VC to Lt (acting Lt Col) John Neville Marshall MC, late Irish Guards, Special Reserve, attached 16th Battalion, The Lancashire Fusiliers:

'For most conspicuous bravery, determination and leadership in the attack on the Sambre-Oise canal, near Catillon, on 4th November 1918, when a partly constructed bridge came under concentrated fire and was broken before the advanced troops of his Battalion could cross. Lt Col Marshall at once went forward and organised parties to repair the bridge. The first party were soon killed or wounded, but by personal example he inspired others and volunteers were soon instantly forthcoming. Under intense fire and with complete disregard for his own safety, he stood on the bank encouraging his men and assisting in the work, and when the bridge was repaired, attempted to rush across at the head of the Battalion and was killed while so doing. The passage of the canal was of vital importance, and the gallantry displayed by all ranks was largely due to the inspiring example set by Lt Col Marshall.'

James Marshall was born in Manchester in 1887, son of a draper, and educated at the Royal Grammar School, Birmingham. He was a most unusual officer, a loner of strange character, who had practised as an unqualified vet in Harlow, Essex. He began the war in the Belgian Army, where his limited veterinary experience seems to have led him being described, and probably employed, as a doctor. Wounded and twice decorated by the Belgians for rescuing the wounded in November 1914, he was discharged and returned to England as medically unfit.

Lt Col James Marshall.

In December 1915, he joined the Irish Guards with a chest full of ribbons from previous service. Without question he was gallant and very brave. His writings reveal a strange belief in destiny and a crusading zeal in which he likens himself to great figures in history. He was wounded many times, although the 10 wound stripes he wore after a wound in 1918 were never authenticated. To his brother officers he was undoubtedly different. His age was open to question (he claimed to be 32, not 27 on his wedding certificate) and there were stories about South Africa. Having won a MC and bar with the Regiment, he was attached to the 16th Battalion, The Lancashire Fusiliers to boost the battalion which had suffered heavy losses. Such was his standing and reputation, he was soon appointed acting Commanding Officer. He was killed in an action of astounding bravery during the 'bounce' crossing of the Sambre-Ouse canal near Catillon (not far from Landrecies) on 4 November 1918, the last set piece battle of the Great War which ended a week later.

Marshall's story is a strange one for he unquestionably was extraordinarily brave, and a very daring and experienced soldier. There is no question that he did not come from the same background as many of the officers, but equally, it is clear that this element was not, in those turbulent times, as important as it is often imagined to be. His competence and leadership are what mattered and that was proven in war. It does seem, however, that there was reluctance in the Regiment to regard Marshall as a shining example. Perhaps Marshall's curious Walter-Mitty personality, his perceived vanity (extra ribbons, extra wound stripes) and his infatuation with his supposed historic destiny, may have, hardly surprisingly, somewhat alienated him from others of a less eccentric temperament. Couple this with his near reckless bravery (He regarded himself the bravest man in the British Army) and it becomes easier to understand how a Victoria Cross winner came to be regarded as so strange.

The poet Wilfred Owen of the 2nd Manchesters, a contemporary in the 91st Brigade, who was killed in the same attack, considered him loud mouthed and brash, and called him the 'Mad Major' and the 'Major of the ten wounds'. Both are buried in Ors Communal Cemetery.

The award of a posthumous VC was announced on 13 February 1919 and presented to his widow at Buckingham Palace on 12 April 1919. His medals are owned by the Regiment and displayed in the Guards Museum.

Lance Sergeant John Moyney

'For most conspicuous bravery when in command of fifteen men forming two advanced posts. In spite of being surrounded by the enemy he held his post for ninety-six hours, having no water and little food. On the morning of the fifth day a large force of the enemy advanced to dislodge him. He ordered his men out of their shell holes, and taking the initiative, attacked with great effect from a flank. Finding himself surrounded by superior numbers, he led back his men in a charge through the enemy, and reached a stream which lay between the posts and the line. Here he instructed his party to cross at once while he and Private Woodcock remained to cover their retirement.

When the whole of his force had gained the south-west bank unscathed he himself crossed under a shower of bombs. It was due to the endurance, skill and devotion to duty shown by this Non-Commissioned Officer that he was able to bring his entire force safely out of action.'

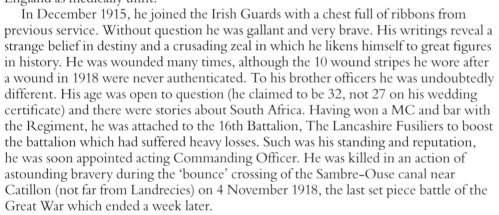

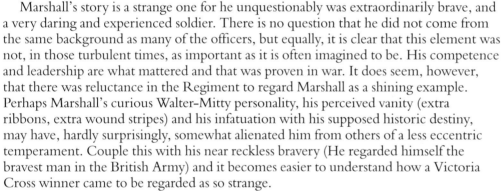

John Moyney was born at Rathdowney, Queen's County Ireland on 8 January 1895. His upbringing was hard and impoverished having left school without qualifications to seek work on a local farm.

He enlisted into the Irish Guards on 6 April 1915 aged 20. In October he was posted to No 5 Company, 2nd Battalion in France. He was appointed L Cpl (unpaid) in February and unpaid Lance Sergeant in September 1916. By late summer 1917 he was Lance Sergeant in No 3 Coy and promoted Sergeant six weeks after his award. In February 1918 he went home on leave with Tom Woodcock to be presented with their VCs. Unfortunately he did not return to duty and on 13 June 1918 was convicted at a General Court Marshal of being absent without leave while on Active Service. He spent the rest of the war as a Guardsman. No reason for going absent was given but it is likely to be linked to his marriage on 17 March 1918 in Roscrea, Co Tipperary, to Bridget Carroll. Meanwhile Tom Woodcock was killed in action during his absence.

On 4 June 1919 he left the Army and returned to Roscrea, to an uncertain future and his country in civil war. In 1929 he joined Great Southern Railway as a porter at Roscrea. He was always plagued by money problems as his family grew to six children and help was constantly being sought.

Inspite of everything, he maintained his association with the Regiment and in the Second World War his son enlisted into the Regiment serving in North Africa with the 1st Battalion where he was taken prisoner. He was delighted that in 1972, his three nephews, the Troy brothers also from Roscrea, joined the Regiment.

He retired as Head Porter at Roscrea in 1960 after 40 years on the railways. He continued to attend regimental functions but he died on 10 November 1980 and was the last surviving Irish VC winner from the First World War.

His medals were bequeathed to the Regiment and are on display in the Guards Museum.

Lance Corporal John Patrick Kenneally

'The Bou feature dominates all ground east and west between Medjez El Bab and Tebourba. It was essential to the final assault on Tunis that this feature should be captured and held.

A Guards Brigade assaulted and captured a portion of the Bou on 27th April 1943. The Irish Guards held on to points 212 and 214 on the western end of the feature, which points the Germans frequently counter attacked. While a further attack to capture the complete feature was being prepared, it was essential for the Irish Guards to hold on. They did so.

Sgt Kenneally on St Patrick's Day.

On 28th April 1943, the positions held by one company of the Irish Guards on the rise between points 212 and 214 were about to be subjected to an attack by the enemy. Approximately one company of the enemy were seen forming up preparatory to attack when L/Cpl Kenneally decided that this was the right moment to attack them himself. Single-handed he charged down the bare forward slope at the main enemy body, firing his Bren gun from the hip as he did so. This outstanding act of gallantry and the dash with which it was executed completely unbalanced the enemy company, which broke up in disorder. LCpl Kenneally then returned to the crest to further harass their retreat.

LCpl Kenneally repeated this remarkable exploit on the morning of 30th April 1943, when accompanied by a Sergeant of the Reconnaissance Corps, he again charged the enemy forming up for an assault. This time he so harassed the enemy, inflicting many casualties that the projected attack was frustrated. The enemy's strength was again about one company. It was only when he was noticed hopping from one fire position to another further to the left, in order to support another company, carrying his gun one hand and supporting himself on a Guardsman with the other, that is was discovered that he had been wounded. He refused to give up his Bren gun, claiming that he was the only one understood that gun, and continued to fight all through the day with great courage, devotion to duty and disregard to his own safety.

The magnificent gallantry of this NCO on these two occasions under heavy fire, his unfailing vigilance, and remarkable accuracy were responsible for saving many valuable lives during many days and nights in the forward positions. His actions also played a considerable part in holding these positions and this influenced the whole course of the battle. His rapid appreciation of the situation, his initiative and his extraordinary gallantry in attacking single handed a massed body of the enemy and breaking up an attack on two occasions, was an achievement that can seldom have been equalled. His courage in fighting all day when wounded was an inspiration to all ranks.'

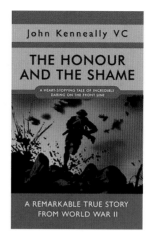

His Autobiography.

John Kenneally with Field Marshal Alexander.

The extraordinary truth is that John Kenneally was not his real name, nor was he Irish. He was born Leslie Robinson in Birmingham and in 1939 joined the Royal Artillery aged 18, was based in London but went absent without leave. Later arrested, he was detained at Wellington Barracks. So impressed was he by his jailers, the Irish Guards, that he applied to transfer, but this was refused by the Royal Artillery. He therefore deserted again and worked with a team of Irish builders who gave him the identity card of John Patrick Kenneally, who had returned to Ireland. With his new identity, he entered the recruiting office in Manchester to join the Irish Guards.

In April 1943, the Allies planned their final assault on Tunis, North Africa but the massive feature of Djebel Bou Azoukaz blocked the way of 24 Guards Brigade. After two days bitter fighting and many casualties the Irish Guards still held the feature, known as the 'Bou' against viscous counter-attacks by the 8th Panzer Regiment. This was the scene for LCpl Kenneally to demonstrate his incredible acts of bravery described above.

Painting of Kenneally for the IWM.

In January 1944, after Tunis, the Battalion took part in the assault landings at Anzio, 30 miles south of Rome, where he was again wounded. On the beachhead, the Battalion lost 32 Officers and 714 men. Only one third of those who left England the year before returned to Chelsea Barracks and the 1st Battalion never fought again as a formed unit.

As demob beckoned, John Kenneally flirted with the idea of joining the Birmingham police, but instead joined the newly formed 1st (Guards) Parachute Battalion and saw service in Palestine in 1947 as a Platoon Sergeant. He bought himself out in July 1948 and ran his own car dealership in the West Midlands before retiring to Worcestershire. He always retained his links with the Regiment, particularly the Birmingham Branch of the Association. He briefly appeared in the news again in 2000 when he wrote to the Daily Telegraph rebuking Peter Mandleson MP for calling Irish Guards Officers "chinless wonders".

He died aged 79 in September 2000 and his medals are displayed in the Guards Museum.

Guardsman Edward Charlton

'On the morning of 21 April 1946, Guardsman Charlton was co-driver in one tank of a troop, which, with a platoon of infantry seized the village of Wistedt.

Shortly afterwards, the enemy attacked this position under cover of an artillery concentration and in great strength, comprising as it later transpired, a Battalion of 15th Panzer Grenadiers, supported by six self propelled guns.

All the tanks including Gdsm Charlton's were hit; the infantry were hard pressed and in danger of being overrun.

Thereupon, entirely on his own initiative, Gdsm Charlton decided to counter-attack the enemy. Quickly recovering the Browning from his damaged tank, he advanced up the road in full view of the enemy, firing the Browning from the hip.

Such was the boldness of his attack and the intensity of his fire that he halted the leading enemy company, inflicting heavy casualties on them. This effort at the same time brought much needed relief to our own infantry.

For ten minutes Gdsm Charlton fired in this manner until wounded in the left arm. Immediately, despite intense enemy fire, he mounted his machine gun on a nearby fence which he used to support his wounded left arm. He stood firing thus for a further

Gdsm Edward Carlton.

A plaque in his home town.

ten minutes until he was again hit in the left arm, which fell away shattered and useless.

Although twice wounded and suffering from loss of blood Gdsm Charlton again mounted his machine-gun on to the fence, now having only one arm with which to fire and reload. Nevertheless, he still continued to inflict casualties on the enemy, until finally he was hit for a third time and collapsed. He died later of his wounds, in enemy hands. The heroism and determination of this Guardsman in his self-imposed task were beyond all praise. Even his German captors were amazed by his valour.

Guardsman Charlton's courageous and self-sacrificing action not only inflicted extremely heavy casualties on the enemy and relieved his comrades from a desperate situation, but also enabled the position to be speedily recaptured.'

What is unusual about this particular award is that it was the last to be awarded in Europe in the Second World War and would not have happened without the recommendation of the enemy.

Eddie Charlton was born in Co Durham in 1920 and the family moved to Manchester in 1935. He volunteered for the Irish Guards in 1940 because he wanted to join the police after the war and the local force were only recruiting ex-Guardsmen.

After basic training he joined the 2nd (Armoured) Battalion as a Sherman tank driver for Lt Barry Quinan of No 1 Squadron under command of Major Mick O'Cock. By April 1945 the Army had crossed the Rhine and 5th Guards Brigade headed north encountering limited opposition. At dawn on 21 April they approached Wistedt from the village of Elsdorf, accompanied by an infantry platoon of the 3rd Battalion Irish Guards riding on their tanks.

As they entered the village Lt Quinan's tank suffered an electrical failure so he transferred to that of his Troop Sergeant ordering Gdsm Charlton, his co-driver, to dismount with the Browning machine gun to provide some local protection as they tried to restart the tank. The rest of the troop and platoon went firm in the village and started preparing breakfast when the Germans surprised them and attacked with fire support from the direction of Wehldorf a village 4km to south west. By the time the order came to withdraw they were all but surrounded with three tanks out of action and having expended their ammunition. Some escaped on foot to Elsdorf but others were captured including the wounded Gdsm Charlton who had put up such strong resistance.

The first indications of the full extent of Charlton's bravery only became apparent when his fellow Guardsmen taken prisoner by the Germans were released a few days later. His comrades and the Germans who captured them also mentioned his bravery.

The Germens' successful dismounted attack had been led by Lieutenant Hans Jurgan von Bulow of the Panzer-Grenadier-Regiment 115 for which he was awarded an immediate Iron Cross, First Class although on 24 April they too were forced from the village. The war ended days later and he himself was taken prisoner.

He voiced his admiration on how brave one solder in particular had been in resisting their assault. This was Eddie Charlton. Gdsm Charlton had been put forward for the award of an immediate Military Medal, which is only awarded to the living. At that point his Company HQ did not know that he had died of his wounds in captivity. One of the conditions of a VC was that the action must be witnessed by two other individuals. Thus uniquely the statements from Lt von Bulow and other German POWs were taken as contributory evidence.

The award was officially announced on 2 May 1946, the last of World War 2 and presented by King George VI to his parents in October 1946. Guardsman Eddie Charlton is buried in the Military Cemetery near Becklingen between Soltau and Celle on the edge of the beautiful Luneburger Heath.

Gdsm Charlton's grave at Becklingen War Cemetery, Soltau, Germany.

His medals were presented to the Regiment and are now displayed in the Guards Museum.

Appendix C
CASUALTIES AND DECORATIONS

THE GREAT WAR

- Strength before mobilization 1914: 997
- Borne on strength through the war: 293 Officers, 9,340 Other Ranks
- Killed in Action or died of wounds: 115 Officers, 2,235 Other Ranks
- Wounded: 148 Officers, approx. 5,000 Other Ranks
- Awards: 4 Victoria Crosses, 14 Distinguished Service Orders, 67 Military Crosses, 77 Distinguished Conduct Medals, 244 Military Medals

THE SECOND WORLD WAR

Bn	Theatre	Officers Killed/Died of Wounds	Officers Wounded	Other Ranks Killed/Died of Wounds	Other Ranks Wounded	Battalion Total	Total Casualties
1st	Norway	7	5	13	23	48	
1st	North Africa	9	16	115	229	369	
1st	Italy	8	16	121	211	356	773
2nd	Hook of Holland	0	0	11	12	23	
2nd	Boulogne	2	1	23	14	40	
2nd	Normandy	7	15	51	96	169	
2nd	Belgium & Holland	3	18	54	100	175	
2nd	Germany	3	3	19	43	68	475
3rd	Normandy	7	6	67	182	262	
3rd	Belgium & Holland	7	28	143	413	591	
3rd	Germany	4	2	42	106	154	1007
Home		1	0	12	21	34	
Other		1	4	4	14	23	57
TOTAL		**59**	**114**	**675**	**1464**	**2312**	**2312**

Awards: 2 Victoria Cross, 17 Distinguished Service Order, 33 Military Cross, 18 Distinguished Conduct Medal, 72 Military Medal, 110 Mentioned in Despatches.

SINCE THE SECOND WORLD WAR

Theatre	Killed in Action
Palestine 1947–1948	10
Aden 1967–1968	10
Northern Ireland	1
Iraq 1994–2007	5
Afghanistan 2006–2014	3

Awards: 3 Distinguished Service Order, 8 Military Crosses, 1 Military Medal, 4 Queen's Gallantry Medal, 40 Mentioned in Despatches.

MEMORIALS

There are over 70 memorials dedicated to fallen Irish Guardsmen in the United Kingdom and Ireland and many others as yet unlisted. Many relate to the Great War, and range from stained glass windows to tablets, brass plaques, paneling, furniture and Stone Celtic crosses. There are more generic ones dedicated to Irish Infantry, the Irish Regiments and the Foot Guards. All Irish Guardsmen killed on active service are remembered in the Book of Remembrance in the Guards Chapel and since 1945 they are named by campaigns on the wall of the Guards Chapel. 'We shall remember them.'

Appendix D

COLONELS OF THE REGIMENT

First

Field Marshal The Rt Hon Frederick Sleigh, First Earl ROBERTS of KANDAHAR and PRETORIA and the City of WATERFORD. VC, KG, KP, PC, GCB, OM, GCSI, GCIE, late Royal Artillery. (*Died in France when visiting Indian troops*)
17 Oct 1900–14 Nov 1914

Second

Field Marshal The Rt Hon, Herbert Horatio, First Earl KITCHENER OF KHARTOUM and of BROOME, KG, KP, PC, GCB, OM, GCSI, GCIE, late Royal Engineers. (*Drowned in HMS HAMPSHIRE en route for Russia*)
15 Nov 1914–5 Jun 1916

Third

Field Marshal John Denton Pinkstone French, 1st Earl of YPRES and HIGH LAKE, KP, PC, GCB, OM, GVCO, KCB, KCMG, late 19th Hussars.
6 Jun 1916–22 May 1925

Fourth

Field Marshal Frederick Rudolph Lambart, 10th Earl of CAVAN, KP, GCB, GCMG, GBE, DCL, LlD, DL, late Grenadier Guards.
23 May 1925–28 Aug 1946

Fifth

Field Marshal The Rt Hon Harold Rupert Leofric George ALEXANDER of TUNIS and ERRIGAL in the County of DONEGAL, KG, PC, GCB, OM, GCMG, CSI, DSO, MC, DCL, LL.D., Commissioned Irish Guards, September 1911.
28 Aug 1946–16 Jun 1969

Sixth

General Sir Basil EUGSTER, KCB, KCVO, CBE, DSO, MC, MA, Commissioned Irish Guards, 1935.
17 Jun 1969–5 Apr 1984

Seventh

General HRH The Grand Duke of LUXEMBOURG, KG, Commissioned Irish Guards, 1942, and served North West Europe.
21 Aug 1984–31 Oct 2000
Promoted to the honorary rank of General by the Colonel in Chief on 17 Mar 95.

Eighth

James Hamilton, 5th Duke of ABERCORN, KG, Commissioned Grenadier Guards, 1964.
31 Oct 2000–17 Mar 2008

Ninth

Major General Sir Sebastian ROBERTS KCVO, OBE, Commissioned Irish Guards, 1977.
17 Mar 2008–10 Feb 11

Tenth

His Royal Highness The Prince WILLIAM, DUKE OF CAMBRIDGE KG, KT
10 Feb 11

Appendix E

SENIOR OFFICERS BIOGRAPHICAL NOTES

General Sir Alexander Godley GCB, KCMG
Transferred to the Irish Guards in 1900. Major-General Imperial General Staff and GOC New Zealand Forces (1910–14); Divisional and Corps Commander Dardanelles and Egypt (1914–16); Commander Army Corps (1916–19); Military Secretary (1920–22); C in C British Army of the Rhine (1922–24); GOC in C Southern Command (1924–28); Governor and C in C Gibraltar (1928–33).

Field Marshal The Rt Hon. The Earl Alexander of Tunis and Errigal in the County of Donegal KG, PC, GCB, OM, GCMG, CSI, DSO, MC
Commanded 2nd Battalion (1917–18); Baltic Landeswehr (1920–21); 1st Battalion (1922–26); Regimental Lieutenant-Colonel (1928–30); Nowshera Brigade, Northwest Frontier (1934–38); 1st Division (1938–40); 1st Corps (1940); Southern Command (1940–42); Burma (1942); Middle East and 18th Army Group (1942–43), Allied Armies, Italy (1943–44); Allied Commander Mediterranean (1944–45); Governor General of Canada (1946–52); Minister of Defence (1952–54); Constable of HM Tower of London (1960–65).

Major-General Charles Haydon CB, DSO★, OBE
Commanded 2nd Battalion 1940. Raised Special Service Brigade (forerunner of the Commandos) and commanded them in the Vaagso Raid in Norway (1943) and that on the Lofoten Islands (1943); Vice Chief Combined Operations (to Lord Louis Mountbatten); Commanded 1st Guards Brigade (1944); British Joint Services Mission, Washington (1944–45); Chief, Intelligence Division Control Commission, Germany (1945–47).

Major-General Gerald Verney DSO, MVO
Commanded 2nd Battalion (1940–42); 32nd Guards Brigade (1942); 6th Guards Tank Brigade (1942–44); 7th Armoured Division (1944); 1st Guards Brigade (1945); Commander Vienna Area (1945–46); 56th (London) Armoured Division (TA) (1946–48).

General Sir Basil Eugster KCB, KCVO, CBE, DSO, MC★

Commanded 3rd Battalion (1945); 2nd Battalion (1947); 1st Battalion (1951–54); Commandant Mons Officer Cadet School (1958); 3rd Infantry Brigade (1959–62); Commandant School of Infantry, Warminster (1962–63); GOC 4th Division, BAOR (1963–65); GOC London District and Major-General Commanding the Household Brigade (1965–68); Commander British Forces Hong Kong (1968–70); GOC in C Southern Command (1971–72); C in C United Kingdom Land Forces (1972–74).

Major-General Sir Robert Corbett KCVO, CB

Commanded 1st Battalion (1981–84); Chief of Staff British Forces Falkland Islands (1984–85); 5th Airborne Brigade (1985–87); Director Defence Programmes, Ministry of Defence (1987–88); GOC Berlin (British Sector) and British Commandant (1989–91); Regimental Lieutenant Colonel (1988–91); GOC London District and Major-General Commanding the Household Division (1991–94).

Major-General Sir Sebastian Roberts KCVO, OBE

Commanded 1st Battalion (1993–1996); Directorate of Land Warfare, Upavon (1996–1999); Director of Public Relations (Army) (1999–2001) Regimental Lieutenant Colonel (1999–2008); Leadership Doctrine Author 2002; GOC London District and Major-General Commanding the Household Division (2003–2006); Senior Army Representative at the Royal College of Defence Studies 2007; Colonel of the Regiment (2008–2011).

Major-General Sir William Cubitt KCVO, CBE

Commanded 1st Battalion (1998–2001); Commandant, Land Warfare School, Warminster (2001–2002); Commander 8th Infantry Brigade, Northern Ireland (2002–2004); Director of the General Staff, Ministry of Defence (2004–2006); GOC London District and Major-General Commanding the Household Division (2007–2011); Regimental Lieutenant Colonel (2008–2012).

Major-General Mark Carleton-Smith CBE

Commanded 22nd Special Air Service Regiment (2002–2005); Commander 16 Air Assault Brigade (2006–2008); Commander Helmand Task Force and Commander British Forces Afghanistan (2008); Director Army Resources and Plans, Ministry of Defence (2009–2011); Director Special Forces (2012–2015); Director Army Strategy (2015–); Regimental Lieutenant Colonel (2012–).

Appendix F

REGIMENTAL
LIEUTENANT COLONELS

Colonel V J DAWSON, CVO
Former Coldstream Officer. On Nile Expedition in 1884/5 with Guards Camel Regt. Present at actions at Abu Klea and El Gubat & Recce of Metammeh.

3 Sep 1900   2 Sep 1905

Colonel R J COOPER, CVO
Former Grenadier Officer. Served in Egyptian war of 1882. Present at engagement at Tel-el-Mahuta and Battle of Tel-el-Kebir. Wounded as Brig Gen CB, CVO 16 Aug 15. Brigade Commander Gallipoli 1915 (wounded). Grandson served E.J.Cooper 1959–1969.

3 Sep 1905   13 Jul 1909

Colonel G C NUGENT, MVO
Killed in Action May 1915

14 Jul 1909   13 Jul 1913

Colonel C FITZCLARENCE, VC
Killed in Action 12 Nov 1914 Polygon Wood, Zonnebeke commanding 1st Guards Bde. Son Eddie served IG. Became 6th Earl of Munster.

14 Jul 1913   11 Aug 1914

Colonel D J PROBY

12 Aug 1914   2 Feb 1917

Colonel The Lord ARDEE, CB, CBE   3 Feb 1917   7 Jan 1918

Colonel Sir John HALL, CBE   8 Jan 1918   20 Mar 1919

Colonel R C A McCALMONT, DSO
While serving in France, was also Unionist MP for   21 Mar 1919   20 Mar 1924
Antrim East from 19 Feb 1913 to Mar 1919. MiD twice.

Colonel W H V DARELL, CMG, DSO
Served in S Africa, Egypt and France throughout WW1.   21 Mar 1924   20 Mar 1928
Died 1954.

Colonel the Hon H R L G ALEXANDER, DSO MC
Retired as Field Marshal The Rt Hon The Earl Alexander
of Tunis KG PC GCB OM GCMG CSI DSO MC DCL   21 Mar 1928   13 Jan 1930
LLD. Died 16 Jun 1969. Father of Shane served 54–58
and Hon Brian 58–60.

Colonel R V POLLOK, CBE DSO
Retired as Maj Gen CB CBE DSO March 1941. Was   14 Jan 1930   18 Oct 1931
GOC Northern Ireland.

Colonel L M GREGSON, OBE
Retired 19 Oct 1935, died by end of year.   19 Oct 1931   18 Oct 1935

Colonel A C G DAWNAY, CBE, DSO
8 MiDs 1914–19. DSO as temp Capt. Died 1937   19 Oct 1935   19 Jul 1936

Colonel J S N FITZGERALD, MBE MC
1st tour. Retired as Colonel CVO Oct 1945. Wounded
twice in WW1; Adjt of 2nd and 1st Bns; took part in   20 Jul 1936   9 Aug 1938
N.W. Russian anti-Bolshevik Campaign 1919 with FM
Alex.

Colonel R B S REFORD, MC
Wounded 1917. Retired as Hon Brig March 1944. Son   10 Aug 1938   1 Sep 1939
served IG. Canadian. 1st university graduate to command.

Colonel the Hon T E VESEY
Father of 6th Viscount de Vesci. Shot 3 times in 11   2 Sep 1939   1 Jun 1942
months in 1914–15.

Colonel J S N FITZGERALD, MBE MC
2nd tour. Retired as Col CVO Oct 1945   2 Jun 1942   15 pr 1945

Colonel C A MONTAGU-DOUGLAS-SCOTT, DSO and Bar

Son of Lord Herbert Andrew M-D-S 01–07. Father of Capt D A served 50–55. Resigned commission in 1927, called up in 1939. Commanded 1IG and 1st Gds Bde in 1944 and 45. Lord Herbert was ADC to Lord Roberts in South Africa and had a DSO for South Africa. Father and son had 3 DSOs between them.

16 Apr 1945   27 Aug 1946

Colonel J O E VANDELEUR, DSO & bar

Retired as Hon Brig Dec 1951. Gentleman-at Arms. Obituary in Times & Telegraph. Captured "Joe's" Bridge over Escaut Canal, led 30 Corps towards Arnhem, played by Michael Caine in *A Bridge Too Far*. Was going to join Cameronians like father, but 5 cousins killed in IG in WW1.

28 Aug 1946   5 Dec 1948

Colonel T W GIMSON

Transferee from North Staffs Regt in 1933. 4 IG Offrs wrote to protest at his seniority over them! Became Adjt 1IG within 2 months.

6 Dec 1948   7 Nov 1950

Colonel D H FITZGERALD, DSO OBE

Retired as Hon Brig Mar 1958. Died Aug 2002. Obituary in *Times & Telegraph*. Wounded on HMT *Chobry*.

18 Nov 1950   6 Oct 1952

Colonel D M L GORDON-WATSON, OBE MC★★

Retired as Brig Mar 1963. Died May 2002. Obituary in *Times & Telegraph*. Son Julian served 1963–66.

7 Oct 1952   28 Oct 1955

Colonel P F I REID, OBE

Retired as Col May 1959. Gentleman at Arms. Died 9 Dec 1994. Obituary in *Times & Telegraph*. Son of Col P L 'Billy' Reid commissioned into the Regiment on its formation. Commandant Guards Depot Aug 1950–Oct 1953.

29 Oct 1955   5 Apr 1959

Colonel H L S YOUNG, DSO
Retired as Hon Brig Dec 1962. Son of Son of Lt G E
S Young KIA 1917. (The picture of the gate at Warley
with 2IG marching out shows Savill in his mother's arms
as old Young leads the Bn out.) Father of young Savill
1963–1967.

6 Apr 1959   23 Jun 1961

Colonel J W BERRIDGE, MBE
Retired as Hon Brig May 1966. Died 26 May 2012.
Grandfather of Capt Will Jenkins who served 2009–2014.

24 Jun 1961   23 Apr 1964

Colonel M J P O'COCK, MC
Retired as Brig CBE MC MA Jun 1974. Stepson of Guy
Tylden-Wright. Stepfather of Col J H O'H Pollock, CO-
96–98. Father-in-law of Maj Gen Sir Robert Corbett CO
81–84. Died June 2007.

24 Apr 1964   11 Jan 1966

Colonel C W D HARVEY-KELLY
Retired as Hon Col MBE Apr 1969.

12 Jan 1966   14 Jan 1969

Colonel J A AYLMER
Retired as Col Oct 1980.

15 Jan 1969   14 Jun 1972

Colonel J G F HEAD, MBE
Retired as Col CBE Apr 1982.

15 Jun 1972   16 Apr 1973

Colonel J N GHIKA
Retired as Brig CBE Aug 1981. Commandant Guards
Depot 1969–1971. Died July 1992. Father of Brig
Christopher 93– . Obituary in Times & Telegraph.

17 Apr 1973   6 Apr 1976

Colonel G A ALLAN, OBE
Retired as Col May 1982. Father-in-law of Capt B P
Hornung 96–90. Died Jan 2009. Obituary in Telegraph

7 Apr 1976   13 Feb 1979

Colonel R T P HUME
Retired as Brig Aug 1987.

14 Feb 1979   29 Sep 1981

Colonel J H BAKER
Retired as Col Sep 1986. MBE for MOD Conservation.
Brother of Capt C B G served 69–75. Gentleman at
Arms. Died 15 Oct 09.

30 Sep 1981   30 Jul, 1985

Colonel Sir WILLIAM MAHON, Bt
Retired Jul 1992. Commandant Guards Depot Dec
1979–Jun 1982. LVO for Quincentennial of Gentlemen
at Arms. Last full-time serving Regimental Lieutenant
Colonel.

31 Jul 1985   29 Jul 1988

Brigadier R J S CORBETT, CB
Retired as Maj Gen Sir Robert KCVO, CB Aug 1994.
served 58–94. Father of Capt Michael served 96–99. Son-
in-law of Brig M J P O'Cock.

29 Jul 1988   17 Mar 1991

Brigadier D B W WEBB-CARTER OBE, MC
Retired as Brig OBE MC Nov 1995.

7 Mar 1991   5 Nov 1995

Brigadier R C WOLVERSON OBE
Retired as Brig 7 Aug 1996.

2 Dec 1995   21 Jul 1999

Major General S J L ROBERTS OBE
Retired as Maj Gen Sir Sebastian Roberts KCVO.
Brother of Majs Cassian served 82–00 and Fabian served
86–12. Father of Capt Julian served 04–10 & Capt
Orlando 06–10. 9th Colonel of the Regiment 18 Mar
2008–11 Feb 2011.

21 Jul 1999   17 Mar 2008

Major General Sir William CUBITT CBE
Retired as Maj Gen Sir William KCVO, CBE. Son-in
law of Martin Pym served 46 – 48. Bro-in-law of Capt
William Pym served 88–93.

18 Mar 2008   17 Mar 2012

Major General M A P CARLETON-SMITH CBE.
Nephew of Maj M V Carleton-Smith 53–70.

18 Mar 2012

Appendix G

DIRECTORS OF MUSIC – REGIMENTAL BAND OF THE IRISH GUARDS

Captain C H HASSELL, OBE

1900–1929

Captain J L T HURD

1929–1938

Major G H WILLCOCKS, MBE, MVO

1938–1948

Lieutenant Colonel C H JAEGER, OBE, LRAM, ARCM, psm
Senior Director of Music, Household Division.

1948–1969

Major E G HORABIN, LDRA, ARCM, psm
Died 2008

1969–1977

Lieutenant Colonel M G LANE, ARCM, psm
Died in service. Senior Director of Music, Household Division.

1977–1989

Major M C HENDERSON, ARCM, psm

1989–1998

Lieutenant Colonel A R CHATBURN, BA, ARCM, psm
Senior Director of Music, Household Division.

1998–2005

Major S C BARNWELL, BBCM, psm
Bandmaster IG 1994–96. Moved to WG Band 2008. Became Senior Director in 2011 as Lt Col.

2005–2008

Major P D SHANNON, MBE, MA, BA(Hons), ARCM, LRAM, psm
Ex Director of Music WG, Senior Instructor Army School of Music. Retired to become Captain of Invalids, Royal Hospital Chelsea.

2008–2011

Lieutenant Colonel R W HOPLA, BA(Hons), ARCM, BBCM, psm
Senior Director of Music, Household Division.

2011–2015

Major B MILLER, BMus (Hons), LLCM (TD), LRSM, ARCM, psm

2015–

Appendix H

REGIMENTAL ADJUTANTS

Lieutenant R C A McCALMONT (Then to Adjt 1IG)	1 May 1903–31 Dec 1903
Lieutenant the Hon J F TREFUSIS	1 Jan 1904–31 Jan 1904
Captain H A HERBERT-STEPNEY	1 Feb 1904–31 Dec 1904
Lieutenant the Hon L J P BUTLER	1 Jan 1905–08 Oct 1905
Lieutenant T A TISDELL	9 Oct 1905–01 Apr 1906
Captain T W B GREENFIELD, DSO	1 Apr 1906–27 Mar 1909
Captain the Viscount de VESCI (1st tour)	1 Apr 1901–03 Jan 1911
Captain P L REID	04 Jan 1911–04 Aug 1914
Captain the Viscount de VESCI (2nd tour)	10 Sep 1914–09 Dec 1917
Major H F WARD	10 Dec 1917–30 Jul 1918
Captain W C REYNOLDS, OBE	01 Oct 1918–10 May 1919
Captain A F L GORDON, DSO MC (1st tour)	11 May 1919–18 Mar 1922
Captain R G C YERBURGH, OBE	19 Mar 1922–21 Jan 1923
Lieutenant R B S REFORD, MC (1st tour)	22 Jan 1923–02 Jun 1926
Major T E G NUGENT, MC	03 Jun 1926–03 Oct 1928
Captain C L J BOWEN	04 Oct 1928–16 Oct 1929
Lieutenant T H H GRAYSON Father of Patrick, Grandfather of Mark.	17 Oct 1929–30 Sep 1931
Major A F L GORDON, DSO MC (2nd tour)	01 Oct 1931–01 May 1934
Major R B S REFORD, MC (2nd tour)	02 May 1934–07 May 1936
Major E R MAHONY	08 Jul 1936–26 Jul 1938
Major R F ROSS	07 Jul 1938–31 Aug 1939
Major A F L GORDON, DSO MC (3rd tour)	01 Sep 1939–01 Jun 1942
Major R C ALEXANDER	02 Jun 1942–01 Jul 1945
Major H L S YOUNG, DSO Retired Hon Brig Dec 1962. Died 7 Feb 2004. Father of Savill served 63–67.	02 Jul 1945–18 Dec 1946
Major J D HORNUNG, OBE MC Uncle of Capt Bernard served 76–90. Later Lt Col Sir John KCVO	19 Dec 1946–25 Mar 1948
Major P F I REID Retired as Col May 1959. Gentleman-at-arms. Died 9 Dec 1994.	26 Mar 1948–01 Jul 1950
Major M J P O'COCK Retired as Brig CBE MC MA Jun 1974. Stepson of Guy Tylden-Wright. Stepfather of Col J H O'H Pollock, Comd Offr.-96–98. Father-in-law of Maj Gen Sir Robert Corbett.	03 Jul 1950–27 Oct 1952

Major J W BERRIDGE   28 Oct 1952–03 Oct 1954
Retired as Hon Brig may 1966.

Major J D CHICHESTER-CLARK   04 Oct 1954–31 Dec 1955
Later Prime Minister of Northern Ireland

Major A B MAINWARING-BURTON   01 Jan 1956–15 Mar 1958
Father of Capts Jeremy 75–80 and Guy 76–79

Major C W D HARVEY-KELLY   16 Mar 1958–03 Jan 1960
Retired as Col Apr 1969. Later made MBE for services to IG welfare in Ireland.

Major J A ALYMER   04 Jan 1960–21 Jan 1962
Retired as Col Oct 1980. CO 1IG Feb 66 – Jun 68 incl Aden.

Major J N GHIKA   22 Jan 1962–19 Jan 1964
Retired as Brig CBE Jul 1992. Died Aug 1981. Father of Brig Christopher 93–.

Major D S GREHAN   30 Jan 1964–27 Feb 1967

Major D J FAULKNER   28 Feb 1967–13 Apr 1969
Served 55–71. Died Mar 93. Father Lt Col W D MC, CO 1IG killed in action Norway
14 May 1940.

Major H C BLOSSE-LYNCH   14 Apr 1969–14 Jul 1971

Major S G B BLEWITT   15 Jul 1971–10 Jan 1974
Later Keeper of the Privy Purse, GCVO.

Major S G O'DWYER   11 Jan 1974–01 Feb 1976
Retired as Lt Col CVO Nov 1987. Private Secretary to Princes Andrew & Edward.
Father of Colonel Michael served 89–13.

Major T C P BROOKE   02 Feb 1976–28 Sep 1977

Major W W MAHON   29 Sep 1977–13 Dec 1979
Retired as Col Sir William Bt Jul 1992. Commandant Guards Depot, Pirbright.
Gentleman-at-Arms. Last Regular serving officer as Regt Lt Col 85–88.

Major R J S BULLOCK-WEBSTER (1st tour)   14 Dec 1979–06 Mar 1983
Father of Maj James served 04–14.

Major H R G WILSON   07 Mar 1983–10 Jan 1985
Retired as Brig Mar 1997.

Major S J H LLOYD   11 Jan 1985–05 Feb 1987
Retired as Lt Col 1993.

Major J B O'GORMAN (1st tour)   06 Feb 1987–10 Nov 1988
Retired as Lt Col Dec 02. Father of Capt Sam served 07–13.

Major R J S BULLOCK-WEBSTER (2nd tour)   11 Nov 1988–08 May 1990
Retired as Lt Col, OBE 1993.

Major A J D SHERIDAN   08 May 1990–05 Jun 1993
Retired as Major 1993.

Major T W J MACMULLEN   05 Jun 1993–01 Nov 1996
Last Regular serving Regimental Adjutant. Son of late Capt Jim MC who served 43–47
Brother of Lt Col Peter 90–.

Lieutenant Colonel (Retd) R J S BULLOCK-WEBSTER OBE (3rd tour)   01 Nov 1996–17 Mar 2008

Lieutenant Colonel (Retd) J B O'GORMAN (2nd tour)   18 Mar 2008–31 Dec 2012

Colonel (Retd) T C R B PURDON OBE   1 Jan 2012
Father of Capt James served 10–13

Appendix I

COMMANDING OFFICERS
1ST BATTALION IRISH GUARDS

Lieutenant Colonel R J COOPER, MVO
2 May 1900–1 May 1904
Former Grenadier. Served in Egyptian war of 1882. Wounded in Gallipoli as Brig Gen CB, CVO 16 Aug 15.

Lieutenant Colonel D J PROBY
2 May 1904–1 May 1908
Transferred from Coldstream

Lieutenant Colonel G C NUGENT, MVO
2 May 1908–13 Jul 1909
Later Killed in Action

Lieutenant Colonel C FITZCLARENCE, VC
14 Jul 1909–13 Jul 1913
Killed in action 12 Nov 1914 Polygon Wood, Zonnebeke commanding 1st Guards Brigade. Son Eddie served 18–45 (27–39 RARO) Became 6th Earl of Munster.

Lieutenant Colonel the Hon G H MORRIS
14 Jul 1913–1 Sep 1914
Killed in Action at Villers-Cotterets.

Major H A HERBERT-STEPNEY (Second in Command)
2 Sep 1914–17 Sep 1914
Killed in Action

Lieutenant Colonel Lord ARDEE
18 Sep 1914–3 Nov 1914

Lieutenant Colonel the Hon J F TREFUSIS, DSO
4 Nov 1914–15 Aug 1915
Killed in Action

Lieutenant Colonel G H C L MADDEN
16 Aug 1915–1 Nov 1915
Killed in Action

Lieutenant Colonel R C A McCALMONT, DSO
2 Nov 1915–2 Mar 1917

Lieutenant Colonel the Hon H R L G ALEXANDER, DSO MC
3 Mar 1917–22 May 1917
Retired as Field Marshal The Rt Hon The Earl Alexander of Tunis KG PC GCB OM GCMG CSI DSO MC DCL LLD. Died 16 Jun 1969. Father of Shane served 54–58, Hon Brian 58–60.

Lieutenant Colonel R R C BAGGALLAY, DSO MC
20 Jun 1918–2 Mar 1919
Retired as Lt Col May 1926

Lieutenant Colonel the Hon T E VESEY
3 Mar 1919–25 Apr 1919
Brother of 6th Viscount de Vesci

Lieutenant Colonel the Hon L J P BUTLER, CMG DSO
26 Apr 1919–14 Jul 1919

Lieutenant Colonel the Hon T E VESEY
15 Jul 1919–13 May 1922

Lieutenant Colonel The Hon H R L G ALEXANDER DSO MC
14 May 1922–20 Jan 1926
Retired as Field Marshal The Rt Hon The Earl Alexander of Tunis KG PC GCB OM GCMG CSI DSO MC DCL LLD. Died 16 Jun 1969. Father of Shane served 54–58, Hon Brian 58–60.

Lieutenant Colonel R V POLLOK, CBE DSO
21 Jan 1926–13 Jan 1930
Retired as Maj Gen CB, CBE DSO March 1941. GOC Northern Ireland.

Lieutenant Colonel the Viscount GOUGH, MC
14 Jan 1930–13 Jan 1934
Father of Lt Shane who served 62–70. First MC in the Regiment, lost an arm winning MC on the Aisne 1914.

Lieutenant Colonel J S N FITZGERALD, MBE MC Retired as Col CVO Oct 1945	14 Jan 1934–19 Jul 1936
Lieutenant Colonel T E G NUGENT, MVO MC Retired as Lt Col Sir Terence (Tim) GCVO. Died 1974.	20 Jul 1936–21 Jul 1936
Lieutenant Colonel R B S REFORD, MC Retired as Hon Brig Mar 1944. Son served 40–45.	22 Jul 1936–9 Aug 1938
Lieutenant Colonel W D FAULKNER, MC★ Commandant of Guards Depot Caterham, Sep 1934–Sep 37 in rank of Maj (hence the historic term Commandant). Killed in Action Norway 14 May 1940. Father of Maj David who served 55–71 – Died Mar 93.	10 Aug 1938–14 May 1940
Lieutenant Colonel E R MAHONY Retired as Brig 1949. Died 1990. Father-in-law of Maj Mike MacEwan 49–58.	15 May 1940–16 Dec 1941
A/Lieutenant Colonel T W GIMSON Retired as Col Nov 1950.	27 Dec 1941–5 Jun 1942
Lieutenant Colonel H S PHILLPOTS, MC	6 Jun 1942–14 Feb 1943
Lieutenant Colonel C A MONTAGU-DOUGLAS-SCOTT, DSO Son of Lord Herbert Andrew M-G S 01–07. Father of Capt D A who served 50–55	15 Feb 1943–27 Apr 1944
A/Lieutenant Colonel T W GIMSON Retired as Col Nov 1950.	23 May 1944–14 Nov 1944
Lieutenant Colonel C R McCAUSLAND, MC Son Marcus served 53–56 Murdered by IRA in NI in 1972.	15 Nov 1944–22 Jul 1945
Lieutenant Colonel H S PHILLPOTS, MC	23 Jul 1945–14 Mar 1946
Lieutenant Colonel D H FITZGERALD, DSO Retired as Hon Brig DSO OBE Mar 1958. Died 2002	15 Mar 1946–17 Jul 1947
Lieutenant Colonel B O P EUGSTER, DSO MC Retired as General Sir Basil KCB KCVO CBE DSO MC. Died 1984. Father of Capt Christopher who served 60–63 & Capt Tim who served 60–65.	22 Jul 1947–23 Aug 1947
Lieutenant Colonel D M L GORDON-WATSON OBE MC Retired as Brig OBE MC (& 2 bars) Mar 1963. Died 20 May 2002 Father of Julian who served 63–71.	24 Aug 1947–19 Jan 1951
Lieutenant Colonel B O P EUGSTER, DSO MC Retired as General Sir Basil KCB KCVO CBE DSO MC. Died 1984. Father of Capt Christopher who served 60–63 & Capt Tim who served 60–65.	3 Apr 1951–13 Jul 1954
Lieutenant Colonel H L S YOUNG, DSO Son of Lt GES Young KIA 1917. Retired Hon Brig Dec 1962. Died 7 Feb 2004. Father of Savill who served 63–67.	5 Aug 1954–30 Jun 1957
Lieutenant Colonel J W BERRIDGE, MBE Retired Hon Brig May 1966. Grandfather of Capt Will Jenkins 09–14.	1 Jul 1957–6 Dec 1959
Lieutenant Colonel M J P O'COCK, MC Retired as Brig CBE MC MA Jun 1974. Stepson of Guy Tylden-Wright. Stepfather of Col J H O'H Pollock CO 96–98. Father-in-law of R J S Corbett CO 81–84.	7 Dec 1959–24 Sep 1961
Lieutenant Colonel R S LANGTON, MVO MC Retired as Col. Died 6 Jul 1992. Father of Col Christopher, served 69 – 01. Grandfather of Maj John served 02–12.	25 Sep 1961–18 Jan 1964
Lieutenant Colonel C W D HARVEY-KELLY Retired as Col Apr 1969. Later made MBE for services to IG welfare in Ireland.	19 Jan 1964–11 Jan 1966
Lieutenant Colonel J A AYLMER Retired as Col Oct 1980. Commanded 1IG in Aden 1967.	7 Feb 1966–26 Jun 1968
Lieutenant Colonel J G F HEAD, MBE Retired as Col CBE Apr 1982.	27 Jun 1968–4 Aug 1970

Lieutenant Colonel R A C PLUMMER   5 Aug 1970–28 Aug 1972
Retired as Brig Dec 1984. Father of Maj John serving 00–. Father-in-law of Maj Matt
Collins 97–11 KIA Afghanistan.

Lieutenant Colonel G A ALLAN, OBE   29 Aug 1972–15 Sep 1974
Retired as Col May 1982. Father-in-law of Capt Bernard Hornung 76–90. Died 15
Jan 2009.

Lieutenant Colonel R T P HUME   16 Sep 1974–27 Jan 1977
Retired as Brig Aug 1987.

Lieutenant Colonel J H BAKER   27 Jan 1977–25 Mar 1979
Retired as Col Sep 1986. MBE. Brother of Capt Charles who served 69 – 75. Died Oct 09.

Lieutenant Colonel D B W WEBB-CARTER, MC   26 Mar 1979–30 Aug 1981
Retired as Brig OBE MC ADC Nov 1995.

Lieutenant Colonel R J S CORBETT   31 Aug 1981–31 Jan 1984
Retired as Maj Gen Sir Robert KCVO, CB Aug 1994. Father of Capt Michael served
96 – 99. Son-in-law of Brig Mick O'Cock who served 58 – 94.

Lieutenant Colonel S G O'DWYER   1 Feb 1984–4 Jul 1986
Retired as Lt Col CVO Nov 1987. Private Secretary to Princes Andrew & Edward.
Father of Col MGC O'Dwyer OBE served 88–13.

Lieutenant Colonel H R G WILSON   5 Jul 1986–14 Dec 1988
Retired as Brig Mar 1997. Uncle of Capt J AC Campbell-Johnston 89–94.

Lieutenant Colonel B W F HOLT   15 Dec 1988–5 Dec 1990
Retired as Col CBE Apr 1998.

Lieutenant Colonel C R LANGTON   6 Dec 1990–30 Jul 1993
Retired as Col OBE Jul 2001 from DA Moscow. Son of late Col R S Langton.
Nephew of Col T C Langton MC. Father of Maj Johnny who served 02–12

Lieutenant Colonel S J L ROBERTS OBE   31 Jul 1993–5 Feb 1996
Retired as Maj Gen Sir Sebastian KCVO 2010. Commanded 1IG on 1st Op
BANNER tour in E Tyrone. Brother of Maj Cassian served 82–00, & Maj Fabian
served 96–12. Father of Capt Julian 05–10 and Capt Orlando 06–10.

Lieutenant Colonel J H O'H POLLOCK MBE   6 Feb 1996–10 Dec 1998
Retired as Colonel Aug 2009. Son of Brig J P O'H served 40–74.

Lieutenant Colonel W G CUBITT OBE   10 Dec 1998–26 Mar 2001
Retired Aug 2011 as Major General Sir William Cubitt KCVO, CBE. Commanded
1IG on Op AGRICOLA. Son-in law of Martin Pym served 46–48. Bro-in-law of
Capt William Pym served 88–93.

Lieutenant Colonel J R H STOPFORD   26 Mar 2001–27 Mar 2003
Retired as Brig Dec 2015. Commanded during Op TELIC 1. Cousin of Capt the
Hon Jeremy Stopford LVO 78–84.

Lieutenant Colonel C P H KNAGGS OBE   5 Mar 2003–13 Feb 2006
Serving as Col OBE. Commanded 1IG on Op BANNER in South Armagh and Op
TELIC 1. Cousin of Lt Col David Foster 73–94.

Lieutenant Colonel M G C O'DWYER MBE   13 Feb 2006–16 Apr 2008
Son of Lt Col Sean O'Dwyer who served 59–87, incl CO 1IG 84–86. Commanded
1IG on Op TELIC 10, Iraq May-Dec 07. Retired as Col OBE 2013.

Lieutenant Colonel B C FARRELL MBE   16 Apr 2008–27 Apr 2010
Retired as Colonel Jun 2011.

Lieutenant Colonel C J GHIKA OBE   27 Apr 2010–2 May 2012
Son of Brig John CBE 51–81. Commanded 1IG on Op HERRICK 13.

Lieutenant Colonel E T BOANAS   2 May 2012–1 Dec 2014
Retired at Lt Col Dec 2015. Commanded 1IG on Op TOSCA 20 in Cyprus.

Lieutenant Colonel I A J TURNER DSO   1 Dec 2014–17 Mar 2017
Nephew of Maj Roger Belson 69–82.

Lieutenant Colonel J A E PALMER MBE (Designate)   17 Mar 2017–

Appendix J

REGIMENTAL SERGEANT MAJORS – 1ST BATTALION

RSM C A BURT
Transferred from Scots Guards. Transferred to Rifle Bde Jan 1905. Retired as WO1 27 Jan 1916.

11 Sep 1900–12 Jan 1905

RSM C A BAYLIS
Retired 1 May 1908.

13 Jan 1905–01 May 1908

RSM J McD MYLES
Retired 16 May 1913.

02 May 1908–16 May 1913

RSM J KIRK, MC
Died from wounds 2 Apr 1916.

17 May 1913–02 Apr 1916

RSM T CAHILL, DCM
Retired 19 May 1922.

03 Apr 1916–24 Apr 1922

RSM C HARRADINE, MBE DCM
Appointed GSM LONDIST 27 Jul 1927. Retired 11 Feb 1935.

25 Apr 1922–26 Jul 1927

RSM P CONNOLLY
Retired 8 Jun 1931.

27 Jul 1927–08 Jun 1931

RSM J F LINNANE, MM
Retired 12 Jan 1935.

09 Jun 1931–12 Jan 1935

RSM J A STACK, MC
Commissioned 12 Aug 1943. Retired Maj (QM) MC 9 Apr 1957.

13 Jan 1935–06 Jul 1940

RSM H F McKINNEY
Commissioned 28 Feb 1943. Retired 9 Jul 1948 Capt (QM) MBE.

07 Jul 1940–27 Feb 1943

RSM B F T PEILOW
Killed in action at the Bou 1943

09 Mar 1943–27 Apr 1943

RSM J McLOUGHLIN
Wounded in action.

27 May 1943–25 Jan 1944

RSM W I ROONEY, MM
Wounded at the Bou 1943, MM Palestine 1938.

26 Jan 1944–23 Feb 1944

RSM F KENNY
Died in Service 9 Jun 1951.

24 Feb 1944–19 May 1944

RSM W I ROONEY, MM
Appointed RSM Guards Training Battalion Jun 1944.
Commissioned 6 Dec 1952. Retired Maj (QM) 21 Jun 1967

20 May 1944–07 Jun 1944

RSM T R KELLY
Retired 14 Jun 1946.

08 Jun 1944–02 Mar 1946

RSM G N HOWE
Commissioned 19 Mar 1951. Retired Maj (QM) MBE.

03 Mar 1946–15 Dec 1949

RSM W I ROONEY, MM
(Third tour)

16 Dec 1949–15 Nov 1952

RSM M MORAN, MM
Retired 15 Jun 1969 MBE.

02 Dec 1952–15 Dec 1954

RSM P L MERCER MBE, MM
Commissioned 5 Jul 1959. Retired Maj (QM) 16 Mar 1971,
MM North Africa.

26 Jan 1955–05 Jan 1959

RSM A BELL
Commissioned 6 Nov 1961. Retired Maj (Regtl QM) MBE 11
Nov 1973

06 Jan 1959–07 Nov 1961

RSM M T O'BRIEN, MM
Retired 4 Jul 1963, MM Anzio.

21 Nov 1961–02 Jan 1963

RSM J STUART
Retired 31 Dec 1965.

17 Jan 1963–31 Aug 1965

RSM V SULLIVAN
Commissioned 13 Jun 1967. Retired Maj (QM) 1 Sep 1975.   01 Sep 1965–13 Jun 1967

RSM J B OFFICER
Commissioned 1 Sep 1968. Retired Lt (SSC) 31 Sep 1969. Died   14 Jan 1967–31 Aug 1968
May 2007.

RSM J F DUFFY
Commissioned 31 Mar 1971. Retired Maj (Regtl QM) MBE 12   01 Sep 1968–31 Mar 1971
Feb 1983

RSM H F GROVES
Commissioned 24 Jun 1974. First Pipe Major to be Regimental   01 Apr 1971–23 Jun 1974
Sergeant Major. Retired Lt Col (QM) MBE 27 Dec 1989.

RSM T J CORCORAN
Commissioned 16 Oct 1976. Retired Maj (IRC) 30 Sep 1982.   24 Jun 1974–15 Oct 1976

RSM D M THOMPSON
Yeoman of the Guard, Retired 22 Mar 1979.   16 Oct 1976–15 Oct 1978

RSM D P CLEARY
Appointed AcSM RMAS. Retired 31 Dec 1987 MBE.

16 Oct 1978–22 Jan 1980

RSM T YOUNG
Commissioned 7 Jul 1981. Retired Maj (QM) 10 Jun 1992.

23 Jan 1980–14 Jun 1981

RSM V F McLEAN
Retired 9 Jun 1988. Cadet Commission 1983. Lt Col OC
Ampleforth College CCF. Retired Aug 09.

15 Jun 1981–8 Jun 1983

RSM R A D KELLY
Commissioned 18 Jul 1986. Camp Commandant LONDIST.
Retired Maj (QM) MBE 8 Jan 1998.

09 Jun 1983–14 Jun 1986

RSM V M McELLIN
Commissioned 12 Jun 1988. Retired Capt 12 Jun 1993.
Appointed Asst Regtl Adj RHQ 1999. Retired 2011.

15 Jun 1986–11 Jun 1988

RSM J J LYNCH
Commissioned 18 Jun 1990. Retired Capt (SSC (LE)) 1 Apr
1996. Maj NRPS Cambridge UOTC.

12 Jun 1988–06 Jun 1990

RSM J C KNOWLES
Commissioned 10 Apr 1992. Retired Maj (QM) MBE 11 Oct 2004.

07 Jun 1990–10 Apr 1992

RSM P J CLONEY
Commissioned (Late Entry) 1 Apr 1995. QM Hong Kong Military Service Corps. Lt Col Staff (QM) Army Training Regt Pirbright 2009. Retired 2011.

11 Apr 1992–27 Jan 1995

RSM M F BRENNAN
Commissioned OC Tonbridge College CCF 1997.

28 Jan 1995–23 Mar 1997

RSM C R BOWKER
Retired as WO1 5 Jul 1999. Son of Sgt Bowker served 1950–60s.

24 Mar 1997–22 Jan 1999

RSM A GARDNER
Commissioned (Late Entry) 8 Apr 2002. QM LONDONS.

23 Jan 1999–21 Jul 2001

RSM J S T MATEER
Commissioned Capt IRC (Late Entry) 14 Mar 2005. QM 1IG.

28 Jul 2001–04 Apr 2003

RSM K T D FOX
Commissioned Capt SSC (Late Entry) 2 Apr 2004. MTO 1IG. QM(T) 09.

05 Apr 2003–17 Mar 2004

RSM S M NICHOLS
Became AcSM RMAS. Commissioned Aug 2007.

17 Mar 2004–11 Jun 2005

RSM J C DONALDSON
Commissioned SSC (Late Entry) 1 Apr 2007. Welfare Officer 1IG. MTO 1 GREN GDS 2009.

12 Jun 2005–5 Jan 2007

RSM P W LALLY
Commissioned SSC (Late Entry) 1 Apr 2009. Recruiting Officer 1IG. Retired Capt (Late Entry) 2011 to become RSM to Royal Hospital, Chelsea.

5 Jan 2007–2 Feb 2009

RSM R A MARTIN
Commissioned 2011, delayed by choice to be AcSM RMAS. Retired Capt (LE) 2012.

2 Feb 2009–17 Mar 2010

RSM S A McMICHAEL
Commissioned (Late Entry) 2014.

17 Mar 2010–16 Dec 2011

RSM J G PARKE
Commissioned (Late Entry) 2014.

16 Dec 2011–17 Mar 2014

RSM B R TAYLOR
Commissioned 2016.

17 Mar 2014–16 Mar 2016

RSM D HINTON (Designate)

17 Mar 2016–

Appendix K

QUARTERMASTERS 1ST BATTALION IRISH GUARDS

Major J FOWLES	23 May 1900–11 Feb 1914
Major H HICKIE, MBE MC	12 Feb 1914–01 Feb 1927
Major P MATHEWS	02 Feb 1927–01 Sep 1936
Major T D McCARTHY, MBE	02 Sep 1936–20 Mar 1941
Major J A STACK, MC	21 Mar 1941–08 Mar 1943
Major H F McKINNEY, MBE	09 Mar 1943–12 May 1945
Major J KEATING, MBE	13 May 1945–19 Mar 1951
Major G N HOWE	20 Mar 1951–26 Jan 1955
Major W I ROONEY, MBE MM	27 Jan 1955–26 Oct 1959
Major J J KELLY, MBE	27 Oct 1959–22 Aug 1962
Major W G JOHNSTONE, MBE DCM	23 Aug 1962–21 Jan 1966
Major P L MERCER, MBE MM	22 Jan 1966–09 Sep 1968
Major A BELL MBE	10 Sep 1968–31 Mar 1972
Major V SULLIVAN	01 Apr 1972–31 Dec 1973
Major J E WILLIAMS MBE	01 Jan 1974–14 Mar 1977
Major J P DUFFY MBE	15 Mar 1977–05 Oct 1980
Major R COWAP MBE	06 Oct 1980–13 May 1983
Major H F GROVES MBE	14 May 1983–23 Feb 1987
Major W E MATTHEWS MBE	24 Feb 1987–1 Jan 1990
Major R A D KELLY MBE	1 Jan 1990–17 Aug 1995
Major J F P FALOONE	18 Aug 1995–24 Mar 2000
Major P J CLONEY MBE	24 Mar 2000–24 Jun 2002
Major J C KNOWLES MBE	25 Jun 2002–11 Jun 2004
Major M PEARS	12 Jun 2004–11 May 2006
Major D J RYAN	12 May 2006–4 Jul 2008
Major P F SHIELDS	4 Jul 2008–27 Mar 2010
Major K D T FOX	27 Apr 2010–5 Sep 2011
Major J S T MATEER	5 Sep 2011–24 Jan 2013
Major P A FAGIN	25 Jan 2013–24 Jul 2015
Major P S NICHOLS MBE	25 Jul 2015–

COMMANDING OFFICERS AND STAFF SECOND AND THIRD BATTALIONS IRISH GUARDS

Formed at Warley Barracks in 1914 as 2nd (Reserve) Battalion. In July 1915 re-designated 3rd (Reserve) Battalion when 2nd Regular IG Battalion formed.

COMMANDING OFFICERS 3RD (RESERVE) BATTALION IRISH GUARDS
Lieutenant Colonel the Lord KERRY
Lieutenant Colonel the Hon T E VESEY

ADJUTANT 3RD (RESERVE) BATTALION IRISH GUARDS
Captain C A S WALKER

QUARTERMASTER (3RD) RESERVE) BATTALION IRISH GUARDS
Major B TINCKLER

REGIMENTAL SERGEANT MAJOR 3RD (RESERVE) BATTALION IRISH GUARDS
RSM G PRICE
Battalion Disbanded 1919, reformed 1941.

COMMANDING OFFICERS – 2ND BATTALION IRISH GUARDS
THE GREAT WAR
18 Jul 1915 – Formed as a Regular Battalion at Waverley Barracks from 2nd (Reserve) Battalion.

Lieutenant Colonel the Hon L J P BUTLER, CMG, DSO	16 Aug 1915–05 May 1916

17 Aug 1915 – Transferred to 2nd Gds Brigade, Guards Division.

Lieutenant Colonel P L REID, OBE	12 May 1916–12 Jan 1917
Lieutenant Colonel E B GREER, MC	13 Jan 1917–31 Jul 1917
Major R FURGUSON	01 Aug 1917–01 Oct 1917
Lieutenant Colonel the Hon HRG ALEXANDER, DSO, MC	02 Oct 1917–05 Nov 1918

8 Feb 1918 – Transferred to 4th Gds Brigade, 31st Division.
20th May 1918 – Transferred to GHQ Reserve. 1919 – Disbanded

2nd WORLD WAR
Battalion reformed as a Regular Armoured Battalion

Lieutenant Colonel J C HAYDON, DSO★, OBE,	15 May 1939–13 Oct 1940
Lieutenant Colonel G L VERNEY, MVO	14 Oct 1940–21 Jun 1942
Lieutenant Colonel C K FINLAY	22 Jun 1942–17 Aug 1944
Lieutenant Colonel G A M VANDELEUR, DSO	18 Aug 1944–07 Apr 1945
Lieutenant Colonel J S O HASLEWOOD, MC	08 Apr 1945–05 Jun 1945
Lieutenant Colonel G A M VANDELEUR, DSO	06 Jun 1945–28 Feb 1946

Lieutenant Colonel D M L GORDON-WATSON, MC	01 Mar 1946–30 Jan 1947
Lieutenant Colonel B O P EUGSTER, DSO, MC	31 Jan 1947–30 Jun 1947

ADJUTANTS – 2ND BATTALION IRISH GUARDS

Captain the Hon T E VESEY	01 Jan 1915–27 Jul 1915
Captain J S N FITZGERALD	28 Jul 1915–15 Dec 1916
Lieutenant P G DENSON	16 Dec 1916–30 Dec 1916
Captain C MOORE	01 Jan 1917–28 Jul 1917
Captain M R HELY-HUTCHINSON, MC	01 Jan 1917–28 Jul 1917
Captain C E R HANBURY	29 Jul 1917–30 Sep 1917
Lieutenant D FITZGERALD	29 Jul 1917–30 Sep 1917
Lieutenant A R PYM	29 Jul 1917–30 Sep 1917
Captain T E G NUGENT	01 Oct 1917–05 Jun 1918
Captain W D FAULKNER	01 Oct 1917–05 Jun 1918

Battalion Disbanded 1919
Battalion reformed as a Regular Armoured Battalion 15 May 1939

Captain J H S PHILLPOTTS, MC	15 Aug 1939–16 Jul 1940
Captain J D HORNUNG, MC	17 Jul 1940–01 Feb 1942
Captain J W BERRIDGE	02 Feb 1942–21 Apr 1943
Captain D A PEEL	21 Apr 1943–22 Mar 1944
Captain A C CRICHTON	23 Mar 1944–4 Aug 1944
Captain R S LANGTON, MC	05 Aug 1944–11 Sep 1944
Captain J V D TAYLOR, MC★	12 Sep 1944–24 Jul 1945
Captain A B MAINWARING-BURTON	25 Jul 1945–22 Aug 1946
Captain D A LAMPARD, MC	23 Aug 1946–03 Jan 1947
Captain J D CHICHESTER-CLARK	04 Jan 1947–30 Jun 1947

QUARTERMASTERS – 2ND BATTALION IRISH GUARDS

Major J BRENNAN	16 Jul 1915–05 Jun 1918
Major R GAMBLE MC	17 Jul 1918–31 Mar 1919
Major J KEATING MBE	15 May 1939–30 Apr 1945
Major A F MCKINNEY MBE	01 May 1945–30 Jun 1947

REGIMENTAL SERGEANT MAJORS – 2ND BATTALION IRISH GUARDS

RSM R GAMBLE, MC	16 Jul 1915–31 Mar 1919
RSM C HARRADINE,MBE,DCM	17 Jul 1918–31 Mar 1919
RSM R HASTINGS	15 Mar 1939–23 Mar 1942
RSM J MCGARRITY	24 Aug 1942–7 Aug 1945
RSM E NYE	08 Aug 1945–30 Jun 1947

COMMANDING OFFICERS 3RD BATTALION IRISH GUARDS

Lieutenant Colonel J O E VANDELEUR DSO	24 Oct 1941–14 Nov 1944
Lieutenant Colonel T W GIMSON	15 Nov 1944–16 Jan 1945
Lieutenant Colonel B O P EUGSTER DSO, MC	17 Jan 1945–21 Feb 1945
Lieutenant Colonel D H FITZGERALD DSO	22 Feb 1945–15 Mar 1946

ADJUTANTS 3RD BATTALION IRISH GUARDS

Captain H D M BARTON	25 Mar 1942–30 Apr 1943
Captain H C NEILSON	01 May 1943–19 Jul 1944

Captain J N FINLAY   20 Jul 1944–13 Mar 1945
Captain J C F QUINN   14 Mar 1945–04 Oct 1945
Captain P A McCALL   05 Oct 1945–15 Mar 1946

QUARTERMASTER 3RD BATTALION IRISH GUARDS
Captain R HASTINGS MBE   24 Aug 1942–15 Mar 1946

REGIMENTAL SERGEANT MAJORS 3RD BATTALION IRISH GUARDS
RSM J E GRANT   24 Oct 1941–11 Sep 1944
RSM G N HOWE   12 Sep 1944–15 Mar 1946
Merged into 1st Battalion in July 1946.

TRAINING BATTALION COMMANDING OFFICERS
Lieutenant Colonel the Viscount GOUGH MC   02 Sep 1939–01 Sep 1942
Lieutenant Colonel L D MURPHY MC   02 Sep 1942–01 Sep 1945
Lieutenant Colonel Sir J F R REYNOLDS Bt MBE   02 Sep 1945–14 Mar 1946
Lieutenant Colonel H S PHILLPOTTS MC   15 Mar 1946–25 Jul 1946

ADJUTANTS
Captain P R J BARRY   02 Sep 1939–28 Jan 1940
Captain J D MOORE   29 Jan 1940–05 Jan 1941
Captain E A S ALEXANDER   06 Jan 1941–24 Mar 1942
Captain E F GUINNESS   25 Mar 1942–11 Aug 1943
Captain A P DODD   12 Aug 1943–02 Jul 1944
Captain P A G RAWLINSON   03 Jul 1944–04 Jul 1945
Captain D F GOODBODY   05 Jul 1945–02 Feb 1946
Captain R MAHAFFY   03 Feb 1946–14 Mar 1946
Captain D LAMPARD MC   15 Mar 1946–25 Jul 1946

QUARTERMASTERS
Captain A ASHTON MBE   02 Sep 1939–14 Mar 1946
Captain R HASTINGS MBE   15 Mar 1946–25 Jul 1946

REGIMENTAL SERGEANT MAJORS
RSM J E GRANT   02 Sep 1939–20 Feb 1941
RSM T KELLY   21 Feb 1941–20 Feb 1944
RSM W ROONEY MM   07 Jun 1944–15 Jul 1946

After a Farewell to Armour parade in Germany on 29 June 1945 the Battalion disbanded in 1947 and personnel merged into the 1st Battalion.

LOCATIONS
1ST BATTALION IRISH GUARDS

Colour code
UK based
Overseas garrison
Operational tour

22 Sep 1900 – Battalion form-up	Pirbright Camp
19 Dec 1900 – 2 Sep 1901[1]	Chelsea Barracks, London
2 Sep 1901 – 1 May 1902	Tower of London, London
26 Nov 1901 – 4 Oct 1902	One section detached to No 2 Coy Guards Mounted Infantry – South Africa. [2nd Section from Jun 02]
1 May 1902 – 12 Jun 1902	Wellington Barracks, London
12 Jun 1902 – 8 Aug 1903	Chelsea Barracks, London
8 Aug 1903 – 27 Sep 1904	Oudenarde Barracks, Aldershot. 1st Bde, 1 Div,
27 Sep 1904 – 10 Oct 1905	Chelsea Barracks, London
10 Oct 1905 – 12 Oct 1906	Oudenarde Barracks, Aldershot
12 Oct 1906 – 1 Oct 1908	Wellington Barracks (Bn HQ & 4 Coys)
2 Oct 1908 – 1 Oct 1909	Victoria Barracks, Windsor
1 Oct 1909 – 4 Oct 1910	Blenheim Barracks, Aldershot (29 Offrs & 829 R+F)
4 Oct 1910 – 5 Oct 1911	Chelsea Barracks, London
5 Oct 1911 – 4 Oct 1911	Tower of London, London
4 Oct 1912 – Aug 1914	Wellington Barracks, London
Aug 1914 – Nov 1918	The Great War
Nov 1918 – Feb 1919	Cologne, Germany, Army of Occupation
1 Mar 1919 – 21 Jul 1919	Warley Barracks, Brentwood, Essex
21 Jul 1919 – Jul 1920	Wellington Barracks, London
Jul 1920 – Jul 1921	Aldershot
Jul 1921 – Mar 1922	Victoria Barracks, Windsor
Mar 1922 – Sep 1923	Tash Kishla Barracks, Constantinople, 1st Gds Bde
Sep 1923 – April 1924	Buena Vista Barracks, Gibraltar
Apr 1924 – Oct 1925	Inkerman Barracks, Woking
Oct 1925 – 23 Sep 1926	Maida Barracks, Aldershot
23 Sep 1926 – 5 Oct 1927	Wellington Barracks, London
5 Oct 1927 – 4 Oct 1928	Chelsea Barracks, London
4 Oct 1928 – 9 Oct 1929	Maida Barracks, Aldershot
10 Oct 1928 – 9 Oct 1930	Tower of London
9 Oct 1930 – 6 Oct 1931	Victoria Barracks, Windsor
6 Oct 1931 – 20 Aug 1932	Wellington Barracks, London
20 Aug 1932 – 29 Aug 1933	Barossa Barracks, Aldershot
29 Aug 1933 – 25 Aug 1934	Chelsea Barracks, London
25 Aug 1924 – 20 Sep 1935	Wellington Barracks, London
20 Sep 1935 – 14 Nov 1936	Chelsea Barracks, London
Nov 1936 – 3 Dec 1938	Kasr El Nil Barracks, Cairo, Egypt
10 Jul – 29 Sep 1938	Nablus, Palestine
16 Dec 1938 – 6 May 1939	Tower of London
6 May 1939 – Apr 1940	Wellington Barracks
Apr 1940 – Nov 1942	Sanderstead/Northwood, London

---

1. Until the outbreak of the Second World War, it was normal to change barrack location every year.

01 Apr – 04 Jun 1940	Norway, 24th Guards Bde [MS *Chobry* sunk]
Jul – Nov 1940	Western Heights, Dover [RAF Battle of Britain]
Nov 1942 – Feb 1943	Ayr, Scotland
Mar – Dec 1943	North Africa, 24th Indep Guards Bde, [The Bou]
Jan – Mar 1944	Op SHINGLE – Italy [Anzio]
May 1944 – Sep 1945	1IG used as UK Holding Bn for 2 & 3IG
Sep – Nov 1945	Hawick, Scotland
Nov 1945 – Mar 1946	Hazlemere Park Camp, High Wycombe. (Combine with 3IG)
Mar 1946 – Mar 1947	Chelsea Barracks, 2 Coys at Tower of London
Mar 1947 – Jun 1948	Palestine. GSM clasp awarded 'Palestine'
Jun 1948 – Apr 1949	Tripoli, Libya
May 1949 – Feb 1951	Chelsea Barracks, London
Feb 1951 – Oct 1953	Llanelly Barracks, Hubbelrath, West Germany
Mar – Jul 1953	Albuhera Bks, Aldershot (for Coronation)
Oct – Dec 1953	Pirbright Camp
Dec 1953 – Mar 1956	Canal Zone, Egypt. GSM clasp awarded 'Canal Zone'
Mar – Jul 1956	Lydd Camp, Kent
Jul 1956 – Jun 1957	Wellington Barracks, London
Jun 1957 – Jun 1958	Shorncliffe Camp, Kent, 1st Gds Bde
Jun 1958 – Nov 1958	Nicosia, Cyprus. GSM clasp awarded 'Cyprus'
Nov 1958 – Nov 1960	Victoria Barracks Windsor
Dec 1960 – Dec 1961	The Barracks, Caterham
Nov 1961 – Jul 1964	Llanelly Bks, Hubbelrath, West Germany
Feb 1962 – Nov 1964	No 3 Coy attached to 2SG in Kenya
Jul 1963 – Oct 1966	Chelsea Barracks, London
Aug 1964 – Feb 1967	No 9 Coy attached to 1SG in Malaysia – Commonwealth Bde. GSM Clasps awarded 'Malay Peninsula & Borneo'
Oct 1966 – Aug 1967	Aden – 24 Inf Bde. GSM Clasp 'South Arabia'
Aug 1967 – Sep 1968	Elizabeth Barracks, Pirbright
Sep 1968 – Mar 1970	Victoria Barracks, Windsor
Apr – Nov 1970	The Barracks, Caterham
Nov 1970 – Nov 1972	Stanley Fort and Lyemun Barracks, Hong Kong
Dec 1972 – Dec 1974	The Barracks, Caterham
Feb – Aug 1973	British Honduras (Belize wef 1 Jun 73) [Bn HQ & 2 Coys]
Dec 1974 – Nov 1977	Buller Bks, Munster, West Germany – 4th Gds Bde (BAOR)
Jun – Nov 1977	No 2 Coy Belize
Nov 1977 – Feb 1980	Victoria Barracks, Windsor
Feb – Jul 1979	Belize
Feb 1980 – Feb 1982	Chelsea Barracks, London
Feb 1982 – Feb 1986	Oxford Barracks, Munster – 4th Armd Bde
Feb 1986 – Jan 1990	Chelsea Barracks, London
Oct 1988 – Mar 1989	Belize
Jan 1990 – April 1992	Wavell Barracks, Berlin
Apr 1992 – Jan 1994	Elizabeth Barracks, Pirbright
Oct 1992 – Feb 1993	Op BANNER – Fermanagh, Northern Ireland
Jan 1994 – Aug 1996	Chelsea Barracks, London
Jun – Dec 1995	Op BANNER – East Tyrone, Northern Ireland
Aug 1996 – Feb 1998	Elizabeth Barracks, Pirbright
Feb 1998 – Aug 2003	Oxford Barracks, Munster, Germany
Feb – Aug 1999	Op AGRICOLA – Kosovo, Balkans
Mar – May 2003	Op TELIC – Iraq – 7 Armd Bde
	(Nos 1 & 2 Coy with the Royal Scots Dragoon Guards battle group)
Sep 2003 – Apr 2006	Wellington Barracks, London
Dec 2003 – Apr 2004	Op BANNER – South Armagh, Northern Ireland
Apr 2006 – Mar 2009	Mons Barracks, Aldershot
May 2007 – Dec 2007	Op TELIC 10 – Iraq – 1 Mech Bde
Mar 2009 – Sep 2011	Victoria Barracks, Windsor
Oct 2010 – Apr 2011	Op HERRICK 13 – Afghanistan – 16 AA Bde
Sep 2011 – Jun 2015	Mons Barracks, Aldershot
Apr 2013 – Oct 2013	Op HERRICK 18 – Afghanistan (No 2 Coy with 1 Mech Bde)
Jun 2015 –	Cavalry Barracks, Hounslow.

IRISH GUARDS REGIMENTAL BIBLIOGRAPHY

'ILLUSTRATIONS OF IRISH HISTORY AND TOPOGRAPHY, MAINLY OF THE 17TH CENTURY'.
Written by Ceasar Litton Falkiner (1863–1908) and published by Longman in 1908. Pages 74–102 cover 'His Majesty's regiment of Guards in Ireland' which the author claims as the original Irish Guards.

A SHORT HISTORY OF THE IRISH GUARDS
A 15 page pamphlet written by Lieutenant Valentine Williams and published in 1918 by Pulman and Sons Limited. It covers the activities of the Regiment in the First World War.

LIFE OF AN IRISH SOLDIER – Reminiscences of General Sir Alexander Godley
Reminiscences of General Sir Alexander Godley GCB, KCMG. Published in London in 1939 by John Murray. 'Alick' Godley was responsible for organising the Mounted Infantry Branch in South Africa, and was present with FitzClarence VC at the Siege of Mafeking. He commanded the ANZAC troops at Gallipoli, and later the British Army of the Rhine. He later became Governor of Gibraltar.

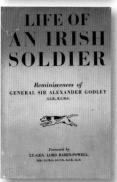

SEYMOUR VANDELEUR
A biography of one of the first officers to join the Regiment. He was killed in 1901 as a Lieutenant Colonel aged 31, having spent nearly all his career on active service. A slightly disjointed book written in the jingoistic style of the day but not everyone has a biography written by their Commanding Officer. His portrait hangs in the Officers' Mess of the Battalion and his medals and sword are displayed at Regimental Headquarters.

THE IRISH GUARDS IN THE GREAT WAR

Published by Macmillan and Co in 1923. Two
volumes by Rudyard Kipling who edited and compiled
them from diaries and papers as a tribute to his son
who was killed in 1915 whilst serving in the 2nd
Battalion.

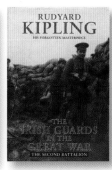
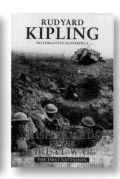

Reprinted with photographs in 1997 by Spellmount Publishers.

MONS, ANZAC and KUT

Published originally in 1919 anonymously by 'An MP'. Aubrey Herbert was one of the most
remarkable Irish Guardsmen of the Great War. The younger son of an Earl, he was the MP
for the Somerset constituency in which he lived but on the outbreak of war, and having
some friends in the Irish Guards, he sneaked aboard the boat which took them to France. He
had bought the necessary uniforms and went on to have an amazing war. He was at Mons,
Gallipoli and the invasion of Iraq; was a skilled linguist who negotiated two vital truces and
was offered the throne of Albania twice. He was wounded at Mons, escaped from German
captivity afterwards, was largely responsible for forcing the Government to investigate the
mismanagement of the Mesopotamian campaign whilst on leave from the war, and yet he has
been largely forgotten. His great-grandson, Lieutenant Colonel Edward Melotte (86–) a serving
Irish Guards Officer, has re-published his memoirs, which Herbert released anonymously in
1919, with additional comment and material. They are not only of great historical interest,
but reveal the inner life of a prominent figure of the generation which went through the most
horrific of wars that changed British society forever. He was immortalised by John Buchan as
Sandy Arbuthnot, the best friend of Richard Hannay in the series of novels which begins with
The Thirty-nine Steps. He first appears in the second book in a field hospital recovering from
wounds received at Loos. Published by Pen and Sword Books.

SPLENDOR & SQUALOR – The Disgrace and Disintegration of three aristocratic dynasties

Written by Marcus Scriven, published by Atlantic Books in 2009. The author, a former
Household Division officer, spent many years researching his four subjects but of interest
to the Regiment is Edward FitzGerald, 7th Duke of Leinster who served along with his
elder brother Desmond in the Micks. Lord Desmond was Adjutant of the 1st Battalion at
the outbreak of the Great War and was killed in a training accident on 3 March 1916 before
commanding the Battalion. He was visiting training accompanied by his padre, Father Lane-
Fox MC and encouraged the padre to throw a grenade. This he did, but dropped it, killing his
next Commanding Officer Lord Desmond, and seriously injuring himself. This resulted in the
title and family assets being passed to his younger brother Edward, the subject in the book. He
too served in the regiment but was discharged from the Army as being unsuitable for military
service. Sadly, he went on to prove the point by leading a feckless life of utter dissolution, dying
in penury having squandered a fortune equivalent to £500 million at today's values.

THE MAN WHO WAS GREENMANTLE – A Biography of Aubrey Herbert

Written by Margaret Fitzherbert, the second daughter of Evelyn Waugh. Her mother was
the daughter of Aubrey Herbert, who wrote 'MONS, ANZAC and KUT' (see above). Half
brother to Lord Caernarvon of Tutankhamen fame, member of a brilliant Balliol generation
which included Raymond Asquith, he was the original of John Buchan's romantic hero Sandy
Arbuthnot in Greenmantle. He dressed as a Mick Officer having borrowed some uniform and
marched to war with the Battalion in 1914. An intrepid traveller and polyglot he was twice
offered the throne of Albania, a man of legendary charm and chivalry. Published by John
Murray 1993.

THE IRISH AT THE FRONT

Michael MacDonagh and published by Hodder & Stoughton in 1916. Written as a tribute to all Irish Regiments in France, Flanders and at the Dardanelles, it is based on letters of regimental officers and men, interviews with the wounded and those invalided home. Although produced barely 18 months into the Great War, the Regiment's contribution is well covered including the Retreat from Mons, the role of the Battalion padre and Michael O'Leary's VC. He was the first Irish VC winner of the war and great propaganda was made of it. It was republished in 2010 by Leonaur Books.

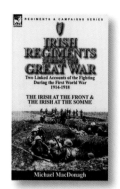

ACTIVE SERVICE DIARY – 21 Jan 1917 – 1 Jul 1917 –
Edward Hornby Shears

Published by his family in 1919, it is the diary of Lt Teddy Shears of the five months he served with 1 IG before being killed, aged 26, at Boesinghe on 4 Jul 1917. Having achieved a 1st in Greats at Oxford he entered the Civil Service but was considered so important it took him months before he was allowed to join the Army. A protégé of Tim Allen, also killed in action with 1IG, he had involved himself in charity work in the East End of London before the war. It is a simple, natural, business like record of the days work demonstrating modesty, compassion and a sense of duty. He is buried at Canada Farm Cemetery, Elverdinghe, near Ypres.

FATHER BROWNE'S FIRST WORLD WAR

Fr Frank Browne SJ, amateur photographer, is best known around the world for his 'Titanic' pictures – he took the last pictures of the doomed liner. He also served with great distinction as an Army chaplain during the Great War. He spent most of the war as Padre with the Irish Guards, was wounded five times and was seriously gassed and much decorated. Every time he recovered from injury he insisted on returning to the Front. His Commanding Officer at the time, who later became Field Marshal Alexander of Tunis described him as 'the bravest man I ever met'. This collection of his photographs published in 2014 by Messenger Publications is really an illustrated history of the Micks during and just after World War One.

MY BOY JACK. The search for Kipling's only son.

Published in 1997 by Leo Cooper Books. Rudyard Kipling's son John was killed in France at Loos in September 1915 but had no known grave and was commemorated at the Loos Memorial to the Missing. 77 years later the Commonwealth War Graves Commission, via an extraordinary piece of intellectual analysis, named a previously unknown soldier buried in St Mary's ADS Cemetery. This is the biography of a Mick Officer who was killed in action aged 18, which lead to his father writing two volumes on the Irish Guards in the Great War as a tribute to his son. David Haig wrote a stage play of the book which was first staged at Hampstead.

THE GUARDS DIVISION IN THE GREAT WAR

By G Headlam. Originally published in 1924. Reprinted by Naval & Military Press Ltd in 2001. 2 vols, 19 maps. IBSN 1843 421240. It is a strictly military record, based on the Divisional, Brigade and Battalion war diaries and supplemented by private diaries and personal narratives Volume 1 covers 1915 – October 1917. Volume 2 continues to the Armistice with Appendices and Index.

A SHORT HISTORY OF THE IRISH GUARDS

It was written by T H H Grayson who was Regimental Adjutant at the time and published in 1931 by Benham and Company. It covers the period from formation to 1927. Written to fill the requirement to study Regimental History as part of the syllabus for the 2nd & 3rd Class Certificates of Education for NCOs' promotion exams. An extra two chapters were added later to cover the period 1928 – 1942. It was republished 2004 by The Naval & Mlilitary Press.

BATTALION DIARY 1st Battalion Irish Guards – PALESTINE July – October 1938.

HISTORY OF THE IRISH GUARDS IN THE SECOND WORLD WAR

Published by Gale and Polden in 1949. Written by Major D J L FitzGerald MC who served with distinction as Adjutant in the 1st Battalion in North Africa and Italy. Very rare in its original form but reprinted in paperback by the Regiment.

HUGH DORMER'S DIARIES

Published in 1947 by Jonathan Cape. The diary of a remarkable Officer covers a period of about a year when he was detached from the Regiment to carry out SOE operations in occupied Europe. He records his sabotage operations behind enemy lines for which he was awarded a DSO. He was killed in action in Normandy while serving with the 2nd Battalion.

'SOME TALK OF ALEXANDER'

Written by Roger Grinstead (a pseudonym) published by Secker & Warburg in 1943. A novel, but a thinly disguised account of life of Guardsmen in a Section in the 2nd (Armoured) Battalion for the two years as it prepared for D Day. A best seller when first published and reprinted five times. Republished in paperback by Read Books on 12 Nov 2006.

'THEY DUG A HOLE'

A follow-up novel to 'Some Talk of Alexander' by Roger Grinstead published in 1946 about life in action in a Section from the D Day landings in Normandy up to Nijmegen.

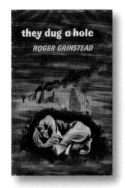

THE MICKS – The story of the Irish Guards

Published by Peter Davies and Pan in paperback and written by Major P V Verney who was a serving officer until his retirement in 1970. This is a very readable account of the Regiment's history from formation until 1968 and an ideal introduction to the Regiment's history to an outsider.

A MAN AT ARMS – Memoirs of Two World Wars – Francis Law

Colonel Hugh Francis d'Assisi Stuart Law DSO OBE MC was born in Dublin, brought up in Donegal, educated in England. He joined the Irish Guards from Sandhurst in 1915. Commissioned before he was 18 years old, he spent his first two years service at the Front without a break. A lifelong friend of Field Marshal Alexander, he led a long and colourful life. Few officers can have seen more action and he was decorated for bravery in both World Wars. He was sent to supervise the peace treaty that extinguished the Ottoman Empire and found himself caught up in Kemel Ataturk's revolution. His memoirs were originally written for his family but were published by Collins in 1983. He died aged 94.

FATHER DOLLY – THE GUARDSMAN MONK

A limited edition published in 1983 by Henry Melland and written by Anthony Wheatley, a former Irish Guards officer. Father Dolly Brookes was a contemporary of Field Marshal Alex in the First War and was Padre to the 1st Battalion in North Africa and Anzio during the Second. His reminiscences as a Mick officer and a Benedictine monk give a most unusual life story, very well and amusingly told. His blackthorn stick is now carried by the 1st Battalion's padre.

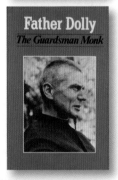

THE HONOUR AND THE SHAME, John Kenneally VC

An autobiography. Published in 1991 by Kenwood as KENNEALLY VC. A very interesting read of a Non Commissioned Officer who won his VC at the Bou. Republished by Headline Review in 2007 as the Honour and the Shame.

ALEX

Published in 1973 by Weidenfeld & Nicolson. Written by Nigel Nicolson who served in the Grenadiers in the Second World War. An excellent biography of the Field Marshal whose life revolved around the Micks even after he achieved High Command.

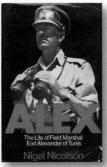

ALEXANDER

Written in 1946 by James A Robinson and published privately by the Banbridge Chronicle Press. A slim volume written to bring into relief the ties which existed between the Field Marshal, and his home at Caledon, Co Tyrone, Northern Ireland. It was written just before he took up the duties of Governor General of Canada. It contains a mine of information and fascinating cameos about him but is emphatically not a military assessment.

ALEXANDER OF TUNIS – A Biographical Portrait

Written by Norman Hillson in 1952 and published by W H Allen. The first proper biography of the Field Marshal published covering his life from boyhood, military career on to becoming Minister of Defence aged 61. He went on to live for another 17 years.

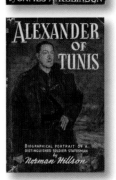

THE ALEXANDER MEMOIRS 1940–1945

Forward by Shane Alexander and Introduction by James Holland.
From the greatest Irish Guardsman. After his first meeting with General Alexander in August 1942, Lt Gen Sir Brian Horrocks wrote that; *'By repute he was Winston Churchill's fire brigade chief par excellence; the man who was always despatched to retrieve the most desperate situations'*. Churchill was in need of a fire chief. Allied forces had been chased back across the desert by Rommel. Alexander brought a new hope to the Desert Rats; he instilled them with his own confidence and thought of victory. Under his command Montgomery was ready to fight and win the Battle of El Alamein. Even as his generals drove the enemy from North Africa, Alexander was planning far ahead for Sicily and Operation Husky; the first seaborne invasion by either side during the war. It was said that before El Alamein the Allies never knew victory and after El Alamein never knew defeat; much of the credit goes to Alexander. For decades his contribution to the British efforts has been overlooked. Here, however, is a comprehensive edition of his personal and candid memoirs, first published in 1961, which includes judgements on such men as Montgomery, Patton and Churchill. He also details his role in leading the withdrawal of the 1st Infantry Division from Dunkirk and the bombing of Monte Cassino abbey. Field Marshal Alexander joined the regiment in 1911 and was Colonel of the Irish Guards from 1946 – 1969. This new edition is illustrated with photographs from Alex's own albums and some previously unpublished supplied by his family. These are the memoirs of one of the greatest British fighting Generals of all time and a Mick.

WITH ALEX AT WAR – From the Irrawaddy to the Po 1941–1945

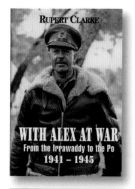

Published by Leo Cooper Books in 2000. Rupert Clarke was Field Marshal Alex's ADC for most of the War so this is an interesting 'fly on the wall' account of WW2 Generalship in action. It is not only an historical account but an invaluable lesson in leadership. It affirms Alex's own record that personal example, firmness of purpose, good manners and total integrity are themselves war-winning qualities.

THE CAMPAIGNS OF ALEXANDER OF TUNIS 1940–1945

There have been at least 6 other books written on Field Marshal Alexander, the last being by his ADC and published in 2000 (With Alex at War). This is the seventh and makes an excellent read. The background to Alex's life up until 1939 is dealt with briefly and the meat of the book concentrates on his qualities as a commander at Divisional level and above but with plenty of references to the Micks. His style of command is compared with the other great Generals of the war and a picture of coolness and bravery in the face of appalling adversity emerges. He was the last man off the beach at Dunkirk, having been especially chosen to be the commander there once it was clear that as much of the BEF had to be evacuated as possible. Churchill and Gort were reluctant to use the man they both considered to be the most able senior British officer, but it is a testimony to Alexander's powers that the evacuation was carried out so successfully – one (non-Army) officer's first question to him at his first O-Group on the beach was whether anyone knew how to conduct a formal capitulation! Alex was later parachuted in to make the best of the disastrous situation which was Burma. His reining in of expensive tactics by his juniors and unshakeable demeanour helped rally a forgotten army. Field Marshal Slim was not a huge fan of his commander though, and this book seeks to examine why that might have been. The Italian campaign is dealt with in most depth and is another tale of strategic steadiness enabling tactical victory, once more though a subordinate strays from Alexander's direction and the results are not disastrous, but certainly not as successful as Alexander's own plan would have been. A well-researched and well-written book, it is an easily-digestible insight into the greatest Mick officer of the war. Written by Adrian Stewart. Published by Pen and Sword in 2009.

Major D M (John) KENNEDY – A Tribute

This is a personal tribute compiled and published privately by the author, Robert Joscelyn, Earl of Roden, a fellow Irish Guardsman. He says *'It is a tribute not only about a half Irish, half Australian boy who loved Ireland, its countryside and people and who went on to become one of the greatest fighting Irish Guards Officers.'* Between 1940–1945, he fought in every battle in which the Regiment was deployed from Norway to Northwest Europe only to be killed in the last months of the war. On the beachhead at Anzio, after desperate fighting, some Irish Guardsmen were captured and the one question they were asked by their German interrogator was *'Where is Major Kennedy?'* He was a legendary figure admired by all who served with him.

THE ARMOURED MICKS 1941–45

Assembled by Capt 'Tinker' Taylor and Capt Sandy Faris and desktop published in 1997, it tells the story of the 2nd (Armoured) Battalion Irish Guards. It is a fine record of personal reminiscences and accounts of many incidents which have become part of the Mick heritage and folklore. The 2nd Battalion had been formed as infantry in 1939. It was with enthusiasm and some trepidation that it converted to tanks when the Guards Armoured Division was formed in 1941. From its inception the 2nd Battalion developed a personality of its own, distinct, not in valour but in character from that of the infantry.

EUROPE'S LAST VC – Guardsman Edward Charlton

After the Battle (magazine) No 49, 1985. It contains additional memoirs of then serving Irish Guards Officers and men as well as captured German Officers which led to the original citation being corrected and up-graded for the last VC awarded in World War II.

A SOLDIER'S STORY – Brigadier J O E Vandeleur DSO

Published privately by the author by Gale & Polden in 1967, it is the memoir of a legendary Irish Guardsman and wartime leader. (Michael Caine played him in the film '*A Bridge Too Far*') It was dedicated 'to my comrades in the Irish Guards. It has been my greatest pride to have been a member of the regiment.'

THE GUARDS ARMOURED DIVISION – A Short History

Written by Major General G L Verney DSO, MVO and published by Hutchinson in 1955. He was a former Irish Guards Officer who commanded 6th Guards Armoured Brigade. The aim was to show the part that units played in the general action of the Division, and the part that the Division played in the Campaign as a whole. It is a curious fact that the Division should now be remembered for the almost unopposed advance to Brussels than for the many hard battles it fought – the Normandy 'Bocage', the Belgium canals, Nijmegen, the Rhineland Battle, and the hard, gruelling and unspectacular actions in Germany.

THE EVER OPEN EYE – B D Wilson

Republished by Melrose Books in 2014. Brian Wilson was a Subaltern with the 3rd Battalion Irish Guards (Mounted Infantry) in North West Europe in 1944 and this is a personal reminiscence of his War and Op Market Garden in particular. His contention is that although the operation was ultimately a failure, the blame cannot be laid at the door of the British troops involved but criticises inadequate generalship for the failure.

FIGHTING WITH THE GUARDS

Published in 1958 by Evans Brothers, London. Keith Briant, already a published author and editor, was commissioned from Sandhurst into the Irish Guards in 1942 and fought in the NW Europe Campaign with 2IG. He retired as a Lt Col in 1951 to return to publishing. The author tells how the Household Brigade began and how it has shaped our history with a spirit and professionalism to turn apparent defeat into victory. The book is divided into four parts. Part I, Men – covers Guardsmen who won the VC in WW2 and includes a chapter entitled 'Up, the Micks!' on Sgt Kenneally's VC at the Bou. Part II – Tradition – traces the history, Part III – Action – is sub-titled Guards in Tanks 1941–1945 and in Part IV he covers the ceremonial side.

HE WALKED TALL – The Story of Canon Michael Casey

Written by Mary Whittle and published in 2002 by Gemini Print (Wigan) Ltd. It tells the life of a much loved Battalion Padre who served in Egypt and Palestine yet afterwards retained his links with the Regiment through the Irish Guards Association in Liverpool. In 2000, a processional cross was presented in his memory by ex Guardsman J J Fitzgerald for use in the Guards Chapel on Regimental occasions.

IRISH GUARDS – 1960

A hardback book produced under the direction of Regimental Headquarters by R K Chollerton in 1961. It is an excellent, mainly photographic, record of the regiment at that time, featuring a picture of every member of the Battalion.

DIPLOMATIC LIGHTWEIGHT – Memoirs of Sir John Curle

Published by AQ & DJ Publications 1992. John Curle joined the Foreign Office in 1939 and almost immediately joined the Regiment having met Bruce Reford, the Regimental Lieutenant Colonel, skiing in Klosters before the war. After a time with the Training Battalion he volunteered for the 5th Bn Scots Guards which was being formed to support the Finns against Hitler. A remarkable unit in that of the 1000 volunteers, 600 were Officers although only 20 were needed. 167 volunteered to join as Guardsmen. Many were founder members of the SAS, LRDG, and Commandos when 5SG was disbanded in March 1940. Recalled to the Foreign Office in 1941. It is fascinating memoir of a full and very interesting career. He died in 1997.

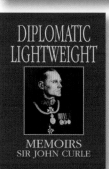

THE STORY OF THE GUARDS

Written by Sir Julian Paget, an editor of the Guards Magazine and first published by Osprey in 1976. Surprisingly, it was the first history of the Household Division as a whole. A coffee table book, it is very readable with excellent illustrations.

ALL THE QUEEN'S MEN

Another history of the Household Division published by Hamish Hamilton in 1977. This time by an outsider, Australian author with Republican tendencies, Russell Braddon, who became more impressed in preparing the book.

THE GUARDS

Published by Arum Press in 1981. Essentially a coffee table book of photographs (aimed at the American market) by American, Anthony Edgeworth with a narrative by British journalist John De St Jorre. The photographs taken on and off duty could not be bettered.

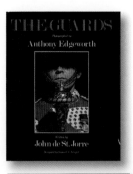

KOSOVO – Irish Guards Battle Group in the Balkans, April – May 1999

Fergus Greer, a renowned portrait photographer, who served as an Officer in the Regiment 1983–87 went to the Balkans as the first photographer to be officially accredited to the MOD as a War Artist. Attached to the Battalion, this book is an intimate photo record of Battalion life on operations, including narrative extracts from his journal.

IRISH GUARDS in KOSOVO

The Battalion produced this excellent 54 page booklet which includes a foreword by the Commanding Officer, Lt Col Bill Cubitt, the Order of Battle, chronology and coloured photographic record of events.

IRISH GUARDS – The First Hundred Years

This excellent, mainly photographic account, published by Spellmount Publishing was produced for the centenary of the Regiment. It is the story, mainly in pictures, of the regiment from its formation in 1900. It captures well all aspects of the formidable spirit of the 'Micks'. A copy was presented to every serving Mick in 2000 to commemorate the centenary of the Regiment.

THE TIMES OF MY LIFE – Sir John Gorman

Published in 2002 by Leo Cooper Books. John served in the 2nd (Armoured) Battalion in North West Europe 1944–45. His MC was legendary, awarded for ramming a German King Tiger tank. His varied career led him into the maelstrom of Northern Ireland politics and Deputy Speaker of the Legislative Assembly. Always a great supporter of the Regiment and participant in Regimental affairs, his son and grandson served as officers after him.

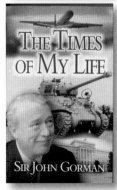

A PRICE TOO HIGH – An Autobiography – Peter Rawlinson

An autobiography by Lord Rawlinson of Ewell written in 1989 and published by Weidenfeld & Nicolson. He was a distinguished Conservative politician and former Attorney General. He devotes a chapter to his seven years in the Regiment during the 2nd World War, a formative period of his life. His love of the Regiment, to which he had strong family connections, comes through in this story of a civilised and compassionate man who lived a full and varied life but sadly died in 2006.

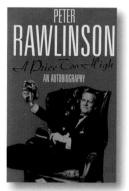

CLASH BY NIGHT: A Commando Chronicle – Brig Derek Mills-Roberts CBE DSO MC

Published in 1956 by William Kimber. Although it is about his exploits as a wartime commando, including the Dieppe Raid, he started his military life as a Mick and his widow presented his Irish Guards cufflinks to the Regiment.

DA CAPO AL FINE – Alexander Faris

Sandy (Alexander) Faris was born in County Tyrone in 1921 in a village surrounded by the Caledon Estate, owned by the father of Field Marshal Alexander. From an early age his musical talent was clear and he pursued a career which saw him conduct some of the greatest musicians and opera singers of the 20th Century, including Pavarotti and Domingo. He wrote the theme tune for the successful television series *'Upstairs, Downstairs'*, and conducted for the Royal Ballet, Saddler's Wells Opera and numerous West End musicals. Before his extraordinary career took off though, he spent three years as an officer in the Irish Guards, commissioning in 1943 and being demobilised in 1946. He was in the 2nd (Armoured) Battalion and was the Signals Officer for the break-out from Normandy, the dash to reach the paratroops in Nijmegen in Operation Market Garden, and saw Brussels liberated and the final surrender of Germany. After the war he lived in London with a fellow Mick officer, Tony de Lotbiniere, and embarked on a hugely successful career as a conductor.

The memoir is very direct, fascinating and funny and will be of huge interest to any music fans and Irish Guardsmen. It was published by Troubadour in 2009.

HE WHO DARED AND DIED – Sergeant Chris O'Dowd MM

This book published in 2011 by Pen & Sword tells the story on Christopher O'Dowd. Brought up in poverty in the West of Ireland, he ran away in 1939 to join the Irish Guards aged 18. After recruit training at the Guards Depot in Caterham he joined the 1st Battalion and participated in the ill fated expedition to Norway. He then volunteered to join the Commandos and saw action in North Africa. Later he was one of the first to join David Stirling when he formed the SAS and was awarded a MM for raids on enemy airfields in 1942 and immediately promoted to Lance Sergeant. Tragically he was killed-in-action with the SAS in July 1943 with 13 others. This is a fitting tribute to a courageous Mick.

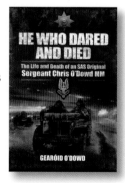

WOLFHOUNDS ON PARADE

A history of the mascots of the Irish Guards. Written by Martin Garrity and Holly Cook in 1997. Published privately by Dogonit, Middleton on Sea. Assisted by RHQ with letters and illustrations, it covers all the dogs up to Cuchulain.

EXCELLENCE IN ACTION. A Portrait of the Guards.

Published in 2008 by Third Millennium Publishing. It is a wide-ranging colour portrait of the Household Division reflecting the tradition of excellence in the context of today's deployment on operations. A coffee table book, it was given to every serving member of the Household Division when published in 2008.

IN THE HEAT OF THE BATTLE – Donough O'Brien

Donough O'Brien served in the 1st Battalion from 1958 to 1962 after his father before him; several of his cousins were also Irish Guardsmen. This, his fifth book, is an anthology of military careers and incidents divided into two halves: those who rose to the occasion and those who did not. It contains over seventy short accounts dealing with skill and bravery from Julius Caesar to Lance Corporal Kenneally IG as well as over confidence and cowardice from Custer to the massacre at My Lai. There is more than a smattering of Irishmen in the book. Apart from Kenneally, Guardsman Charlton VC, Field Marshal Alexander and the Regiment get several mentions too. *In the Heat of Battle* is broken down into stories of 2–10 pages, grouped by categories. An informative, entertaining and gripping book. *In the Heat of Battle* was published in 2009 by Osprey.

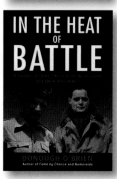

'Jiggs' – Colin Dean

A biography of Lieutenant Colonel 'Jiggs' Jaeger OBE, Mus Bac, LRAM, ARCM, psm. He was undoubtedly one of the most charismatic, talented and popular characters ever to serve with the Regimental Band. He was brought up more or less as an orphan and joined the army as a 14 year old Band Boy in 1927. He went on to be appointed as Director of Music of our Band in 1949 and served with it for 19 years. He was a hugely popular character. Published in 2013 by Parapress. Colin Dean was for many years administer of the Regimental Band and an acknowledged expert on Military music.

AROUND THE WORLD IN 80 YEARS – Brian Glibart-Denham

Brian served in the Regiment from 1954 to 1993 as had his father who was killed on the *Chobry* in Norway in 1940. This is a light hearted personal account of his eclectic and exciting life. He saw active service against the Mau Mau in Kenya, rioters in Aden, and revolutionaries in Cyprus. He has toured Argentina and Brazil cricketing, run his own delicatessen near Harrods, dealt with property in London and Greece, hot air ballooned over the desert, and travelled extensively and ruggedly to the most exotic corners of the world. He became involved with and sailed the Tall Ships, served as a Middle East, has worked as a North Sea oil rig roustabout, and in his 70s trekked to Mount Everest base camp. Typically of Brian, all proceeds from the book, published by Matador, which is obtainable from Regimental Headquarters, go to Regimental Benevolent Funds.

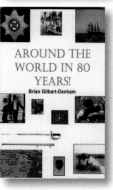

Appendix O

DIRECT ENTRY IRISH GUARDS OFFICERS SINCE THE END OF NATIONAL SERVICE

(in reverse order of arrival in the Battalion)

Names are given as used on joining the Regiment, not titles and appointments received later.
Legend:
+   Related to another Irish Guards Officer.
T   Transferee into Regiment from another unit, so not the year they commissioned.
★   Gap Year Commission or Short Service Limited Commission.

2015
McGrath R C   +
Orchard T P
Knight J J K   +
Craig-Harvey C H   +
Jones F M

2014
Mulira C W E K   T
Jerram D A
Connolly J M
Bell C E L
Nunn H C N   +
Moore W M W

2013
Grant R G F
Hamilton M C W   +
Stodal D J C
Ronan J J G

2012
Larkin H G R
Rostron O G
Pumphrey D L   +
Foggin E P M
Nassau HRH Prince
    Wenceslas of   +
Habsburg HS&IH Archduke
    Alexander of Austria   +
Leigh C F A

2011
Hamilton A J   +
Floyd A E
Graham-Watson F N
Simpson F F J

2010
Pope J R M
Drummond-Brady F M   +
Khashoggi N A C
Purdon J C R B   +
Gore R StJ E

2009
Liechtenstein HSH
    Prince Josef-Emanuel of   +
Jenkins W H R   +
MacDermot T P   +
Roffe-Silvester E J

2008
Sprake G C
Leonard B F O
Gair C W J
Campbell A C S
Collis H J N   T
de Stacpoole G E S D   +
Evans D T   T

2007
Dooher M F L
Evans T D
Kennard A D S   +
O'Gorman P S G   +
Gaggero N J   +

2006
Roberts O T A   +
Allman-Brown C A
Irwin-Clarke B J
Prior A J L
Howard C G G

2005
Murphy G T
Solly N S
Maunder-Taylor W R
Aitken G P H
Rogers T P T

2004
Bullock-Webster J H R L   +
Sands H J M   ★
Oakley T D H
Roberts J J J L   +
Pennington B T A
Lambe C J W
Money R P   T

2003
Dickinson H A H   +
Wolseley S G H C
Doherty O B
Williams C E V

2002
Radclyffe C P T
Reutter G L T H P   ★
Roffe-Silvester E J   ★
Ferrier N O C
Durdin-Robinson A J L

2001
O'Connell D C M
Hawley W A B
Langton J S   +
Orde-Powlett T P A

2000
Townley J P F
Lance P C   +
Dickinson H A H   +
Smythe B P
Cosby A J A   +
Plummer R J   +
Sincock C E W
Palmer J A E

1999
Magan E W M
Moulton J D
Brennan N P
Rosco W J F   +
Erasmus J V   +

1998
Turner I A J
Olsen T A L
Scott-Kerr J W
Cubitt W G   +T
Jones E N
Gay N P T
Rous R W J
Ormerod P M P   +
Keilthy P N

1997
Offer J S
Tulloch D C D   ★
Wills A J
Simpson G J M
Grayson M P M   +
Hopkirk W J
Coote T C

1996
Reddington J M
Stewart M R N
Collins M J
Corbett M D S   +
Light G C
Nunan M W

1995
de Rouet W J
Roberts F A D L   +
Kendell M M
Orrell J B J
O'Reilly C

1994
Lythe J E
Hymans N A
Chapman A N C
Lytle J J B
Melaniphy E G P
Orme-Smith J D
Pampanini S G

1993
Boanas E T
Webb J F
Wilkinson D G L
Walker C R V
Ghika C J   +
Tulloch R H E D   +★

1992
McBrien J M B
Wheeler P R D
Shanagher S P B
Mayhew P O

1991
Lockwood R A   +
Lloyd-Thomas G H R   +
Craig-Harvey C A   T
Holt H A B
Wilson E K   +

1990
Churchill J W
MacMullen P C A   +
Taylor S P P
Farrell B C

1989
Vigors T A M
Jenson N W
O'Dwyer M G C   +

Strauss D T
O'Connor T N T
Dawson-Damer Hon E L S +
Campbell-Johnston J A C   +

1988
Pym W A C   +
Hannah D M
Wallace P J J W
Nutting W F   +
Jarvis P R
Patrick J H L

1987
Venning N R
Burgess C N N
MacEwan A C B   +
Tett C J

1986
Segrave S O'N+
Morris-Adams C R
Melotte E J F V
Carleton-Smith M A P   +
Redmayne C G M
Quilter G R C
Owen S P   T

1985
Young R J P
Shapland H C M
Sharp R J T
Harris J C J
Colborne-Malpas T W

1984
Millar S D B   +T
Pratt J C R
Blakey W D
Bassett G A C
Gibbs P J   +
Carter H L S
Boyle R A R   +
Beeley A P M   +
Bonham-Carter T D   +
Matthews G C
MacKean S C R   T
Middlemiss M

1983
Greer F J M   +
Hand J P

1982
Roberts C B L L   +
Shaw R C O'M   +
Knaggs C P H   +

Howard-Allen H
Moriarty G M

1981
Gunston J   +
Hall N J

1980
O'Connell M D C
Robinson G C   +
Stopford J R H   +
McGrath C A   +
Haynes J T
Grotrian J B

1979
Gibbs D F   +
Lowther-Pinkerton A J M
Sieff M D
Hornung C   +★
Gaggero J P G   +

1978
Wheatley D M D A   +
Richardson M K O   +
Morrissey M P   +
Stopford Hon J N   +

1977
Donegan S P
Windham A G R
Downward J P
Frewen R E J
Nicholson M M
Roberts S J L   +
MacMullen T W J   +
Beeley R F G   +★

1976
Parshall H A C
Jeffries P A D   +
O'Brien L E   +
Hornung B P   +
Mainwaring-Burton G A   +
Boyle R E J

1975
Mainwaring-Burton J J   +
Purcell H M
Sugden J M
Robertson S W   +
Laband J R
Sheridan A J D
Buckmaster H G
Tandy P S O'C

de Stacpoole D H O   +
Bowen J W   +★
Lloyd S J C   T

1974
Smith M D L
Hill D A McC
Moore D M
Thorn J P   +
Birtwistle M D A
Pollock J H O'H   +
Morgan N J
Johns P N C

1973
Ramos J S de P
Foster D C G
Solly P C C   +
Coc J H R
Bellew C J   +★

1972
Grimshaw R H+
Holt B W F
O'Farrell B W
Robertson L H

1971
Robertson I K F   +
Dorman R O   +
Brownlow W J
Gorman J C   +
Boyd R McN   +

1970
Shakerley P G D
Mellor J C M
Roche T O'G

1969
Windham J J
Markes E C
Langton C R   +
Hungerford J P
Purdon T C R B+
Kennard J D   +
Belson R W
Long D W M

1968
Warrender M J V   +
O'Gorman J B   +
Baker C B G   +
Wilson H R G   T
Gardner N C E
Sharman M F

1967
Russell J D A
Bevan M C
Harclerode H M P D

1966
Gubbins B E T
Weldon A W
Carleton-Paget D D B   +
O'Reilly P B

1965
Aikenhead C D   +
Keigwin R T   +
Bullock-Webster R J S   +
Ormerod M N   +
Chesterton M S   +
Foster A N

1964
Vincent, Sir William Bt
Bigham Hon Andrew

1963
Gordon-Watson J M   +
Davies C C S
Thomson-Moore C N R
Corbett P M   +
Bellew Hon B E   +
Trusted T J
FitzHerbert E H T
Young G T S   +

1962
Wilson R A   +
Villiers-Stuart P D
Couchman J M D
Forward R S D
Grayson P T F   +
Reynolds J J   +
de Courcy J
Wolverson R C
Gough, Viscount   +
Bellingham A M
Eugster T B E   +

1961
O'Dwyer S G   +
Brown C R
Cole A J G   +

1960
Webb-Carter D B W
Cooper J K Fitz-G
McGillycuddy of the Reeks
Mahon W W

GALLANTRY, LEADERSHIP AND BRAVERY AWARDS SINCE 1945

Distinguished Service Order (DSO)
Awarded for highly successful command and leadership during active operations.

Colonel H A B Holt OBE	Afghanistan	2010 (detached)
Lt Col C R V Walker	Afghanistan	2010 (Comd 1 Gren Gds)
Major I A J Turner	Afghanistan	2011

George Medal (GM)
Awarded to military personnel for those acts which would not normally be granted, such as acts of exemplary bravery not in the presence of the enemy.

Lieutenant J C Gorman	Hong Kong	1970 (Kotewall Rd Disaster)

Most Excellent Order of the British Empire – Military Division

Commander (CBE)

Colonel B W F Holt	Northern Iraq	1983
Brigadier W G Cubitt	Northern Ireland	2005
Brigadier M A P Carleton-Smith OBE	Afghanistan	2008

Officer (OBE)

Lt Col D M L Gordon-Watson	Palestine	1948
Lt Col (Temp) T H H Grayson	Egypt	1951
Lt Col C R Langton	Northern Ireland	1993
Lt Col T C R B Purdon MBE	Northern Ireland	1994 (Comd 1 WG)
Lt Col W G Cubitt	Kosovo	1999
Lt Col M A P Carleton-Smith	Iraq	2004 (detached)
Lt Col C J Ghika	Afghanistan	2011

Member (MBE)

Maj M McN Boyd	Cyprus	1959
Maj J G F Head	Borneo	1966
Capt T C R B Purdon	Rhodesia	1980
Capt M Middlemiss	Northern Ireland	1990
Maj A J M Lowther-Pinkerton	Columbia	1990 (detached)
Maj C A McGrath	Northern Ireland	1994
Maj M A P Carleton-Smith	Kosovo	1999 (detached)
Maj B C Farrell	Kosovo/Macedonia	1999
Maj D M Hannah	Sierra Leone	2002
Maj P C A MacMullen	Iraq	2003
Maj E J F V Melotte	Iraq	2004
Capt J A E Palmer	Iraq	2007
Maj M R N Stewart	Libya	2014
Carleton-Smith	Kosovo/Albania	Middlemiss 1990 (detached)

British Empire Medal (BEM)

After 1993 it lay in abeyance until but brought back, for civilians only, in June 2012 for the Queen's Diamond Jubilee. All Military are eligible for the MBE instead.

Gdsm S B O Little	Palestine	1948
Gdsm P Owens	Palestine	1948
Gdsm Trafford	London	1978 (Chelsea Bks Bomb)
Sgt Murphy	London	1978 (Chelsea Bks Bomb)
Sgt Cullen	London	1978 (Chelsea Bks Bomb)
Sgt Bond	London	1981 (Iranian Embassy Siege)

Note: In 1993 Honours and Awards to Service Personnel underwent a major revision, when the practice of having some categories of awards, different medals for Officers and Other Ranks was discontinued. That is why the Military Medal is no longer awarded to Other Ranks, who instead, were eligible for the Military Cross.

Military Cross (MC)

Awarded in recognition of exemplary gallantry during active operations against the enemy on land.

Maj P A McCall	Palestine	1948
Capt D B W Webb-Carter	Aden	1967
Lt D C M O'Connell	Iraq	2003
Lt The Hon T P A Orde-Powlett	Iraq	2003
Gdsm A L Branchflower	Iraq	2003
CSgt Kincaid	Iraq	2007 (detached)
LSgt J S Cooke	Afghanistan	2008 (detached Gds Para)
LSgt M P Turrell	Afghanistan	2009 (detached WG)

Military Medal (MM)

Sgt Lewis	Aden	1968

Queen's Gallantry Medal (QGM)

Awarded to military and civilian personnel for 'exemplary acts of bravery' at a level below that of the George Medal, not in the presence of the enemy.

LCpl S D Campbell RVM	Iraq	2003
Gdsm L Wheeler	Iraq	2003
WO2 (CSM) P J Campbell	Iraq	2007
LSgt K W Thompson	Iraq	2007

Mentioned-in-Despatches (MiD)

It is the oldest form of recognition for gallantry within the UK Armed Forces. Technically is one whose name appears in an official report to higher command describing a gallant or meritorious action in the face of the enemy. A single bronze oakleaf emblem is worn on the medal.

Lt Col A L W Koch De Gooreynd	Palestine	1948 (twice awarded)
Maj R C Aikenhead	Palestine	1948
Maj J W Berridge	Palestine	1948
Maj J A H Hendry	Palestine	1948
Capt R S Langton MC	Palestine	1948
Capt D A Lambert	Palestine	1948
Capt N G H White	Palestine	1948
Capt E C Whitely	Palestine	1948
Lt J B Gillow	Palestine	1948
WO2 I I Kelly	Palestine	1948
WO2 A A Mahoney	Palestine	1948
Sgt M A Wrafter	Palestine	1948
Sgt G Walsh	Palestine	1948
Sgt R C Woodham	Palestine	1948
Sgt F J Cox	Palestine	1948
LSgt S Hill	Palestine	1948
LCpl S V Cummins	Palestine	1948

Gdsm S Fletcher	Palestine	1948
Gdsm S W Hardy	Palestine	1948
Gdsm C T Wallace	Palestine	1948
Gdsm H W Barr	Palestine	1948
Gdsm S W Hardy	Palestine	1948
Gdsm T Tranter	Palestine	1948
Gdsm V W Trinder	Palestine	1948
Maj J G F Head	Cyprus	1958
LSgt F G Boyd	Borneo	1964
Maj B A S Barnes	Borneo	1965
Gdsm T Bell	Aden	1967 (Posthumous)
Lt D W M Long	Northern Ireland	1973 (with AAC)
Maj J B O'Gorman	Northern Ireland	1986
Capt C A McGrath	Northern Ireland	1992
LSgt M D Swift	Northern Ireland	1993

From 1993 it became a silver oakleaf emblem reserved for gallantry during active servive.

Sgt J P Gribben	Former Yugoslavia	1999
Sgt T A Meadows	Former Yugoslavia	1999
LSgt G P O'Neill	Iraq	2007
Capt C W J Gair	Afghanistan	2011
Lt R StJ E Gore	Afghanistan	2011
Gdsm C M Tobin	Afghanistan	2011
Lt A E Floyd	Afghanistan	2013
Gdsm G Boyce	Afghanistan	2013

Queen's Commendation for Brave Conduct (QCBC)
Awarded for bravery entailing risk to life and meriting national recognition, but not at the level of the QGM

Sgt G Johnston	Aden	1966
Gdsm P Kennedy	Hong Kong	1972 (Kotewall Rd Disaster)
Maj H C Shapland	Northern Ireland	1993
WO2 (CSM) S Moffatt	Northern Ireland	1993

Queen's Commendation for Bravery (QCB)
Replaced QCBC in 1994. Acknowledges brave acts in non-warlike circumstances entailing a risk to life. A silver spray of laurel leaves is worn on the medal ribbon.

WO2 (CSM) J M Thompson	Northern Ireland	1994
WO1 (RSM) A Gardner	Kosovo	1999
Sgt D J Browne	Northern Ireland	1999
Gdsm M W H McMurtry	Afghanistan	2011

Queen's Commendation for Valuable Service (QCVS)
Recognises meritorious service during, or in support of operations. The emblem of a spray of silver oak leaves is worn on the medal ribbon.

Capt H A B Holt	Colombia	1997 (detached)
Maj C A Craig-Harvey	Kosovo	1999
Maj D M Hannah	Democratic Republic of the Congo	2000
Maj M A P Carleton-Smith MBE	Former Yugoslavia & Albania	2000 (detached)
Sgt L A M J O'Connor	Northern Ireland	2004
Col C P H Knaggs OBE	Afghanistan	2006
Maj J A E Palmer MBE	Afghanistan	2013

Joint Commanders' Commendation

Capt D M Hannah	Bosnia	1994
WO2 Bonner	Kosovo	1999
Gdsm Bradford	Kosovo	1999

LSgt Purtell	Kosovo	1999
Capt J D Moulton	Iraq	2003
LSgt W J Lyttle	Iraq	2007
LSgt F M Whelan	Iraq	2007
Maj M R N Stewart	Afghanistan	2011
LCpl A J Morgan	Afghanistan	2011
Gdsm S J McCormack	Afghanistan	2011
Gdsm J T Rainey	Afghanistan	2011
LSgt C Fitzgerald	Afghanistan	2013

Commander British Forces' Commendation – Kosovo

LSgt Brettle	Kosovo	1999
LSgt Dyer	Kosovo	1999
CSgt Haines	Kosovo	1999

GOC's Commendation – Northern Ireland

Maj C B L L Roberts	Northern Ireland	1994
Lt S G Pampanini	Northern Ireland	1995
LCpl C Laverty	Northern Ireland	2004
Gdsm J Wilson	Northern Ireland	2004

GOC's Commendation, Multi-national Division – South East Iraq

Cpl Hogan	Iraq	2007
Gdsm Bierley	Iraq	2007
Gdsm Sinnott	Iraq	2007

Commander Task Force Helmand Commendation – Afghanistan

CSgt J J Gavin	Afghanistan	2011
LSgt Hobson	Afghanistan	2013
LCpl Quinlan	Afghanistan	2013

Commander-in-Chief's Commendation

Capt S G O'Dwyer	Aden	1967
LSgt P A McGowan	Aden	1967
Sgt T Melia	Aden	1967
Sgt J Mayne	Aden	1967
LSgt L Mills	Aden	1967
LCpl P A Mooney	Aden	1967
LCpl Tighe	Aden	1967
Gdsm E J Robinson	Aden	1967
Gdsm W R Rea	Aden	1967
Gdsm McKenna 07	Aden	1967
Gdsm Kelly 38	Aden	1967
Gdsm A O'Neill	Aden	1967
LCpl A Moffett	Oman	2002 (APC rescue)
Gdsm C H Hegarty	UK	2002 (Apprehended assailant)

US Army Legion of Merit

Brig C J Ghika	Iraq	2015

US Army Commendation Medal

Capt C A McGrath	Iraq	1991

US Army Bronze Star Medal

Lt Col C A Craig-Harvey	Iraq	2008
Col J H Stopford	Iraq	2014

Appendix Q

IRISH GUARDS WOLFHOUNDS

The Irish Wolfhound was the ancient hunting dog of the legendary Irish warriors led by Fionn MacCumhaill so it was appropriate that on 15 Aug 1902 the Irish Kennel Club should hold a competition to find a suitable dog for the newly formed regiment. The newspapers reported the following day of the Kennel Club Show at Crystal Palace, London.

Brian Boru.

> *'The principle attraction at the Crystal Palace yesterday was the competition instituted by the Irish Wolfhound Club for the honour of presenting a hound to the Irish Guards suitable for being trained as a regimental dog. The club had arranged to purchase the selected hound for 30 guineas, and this price somewhat restricted competition on the whole, the eight hounds brought before the judges were very fair specimens of the breed, the winner, Mrs A J Gerard's (Malpas) Rajah of Kidnal, two and a half years old, and a frequent winner in good company, being in the opinion of the judges, a cheap hound and one best fitted by age, promise, and appearance to be handed over to the regiment..... Mrs Gerard handed over the young hound to Lieutenant the Hon Mervyn Wingfield and Captain Fowles (Quartermaster) of the Irish Guards and the hound left the Crystal Palace in charge of four non-commissioned officers and two drummers, the interesting ceremony and presentation creating great enthusiasm.'*

Rajah of Kidnal was immediately re-named **Brian Boru** by the Regiment, but affectionately known as '**Paddy**', and given the Regimental Number 1463. He appeared on St Patrick's Day in 1908 with his successor, **Leitrim Boy**, who was presented by 8th Viscount Powerscourt, a serving officer, who as Hon Mervyn Wingfield collected Brian Boru at the Kennel Club in 1902. **Leitrim Boy** continued until 1917 when he was replaced by **Doran** of whom very little is known.

Leitrim Boy.

The next dog was **Cruachan (of Ifold)** whose picture, painted by Mrs Horace Colemore hangs in the Officers' Mess. He was winner of the Height Cup at the Irish Wolfhound Show in 1924. The same year the Officers of the Regiment presented the Irish Guards Challenge Shield to be competed for at the Irish Wolfhound Club's Annual Show. It is awarded to the Best Hound of opposite sex to the winner of the Graham Shield. (Capt George Graham founded the Irish Wolfhound Club in 1885 and saved the breed from extinction following the Irish Famine of 1845.) The silver collar presented in return by the club and used by **Cruachan** is now in the Guards Museum.

Major General R V Pollok CBE DSO, who commanded the Battalion in 1917–18 and 1926–1930 and was Regimental Lieutenant Colonel from 1930–31 recalled in 1968:

> *I was in command when Mrs Horace Colemore painted the picture of Cruachan. The Battalion was stationed in Maida Barracks, Aldershot in 1924. I cannot remember what Mrs Colemore was paid for the picture or who paid. Mrs Colemore stayed with us while she was doing the picture. Gdsm Cahill was in charge of the hound, but he lived in the house with us and my wife really looked after the dog, which became a great pet.*
>
> *Unfortunately, as the dog got older he took to killing other dogs, a common complaint with Wolfhounds apparently. One day, when out in Hyde Park, he savaged the Italian Ambassador's Greyhound. I had to attend the Italian Embassy to apologise. I was shown into the room,*

Doran.

Cruachan.

where I saw a very lovely lady who described herself as the 'canine nurse'. Shortly afterwards, a still more lovely lady came in who said she was the 'canine night nurse'. After that His Excellency arrived and I apologised. A few weeks later the Italian dog was being exercised again in Hyde Park, by his lovely but idiotic canine nurse, when Cruachan made a dive for the dog and killed it. After that Cruachan had to do his exercise in Battersea Park.

Next time the Battalion were in Aldershot, I had to take Cruachan to the sick lines and he was painlessly destroyed in 1931. He had got old and very unreliable with other dogs.

My wife and I was very fond of Cruachan. I hated him being a Regimental Pet and when he died I made no attempt to get a replacement.'

Irish Guards Challenge Shield.

Hence for 32 years there was no Regimental Pet. **Pat** succeeded in 1951 but unfortunately he had to be put down in 1954 due to disease, having spent little time with the Battalion who were abroad in West Germany most of his service. The first three Wolfhounds were all painted by Heywood Hardy and their portraits hang in the Officers' Mess. The portrait of **Pat** is shown with his handler, 'Boy' Sullivan, who later went on to be Drum Major of the Battalion. He was the last Drummer Boy handler as that form of entry into the Army ceased in 1957 with the first intake of the Junior Guardsmen's Company in 1958.

Pat.

Shaun (Rory of Ballygran) succeeded **Pat** in 1959. He belonged to an officer in the 11th Hussars in Omagh, Northern Ireland who offered him to the Regiment when his Regiment was posted abroad. In 1960 he was presented with a scarlet cape by the Irish Linen Guild to be worn on ceremonial occasions. A cape of the same material is still worn today on specific occasions when Home Service Clothing is worn.

On 26th July 1961 the official status of the dog was changed by the Ministry of Defence from regimental 'pet' to regimental 'mascot'. He joined a select group in the Army of two Drum Horses, two Shetland Ponies, two Goats, a Ram and an Indian Black Buck who are officially approved as mascots and therefore entitled to free veterinary services as well as transport and quarantine at public expense. Unfortunately, food was not included until 1979.

In 1966 the Irish Wolfhound Club honoured the Regiment by inviting the Regimental Lieutenant Colonel to become President in succession to the late Princess Royal. A previous president in the 1920s was the Earl of Cavan, 4th Colonel of the Regiment. The Lieutenant Colonel in post has continued to hold this honorary appointment.

Field Marshal Alex with Fionn (left with LCpl O'Toole) and Cormac at the Guards Depot, Alexander Barracks, Pirbright on St Patrick's Day, 1977.

Shaun.

Shaun, appearing with his successor **Fionn**, walked off his last parade to '*Auld Lang Syne*' on 26 September 1967. He retired to a family in Scotland with very strong regimental connections. He died peacefully in 1970 and was buried, wrapped in his blanket, in a glade at Easter Moncrieff. 'Flowers of the Forest' was played on the pipes, a libation of whiskey was pored into his grave and his tombstone simply says 'SHAUN, IRISH GUARDS, DIED 1970".

Fionn (Samanda Silver) was presented by the Irish Wolfhound Club together with a new silver collar. He served until April 1976 when he retired to Epping Forest. However, from 1970 to 1977 the Battalion was mostly serving abroad in Hong Kong, Belize and West Germany,

Cormac.

Fionn.

Connor.

Malachy.

so **Fionn** lived at the Guards Depot at Pirbright, although he played his full part in recruiting and ceremonial events.

Cormac (of Tara), the 8th wolfhound, was presented by a breeder, Miss Margaret Harrison, as a 6 month year old puppy in February 1977. His first parade was St Patrick's Day at Pirbright when he was presented with his shamrock by Queen Elizabeth The Queen Mother. He continued to serve the Regiment until 1985, although he remained in England when the Battalion was posted to Germany in 1982.

His successor, **Connor** was also presented by Miss Harrison and welcomed into the Regiment on 17th Jan 1985 by the Queen Mother at Clarence House. He was succeeded in turn by **Malachy** in 1990 as the Battalion returned from Berlin. He developed some endearing habits and his own Mickish sense of style such as nonchalantly leaning against his handler during quiet moments on parade. Unfortunately **Malachy** was a very short-lived mascot and died in 1994 of complications after dental surgery. The Battalion had returned from Northern Ireland at the time and had just gone on leave. The first morning of leave dawned to reveal a dead mascot whose body had to be frozen in the food store much to the surprise of the Master Cook on his return from leave.

Cuchulain.

Aengus.

Cuchulain arrived in 1995 but he had to be put down in July 2000 due to heart problems, which often affect Wolfhounds because of their size and the strain it puts on their circulation. **Aengus** replaced him in the same year but also sadly died young in 2003 after the move from Münster, Germany back to London.

Just before Christmas 2003, **Donnachadh** (pronounced '**Dunnock**'), the new Regimental Mascot, was handed over to Drummer Clerkin, his handler. Drummer Clerkin had been away for a while, learning about all things canine on the military dog handler's course whilst **Donnachadh** was being prepared, by the breeders, for his move to the Regiment. This fine-looking hound was given by Keith and Mary Pursgrove of Rougesmoor Irish Wolfhounds and Deerhounds. The name **Donnachadh** is

Domhnall.

Conmael.

Donnachadh.

steeped in history. The original bearer was the younger son of Brian Boru, the last great High King of Ireland. **Donnachadh** died of heart failure and was succeeded in September 2006 by Fergal.

Fergal.

Fergal was donated by Mr Ben Baker, an American friend of the Regiment, and acquired from Cunaardri Irish Wolfhounds in Co Tipperary. He died tragically in an accident in Liverpool in November 2007. Mrs Elizabeth Hanley, the breeder generously offered to replace him with a two year old half-brother of **Fergal**. He was named **Conmael** and in 2012 **Conmael** retired back to Mrs Hanley in Co Tipperary. He settled in immediately, reclaiming his bed from his father.

On 5 October 2012, the Republic of Ireland's Irish Wolfhound Association generously presented the Regiment with a three month old puppy named **Domhnall** (pronounced **'Donal'**) at the British Ambassador's Residence in Dublin. In April 2014 during the State Visit to Britain by the President of Ireland, Michael D Higgins, presented a new red cape to **Domhnall** at Windsor Castle. The gift was unexpected and the presentation stole the show from the Grenadier Guards Guard of Honour much to their annoyance.

BRIAN BORU	1902–1910	CONNOR	1985–1990
LEITRIM BOY	1910–1917	MALACHY	1990–1994
DORAN	1917–1924	CUCHULAIN	1995–2000
CRUACHAN	1924–1929	AENGUS	2000–2003
PAT	1951–1954	DONNACHADH	2003–2005
SHAUN	1959–1967	FERGAL	2006–2007
FIONN	1967–1977	CONMAEL	2008–2012
CORMAC	1976–1985	DOMHNALL	2012

New Cape for the Wolfhound. In April 2014, the President of Ireland made a state visit starting at Windsor. The Regiment had no involvement until the President Michael D Higgins indicated he would like to present Domhnall with a new red cape. The very smart Grenadier Guard of Honour did not feature in the press.

Appendix R

QUARTERMASTERS, DIRECTORS OF MUSIC AND LATE ENTRY OFFICERS

Historically, it was the case that Warrant Officers in the Regiment were commissioned to undertake roles like Quartermaster within the Battalion. These were originally selected and appointed by the Regimental Lieutenant Colonel but nowadays individuals are recommended by the Regiment but compete for the promotion across the Infantry. Their experience and expertise nowadays is much more widely used within the Battalion and wider Army in areas other than the Quartermasters' department including welfare and career management. Their service in the ranks is widely appreciated and they are entitled to serve until aged 55. Generally, about 5 of the 30 regimental officers serving in the Battalion will be what is termed Late Entry officers. Listed below are those who have served in the Regiment since 1945 although some of the early ones were commissioned before that date.

Name	Year	Type of Commission	Name	Year	Type of Commission
T D McCarthy, MBE	1933	QM	M J Henderson	1990	DOM
G H Wilcocks, MBE	1933	DOM	J J Lynch	1990	SSC(LE)
A Ashton	1938	QM	M Burns	1990	SSC(LE)
J Keating, MBE	1939	QM	L K Windle	1990	SSC(LE)
R Hastings, MBE	1942	QM	J C Knowles	1992	SSC(LE)
H F McKinney, MBE	1943	QM	A E Smith	1994	SSC(LE)
J A Stack, MC	1943	QM	P J Cloney	1995	SRC
C H Jaeger	1948	DOM	G C Lumb	1996	SRC
G N Howe, MBE	1951	SSC	S Devitt	2001	SSC(LE)
T E Coppin, MBE	1951	SSC	D J Ryan	2001	SSC(LE)
W I Rooney, MM	1952	SSC	A Gardner	2002	SSC(LE)
J J Kelly, MBE	1955	Staff QM	S Boyd, MBE	2002	SSC(LE)
W G Johnston, DCM	1957	SSC	P F Shields	2002	SSC(LE)
P Mercer, MBE, MM	1959	SSC	M Pears	2002	SSC(LE)
A Bell,	1961	SSC	W J Duggan	2004	SSC(LE)
V Sullivan,	1967	QM	K T D Fox	2004	SSC(LE)
J E Williams, MBE	1968	Staff QM	R J Wilmont, MBE	2006	SSC(LE)
E G Horabin	1968	DOM	P S Nichols, MBE	2007	SSC(LE)
G R Hooton, MBE	1971	SRC	G S Johnson, MBE	2007	SSC(LE)
J P Byrne	1971	SSC	J C Donaldson	2007	SSC(LE)
J P Duffy	1971	QM	F W Howell	2008	SSC(LE)
A W Cunningham	1972	SSC	P W Lally	2009	SSC(LE)
E Keating	1973	SSC	P A Fagin	2009	SSC(LE)
F H Groves	1974	QM	P D Shannon	2009	DOM
W E Matthews, MBE	1974	QM	L J McNaughton	2010	SSC(LE)
R Cowap, MBE	1974	QM	W Buckley	2010	SSC(LE)
T J Corcoran	1976	SRC	R A Martin	2010	SSC(LE)
G W Pidgeon	1976	SSC	R W Hopla	2011	DOM
M G Lane	1977	DOM	D D Johnston	2012	SSC(LE)
T Connor	1978	SSC	D R Brettle	2014	SSC(LE)
T H Young	1979	QM	M I Butler	2014	SSC(LE)
H V Meredith	1980	SSC	K Fletcher	2014	SSC(LE)
D Wilkinson	1980	SSC	S A McMichael	2014	SSC(LE)
J Clegg	1980	Reg (LE)	J G Parke	2014	SSC(LE)
C M Butterworth	1982	SSC	R Sixsmith	2015	SSC(LE)
V F P McLean	1983	SSC	B R Taylor	2015	SSC(LE)
R A D Kelly, MBE	1986	Reg QM	B Miller	2015	(DOM)
W J O'Keeffe	1986	SSC	D G McKernan	2016	SSC(LE)
V M McEllin	1988	SSC (LE)	M Flynn	2016	SSC(LE)
J F P Faloone	1988	Reg (LE)	S Nelson	2016	SSC(LE)
M E J O'Neill	1988	SSC(LE)			

Legend: Types of Commission

QM – Quartermaster	SRC – Special Regular Commission	SSC(LE) – Late Entry
DOM – Director of Music	SSC – Short Service Commission	Reg(LE) – Regular (Late Entry)

INDEX

*(Page numbers in **bold type** indicate an illustration)*